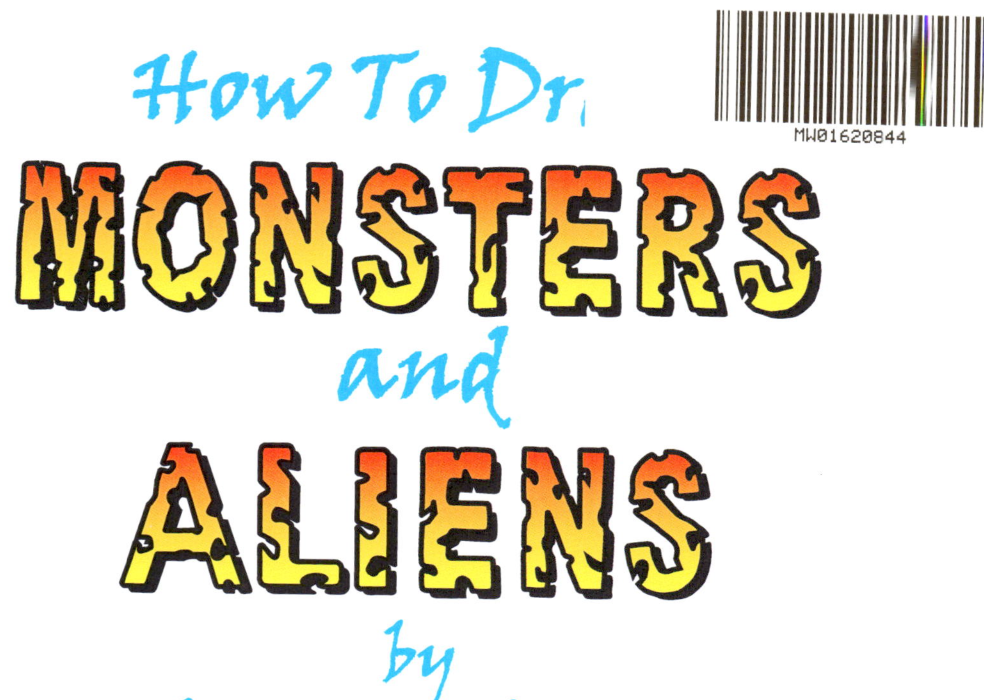
How To Dr
MONSTERS
and
ALIENS
by
Spencer Nelson

About the Author

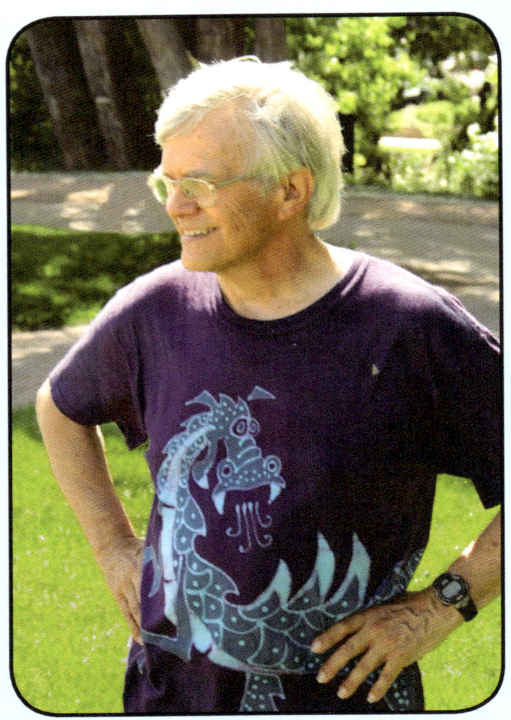
Photo by Bryce Pratt — crawlingspidergallery.com
T-shirt from Grebebatik.com

Spencer Nelson has loved to draw all his life. Born and raised in Idaho, his talents brought recognition even in elementary school. As a teenager he received awards in city and state-wide art competitions. He spent hours drawing space ships, fantasy art of all sorts, and comic strips — some in 3D!

A passion for the movies drew him to study filmmaking at the University of Southern California. He subsequently made award-winning TV commercials, business films and training films for a dozen years.

In the early 2000's, after a much-too-long break designing machines, he turned his attention to his true calling: art and writing. His paintings and commissioned portraits are displayed in living rooms throughout the country.

Recognizing a universal interest in weird creatures among the young and not-so-young, he revived his own childhood fascination and set out to create this book. Doing so has, for him, been enormous fun — bringing back the joy he felt as a youngster when he sat before a sheet of paper, opened a box of crayons, and went to work.

He currently lives in Broomfield, Colorado.

How to Draw Monsters and Aliens
Second edition / Version 2.0 / February 25, 2014

All illustrations by Spencer Nelson except where noted.

Manufactured in the United States.

Published by Wildflower Creative
265 Laurel Street #6, Broomfield Colorado 80020

ISBN: 978-09888173-0-2

Library of Congress Control Number: 2013934393

Visit www.spencerWnelson.com where you may acquire more ideas and info relating to this book, including a list of sources and prices for materials, *and* see more of the author's artwork!

To Patty Bartlett Taylor...

...my tenth-grade high school teacher who very long ago allowed me to attempt to write a book in place of submitting book reports. I hope that with this book she will consider the assignment complete.

Acknowledgments

There is not enough space to thank all the people to whom I owe thanks for moving me along on my art career in general, and this book in particular. I shall mention but a few, with hope that those on earth and in heaven will know of my gratitude:

To the neighbors in Boise, Idaho, who brought me reams of paper to draw on and who patiently critiqued my grade-school level work. To my late Aunt Jean and grandmother Jeannette, who provided a treasure of artist supplies in my high school years and who continuously praised my creations and nourished my interests .

To the many teachers who taught me not only what was in books, but more importantly, what was inside *me*.

To Rhonda Lyles for her encouragement. To my children, Shane and Cimarron, who *demanded* that I do my art. To Judith Mohling, Alice MacDonald, Joe Horn, Ashley Eder, Jenni Skyler, Diane Dandeneau, Ramona Sowa and countless other friends and counselors who have provided valuable feedback and continuously supported my sensitive ego.

And finally to Peg Finucane and Courtney Sowa for correcting numerous errors and making this work readable — a most humbling experience for the author.

—Spencer Nelson

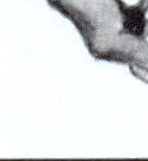

Contents

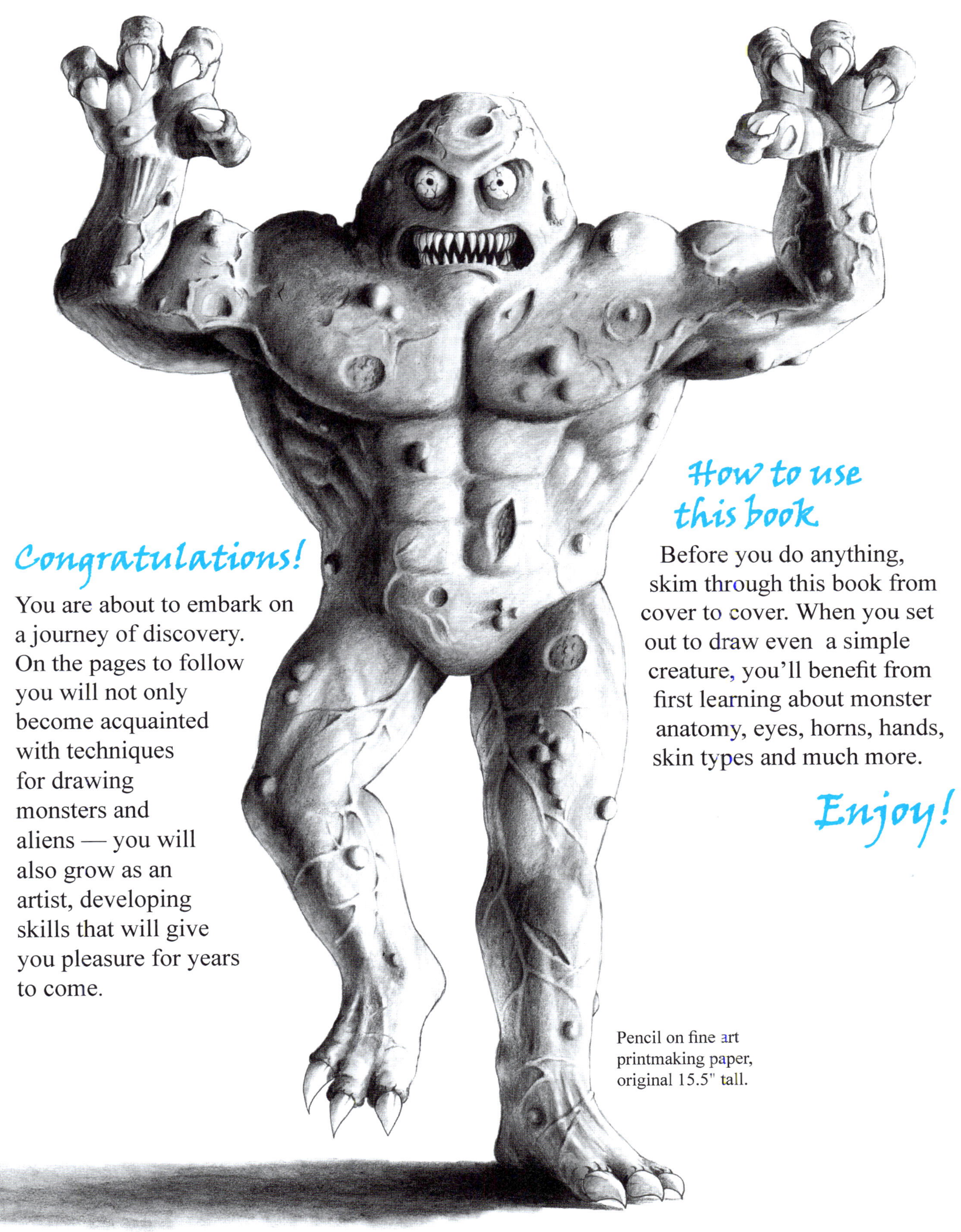

Congratulations!

You are about to embark on a journey of discovery. On the pages to follow you will not only become acquainted with techniques for drawing monsters and aliens — you will also grow as an artist, developing skills that will give you pleasure for years to come.

How to use this book

Before you do anything, skim through this book from cover to cover. When you set out to draw even a simple creature, you'll benefit from first learning about monster anatomy, eyes, horns, hands, skin types and much more.

Enjoy!

Pencil on fine art printmaking paper, original 15.5" tall.

An Extremely Brief HISTORY of Monsters and Aliens

Monsters have occupied the human imagination for thousands of years. In the 2,800 year-old tale *The Odyssey*, for example, heroic Odysseus and his men are attacked by a six-headed monster and a man-eating giant. People believed until recent times in the existence of sea serpents. Folks have long insisted they saw Scotland's Loch Ness monster, though scientists have failed to locate the elusive beast in that country's famous lake.

The monsters best known throughout history, in nearly every culture on earth, are dragons. Perhaps the most famous story is that of medieval knight St. George, who slayed a dragon and saved the life of a grateful maiden in the process. While dragons were generally feared in the West, they have been perceived as good and beneficial in China.

The idea that **aliens** might exist was not taken seriously by most people until the sixteenth and seventeenth centuries, when Copernicus theorized that the earth was not the center of the universe and Galileo studied planets with the newly invented telescope. Educated people soon began to ponder the possibility of life beyond earth. Life was thought to exist on the moon and even the sun. As late as the 1950's, intelligent life on Mars and Venus was considered possible.

In 1898 science fiction writer H. G. Wells penned *The War of the Worlds* about an invasion of earth by creatures from mars — "Martians". In 1938 the story inspired a fictional radio "newscast" by 23-year-old Orson Wells that scared a great many people who thought the invasion was real.

An alien is rumored to have crash-landed near Roswell, New Mexico in 1947. This sparked beliefs in UFO's, tales of alien abductions, and lasting debate. Credible evidence of the alien and his spacecraft is absent.

Monsters and aliens began appearing in movies soon after the motion picture camera was invented. In a 1902 silent film, *A Trip to the Moon*, explorers are propelled to the moon in a capsule shot from a large cannon and have combat with moon inhabitants called "Selenites". A film serial in 1936 pitted hero Flash Gordon against villain Ming the Merciless on the planet Mongo.

In the 1930's and 40's, audiences watched monster movie classics like *King Kong* and *Frankenstein*. The 1950's brought forth movie creatures spawned by nuclear testing in films such as *The Beast from 20,000 Fathoms*, *Them!* and the ever-popular *Godzilla*. 1951 saw the production of *The Thing from Another World*, a terrifically scary movie and favorite of this author, about a man-like creature who arrives to populate earth with his own kind.

Special effects used to produce early movie creatures were initially crude, but today computer-generated imaging (CGI) is routinely employed to create monsters and aliens that are very believable — helping to explain, perhaps, their continued popularity in film and television.

In many of the early films, monsters were often viewed as sad creatures who can't help what they are. Audiences tended to feel sorry for them. No one could be happy watching King Kong's unfortunate demise. In recent years monsters are sometimes seen in a favorable light, occasionally depicted as harmless and even appealing, as is *Sesame Street's* Cookie Monster and the stars of the Disney/Pixar movie *Monsters, Inc.*

Aliens have almost always been portrayed as beings bent on enslaving or wiping out humanity. This image was countered when gentle, peaceful aliens visited our planet in 1977's *Close Encounters of the Third Kind* and again when *The Extraterrestrial* warmed the hearts of millions.

The fact remains, however, that most monsters and perhaps some aliens would have no qualms about tearing you to pieces.

* * *

MATERIALS

The enormous variety of materials with which you can draw and paint your monsters and aliens includes:

- Inexpensive and inferior
- Inexpensive but good quality
- Expensive and high quality

It's great if you can afford the high quality stuff, but if you can't, go the "Inexpensive but adequate" route: **you do NOT need to spend a fortune on a whole bunch of costly art supplies to create cool creatures!**

The drawings on this and the next page illustrate how few artistic tools you can get away with. You'll learn how to use them later in this book.

This lovely creature was created with seven Prismacolor® brand colored pencils on inexpensive but decent quality Norton "Kids Art®" drawing paper.

Colors used were yellow, green, dark green, light blue, and magenta. They were blended together to create in-between shades. White and black pencils were used for lightening and darkening. Colors were smoothed with a colored pencil blender.

The original drawing is 16″ wide.

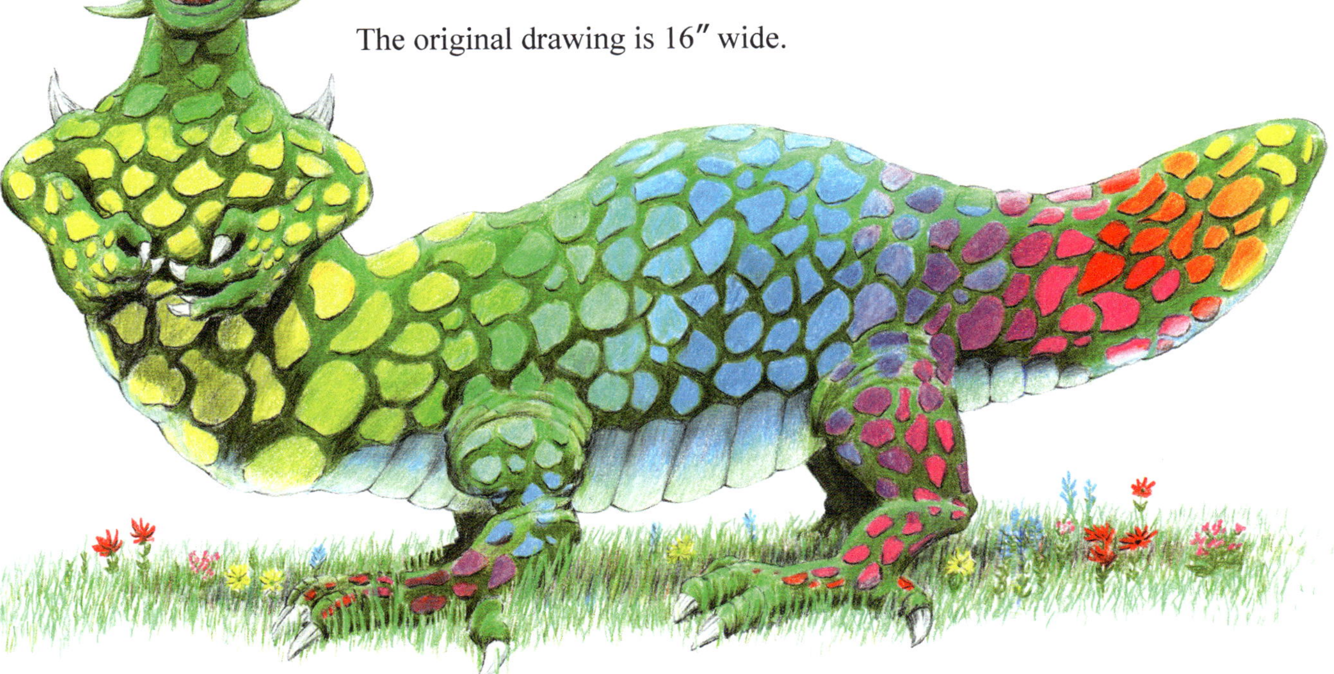

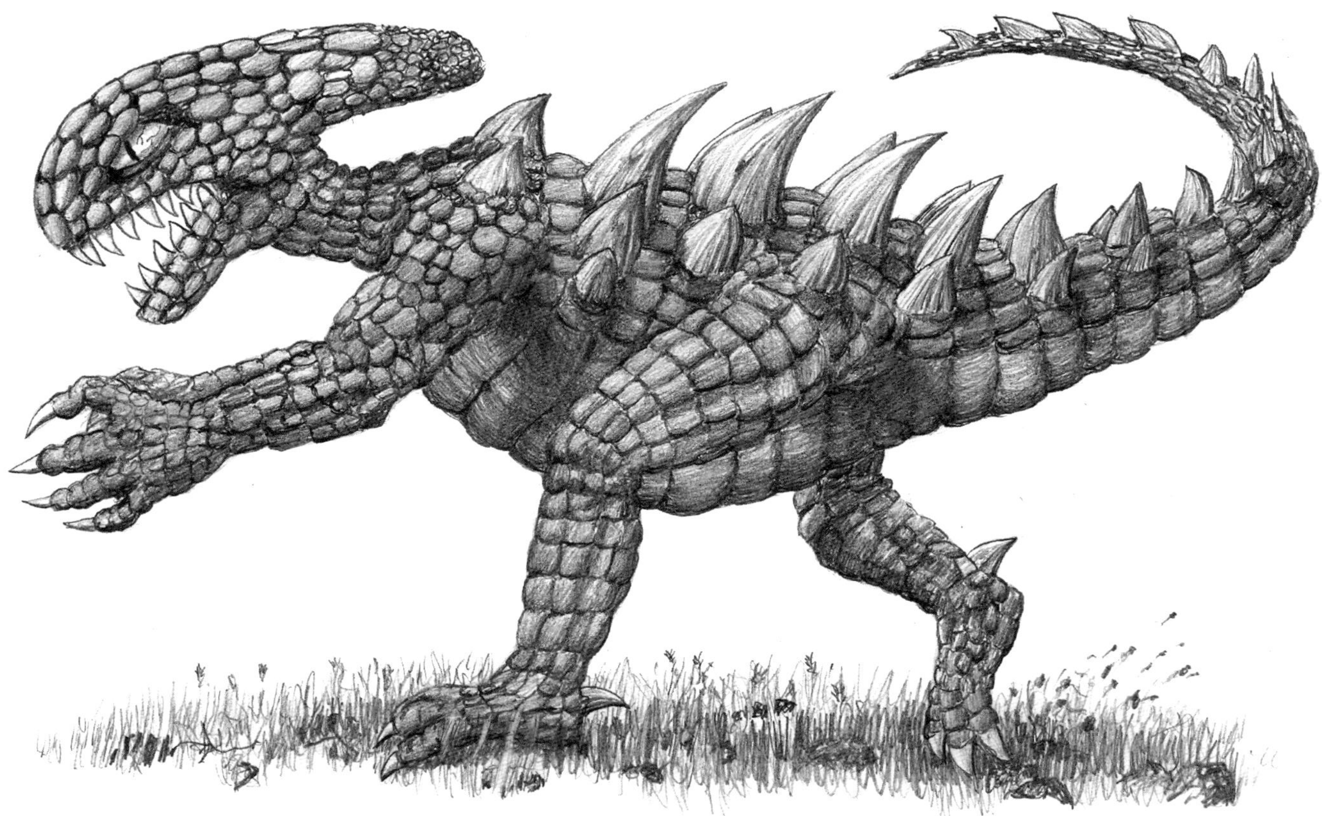

This guy was drawn with a single number 2 school-type pencil on ordinary, inexpensive "bright white" ink-jet printer paper.

This monster was drawn with two moderately priced Foray™ brand ball point pens — a 1.0mm "medium point" and a 0.5mm "ultra fine point" on "bright white" ink-jet printer paper.

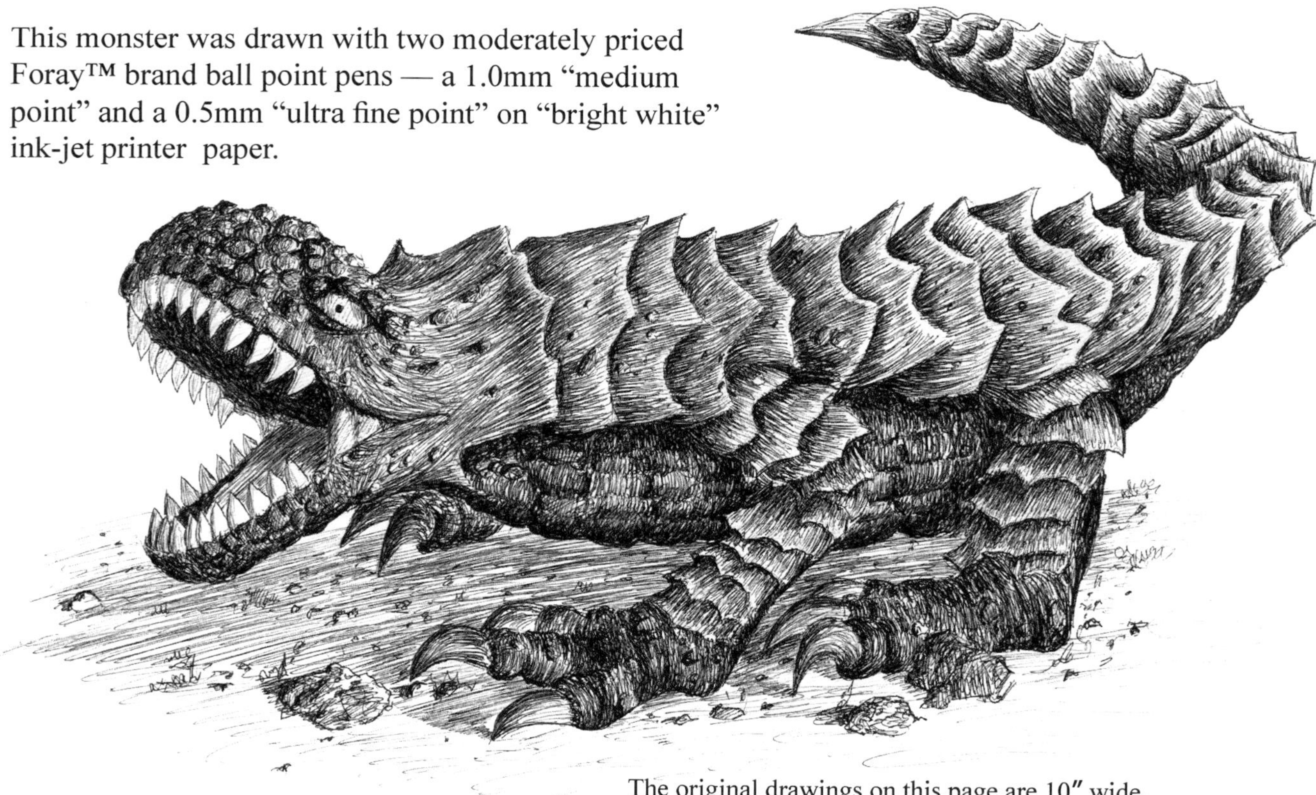

The original drawings on this page are 10″ wide.

Drawing Pencils

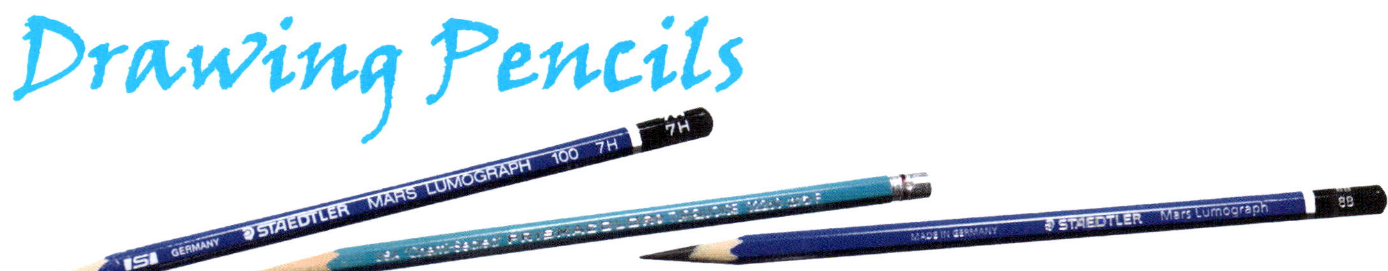

Drawing pencils are offered in a wide range of leads that can be used to produce different shades of gray plus black. The "H" leads are hard and produce lighter lines. The "B" leads are soft and produce darker lines. The "F" and "HB" leads are in-between.

As was demonstrated on the previous page, one middle-grade pencil, such as an HB, can produce both light and dark lines, depending on the force you apply. However, the *quality* of the lines will be different: those produced with H leads will be thinner and sharper than those produced with an HB lead, and those made with a B lead will be thicker and more fuzzy. You will not be able to produce the kind of really dark or black lines with an HB lead that you can with the softer B leads, especially the 7B and 8B's.

Staedtler Mars Lumograph and Sanford graphite pencils are of high quality.

It is not necessary to acquire all sixteen to twenty shades available to produce good drawings. A suitable "palette" *might* include these six shades:

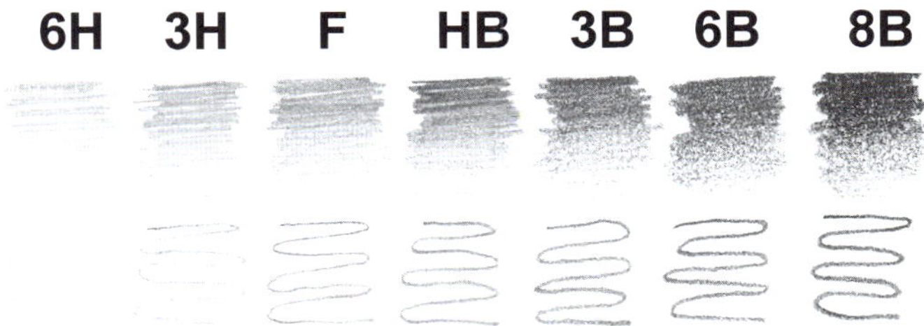

These samples were created with Staedlter pencils. Other companies' 7B and 8B leads may or may not be as dark as Staedlter's.

Producing Very Dark and Black Areas

The "lead" in H and B pencils is actually a combination of **graphite** and clay. When graphite is applied to paper with some force, it can produce an unwanted shiny, glossy surface that reflects light in an unpleasant way when viewed at a certain angle. It will likely NOT appear as dark as you wish.

To produce a very dark area that is not shiny, DO NOT press hard with a 6B or harder lead; instead, use a 7B, 8B, or carbon pencil. (A disadvantage of carbon is that it tends to leave black flecks on the drawing that can smear easily and be somewhat difficult to remove.)

Carbon (not shiny)

8B (slightly shiny)

6B (very shiny)

In this photograph of pencil tips, you can see that the 6B lead is shiny, the 8B less so, and the carbon lead not shiny at all. When you shop for pencils, check out the appearance of the lead in the pencil — some pencils may be labeled "black" or "jet black" or "ebony", but they may still make shiny, not-very-black surfaces.

PENCIL LEADS:

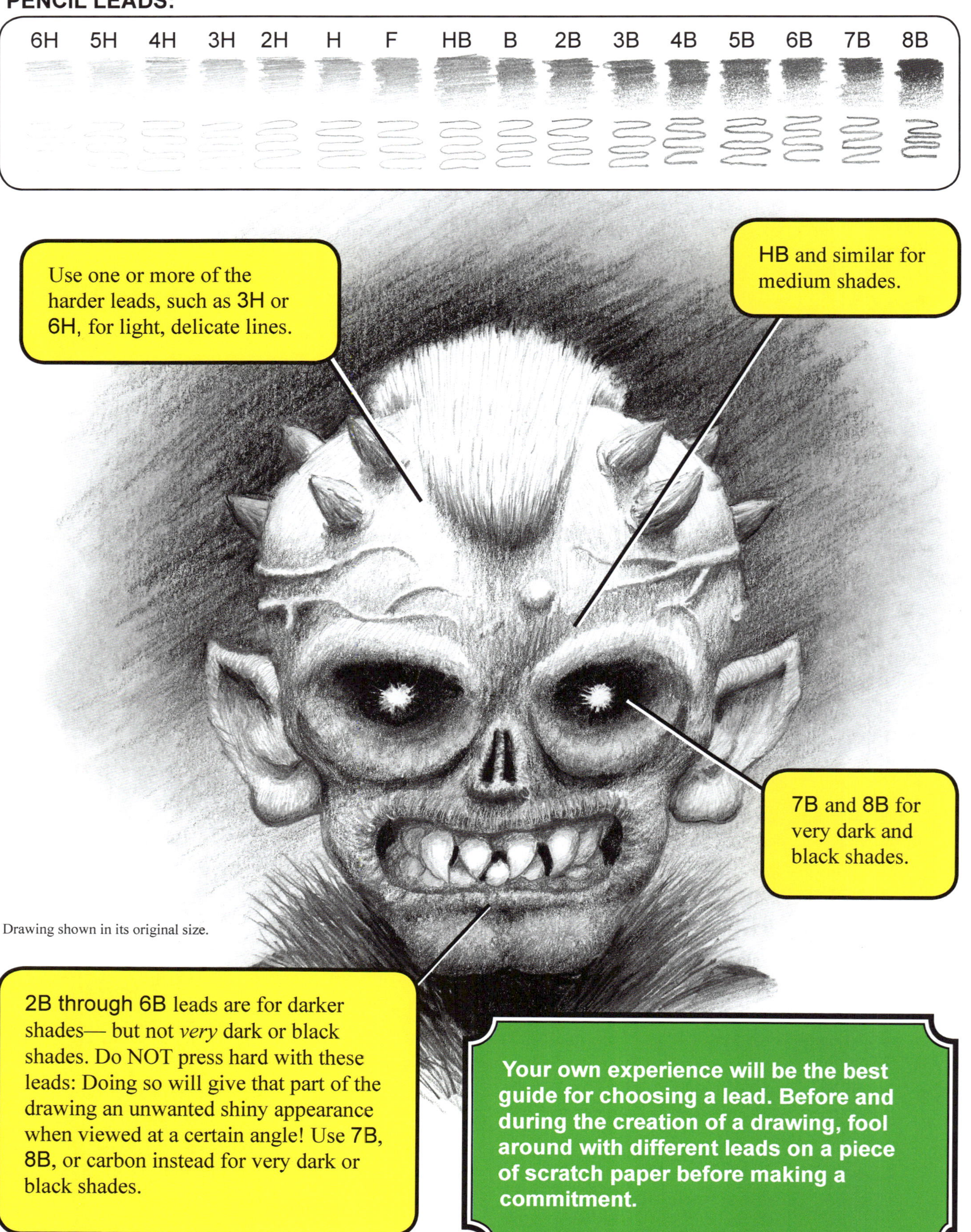

Drawing shown in its original size.

Mechanical Pencils and Lead Holders

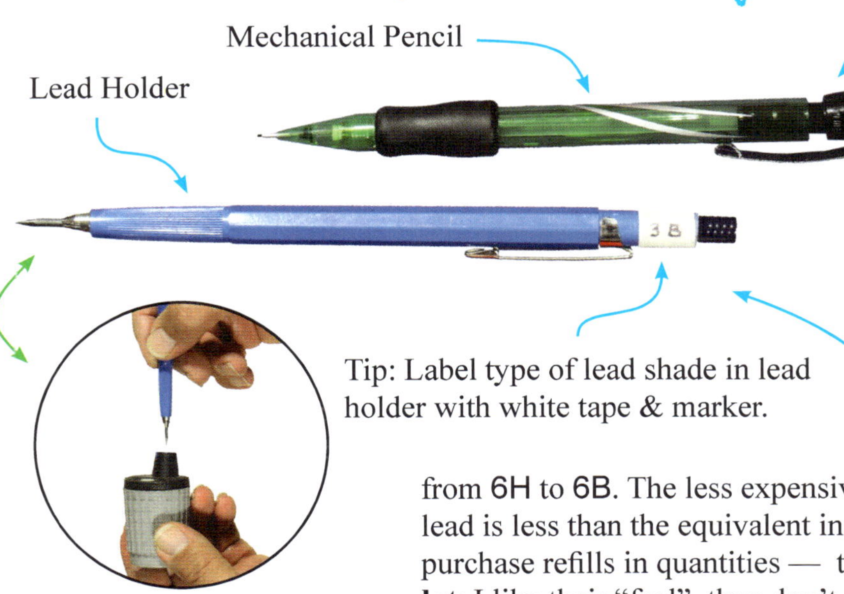

Mechanical pencils hold thin leads — 0.5 mm and 0.7 mm sizes with HB leads are common and recommended. Mechanical pencils are good for making thin lines and for general sketching. (TIP: rotating the pencil as you draw will keep the lines extra sharp.)

Tip: Label type of lead shade in lead holder with white tape & marker.

Lead holders hold thick 2.0 mm diameter leads in shades from 6H to 6B. The less expensive holders are good enough. The price per lead is less than the equivalent in a wood pencil, but it may be necessary to purchase refills in quantities — two or twelve per pack. **I use lead holders a lot**: I like their "feel", they don't get short, and their leads can be brought to a very sharp point with a good lead pointer. They are available at art supply and hobby stores. You may need to go online to find the harder and softer leads (e.g., 6H and 6B). The Sanford brand may offer the widest variety.

Hand-held lead pointers can bring 2.0 mm diameter leads to a very sharp point.

Erasers

Drawings created with the sort of lead pencils discussed on this and the previous two pages are often said to be "graphite" drawings.

When using lead (graphite) pencils...

YOU NEED A Kneaded Eraser!

Unlike most erasers, kneaded erasers do not leave annoying particles, or "crumbs". They do a great job of erasing large areas — especially useful for cleaning up the white portion around the drawing. They are easily molded into moderately sharp points for more precision. They are inexpensive and available in a variety of sizes. (Get the largest you can.) Next to pencils themselves, a kneaded eraser will likely be your most valuable tool when creating grayscale drawings.

Pencil erasers and the erasers at the end of mechanical pencils work well for small areas, though they'll leave eraser crumbs. (See next page.)

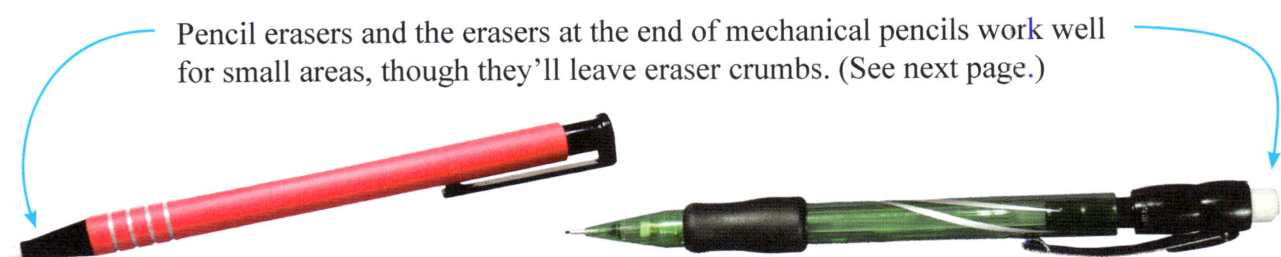

To Remove Eraser Crumbs:

Erasing areas of drawings almost always creates eraser crumbs (except when kneaded erasers are used).

CAREFUL! Removing crumbs with your fingers may smear the drawing. Attempting to blow them away risks spitting on your masterpiece!

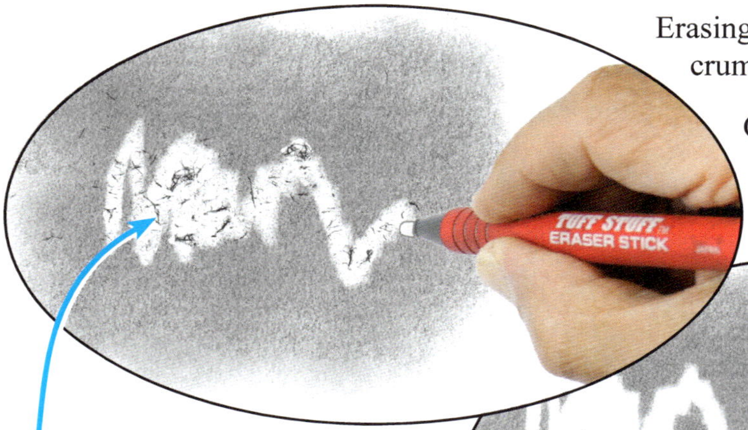

TUFF STUFF ERASER STICK

Eraser crumbs

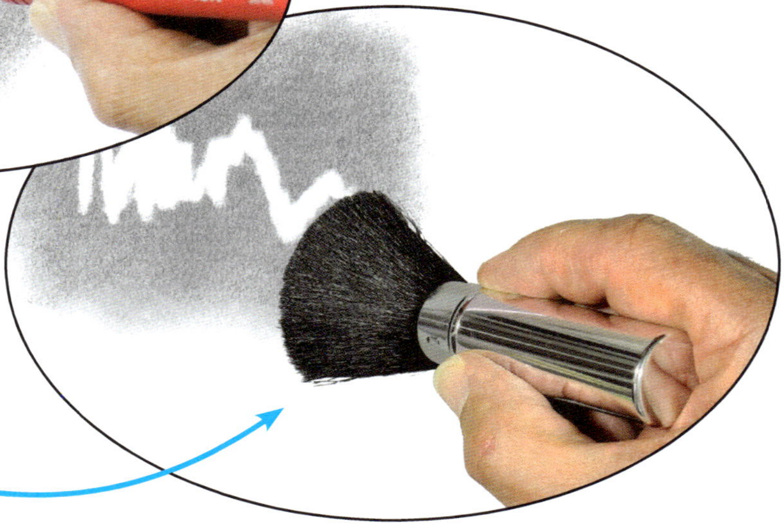

Use A *very soft* brush to remove crumbs. A makeup brush, available at cosmetic counters, works very well.

Paper

Paper is available in a range of surface textures, from very smooth to very rough. The surface you choose will affect the look of your drawing. When you apply a pencil with light to medium pressure, the "grain" of the paper will show: the rougher the surface, the more grainy its appearance.

Smooth surfaced paper, typically designed for pens or computer printing, allows you to create sharp lines with regular lead and colored pencils. However, you can lay down more intense, richer shades with **medium grain** drawing paper while still making lines that are reasonably sharp.

Medium grain drawing paper is recommended for most regular lead and colored pencil use.

The grainy texture of heavy, rough surfaced paper, such as that often used for watercolor paintings, will show through despite your best efforts and will likely be distracting.

Different levels of graininess are illustrated on the next page.

Your paper should allow for vigorous, complete erasing without the paper being damaged. It should be fairly thick: paper labeled 115 gsm or higher is thick enough for most drawings. (gsm = **g**rams per **s**quare **m**eter.)

Artists are not united in their choice of specific brands: **Stonehenge** and **Canson** drawing papers were used for many of the illustrations in this book and I recommend them, especially Stonehenge. Some artists recommend Strathmore 400 series and BFK Rives paper.

Ironically, **fine art printmaking paper**, though not designed for drawing, does in fact provide an **excellent surface for pencil drawing**. It can, however, be rather expensive. I have used fine printmaking paper for my professional portraiture work. (Not to be confused with computer print paper!)

Inexpensive drawing papers found at big box stores such as Target may be entirely adequate — as long as they are acid free.

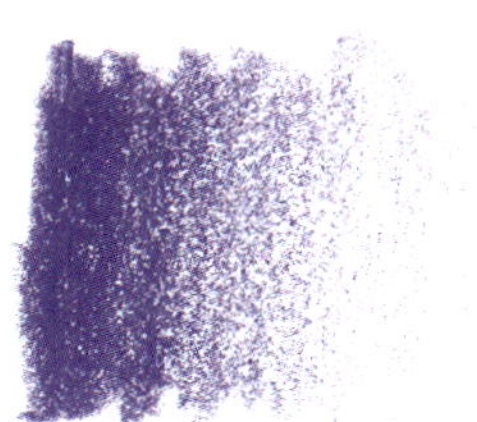
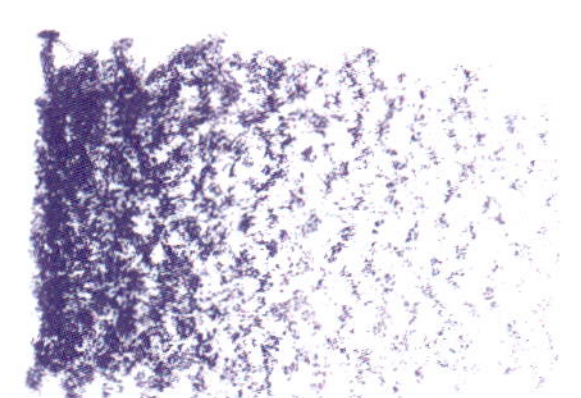

Colored pencil on...

Very smooth surfaced paper

Computer printing paper

Medium grain drawing paper

Watercolor paper

ACID-FREE PAPER

If you want your artwork to last, be sure your paper is labeled "acid-free" or "rag"— otherwise it may become yellow, brittle, and appear stained over time. If you are unsure, ask a knowledgeable sales person for guidance.

Most art paper is acid-free these days, except for paper labeled "newsprint".

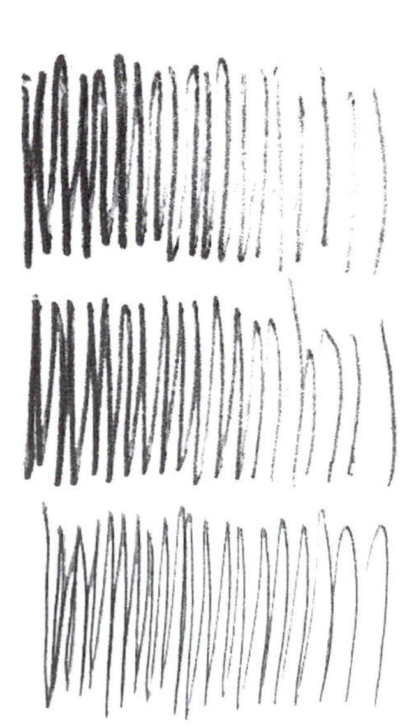

Ball point pen on...

Medium grain drawing paper

Computer printing paper

Smooth surfaced paper for pens

Ball point pens, and many other pens, work best on smooth surfaced paper designed for ink, including good-quality computer paper.

Such paper also works well with HB lead pencils when *only* sharp, clear lines are desired.

Pen samples on the left are enlarged 150% so you can more easily see the difference.

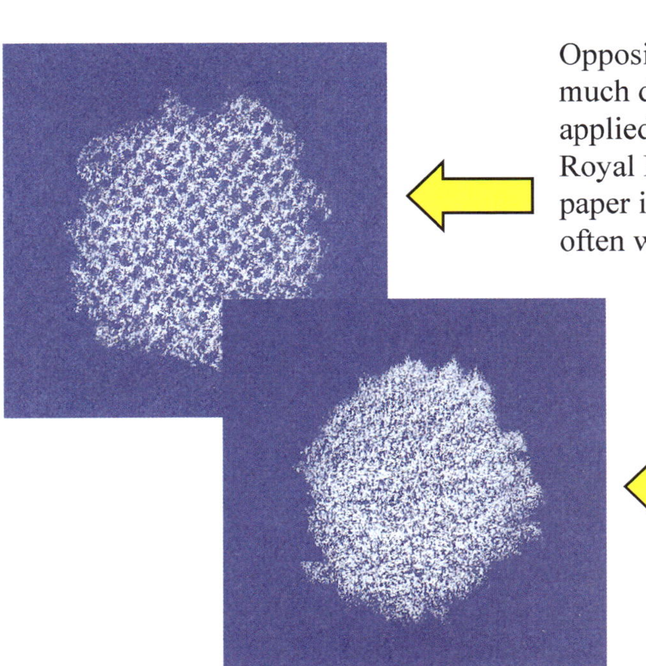

Opposite sides of the same sheet of paper can produce much different results. Here white colored pencil was applied with moderate pressure to Canson Mi-Tientes Royal Blue pastel paper. Note the rough texture. Pastel paper is designed for use with pastels (colored chalk), but often works well with graphite and colored pencils as well.

The same color was applied to the opposite side of the paper. The texture is much smoother. Unless you *like* a rough texture, I suggest you seek out the smoother side.

The opposite sides of some ordinary white drawing papers can also produce different results.

Colored Pencils and Color Sticks

Most of the illustrations in this book were created with Prismacolor® premium grade colored pencils, alone or in combination with markers and water based paints. Although some media, such as pastels and oil colors, can be applied more quickly and *possibly* result in more impressive creations, colored pencils are more affordable, easier to control, non-toxic, and create little mess.

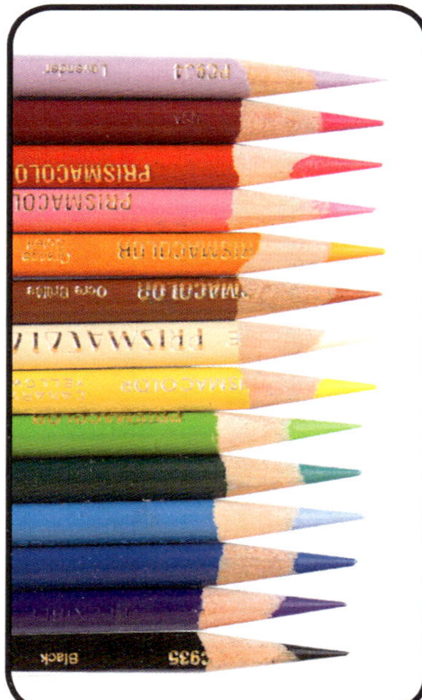

Prismacolor brand soft lead pencils are available individually or in sets of 12, 24, 48, and more than 130 colors. It's nice to have a variety, but you don't need a whole bunch — I have more than a hundred different colors, many of which are rarely used or not used at all!

They are easily sharpened with a standard or electric pencil sharpener.

Less expensive student grade* "Scholar Art Pencils" are available, but only in sets.

Learn more about colored pencils and blenders by visiting www.prismacolor.com.

Student Grade

is a term often applied to art materials that are more affordable to people with tight budgets, (e.g., students). Such materials, typically available from reputable manufacturers, are lower in quality than regular materials, but are often satisfactory.

Thin lead colored pencils, such as Prismacolor® Verithin® pencils, have leads that are harder than those shown above. Although they can be brought to a sharper point, stay sharp longer, and break less easily, they do not produce the same deep rich colors. They should be used only when very thin lines and the filling in of small areas is required. As an alternative, you should consider fine point markers mentioned on page 19.

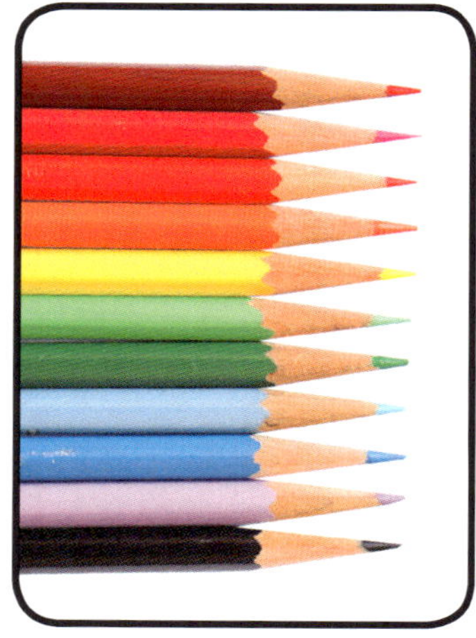

Prismacolor Art Stix are thick blocks of solid color. They are good for coloring large areas quickly but not so great if you want to saturate the paper with pigment so the white "flecks" of paper underneath do not show.

Colored Pencil Blender

Blenders are great for smoothing out and blending colors created with colored pencils. They look like colored pencils but have no pigment (color).

They are especially useful for giving the color on the paper a more saturated paint-like appearance.

Notice here that white "flecks" of the paper show through the not blended samples much more than with the blended samples.

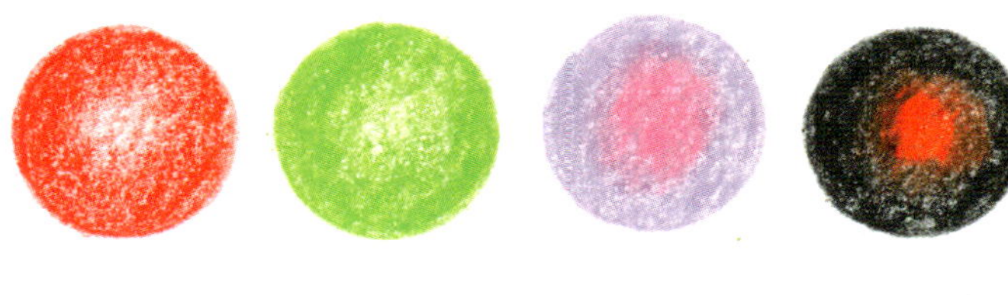

Not blended.

You can also blend with white and colors that are lighter than the colors you are blending; in fact, that is often recommended. (See page 48.)

You'll see examples of blending in the illustration on pages 49 - 50 and in other illustrations throughout this book.

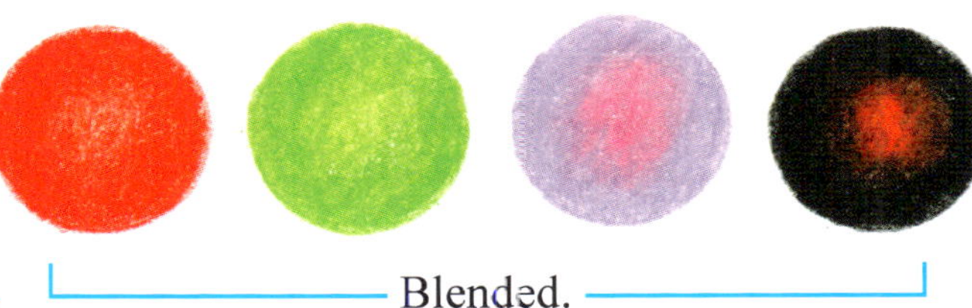

Blended.

The original spheres are 1" in diameter, colored pencil on Canson drawing paper.

Pencil Extenders

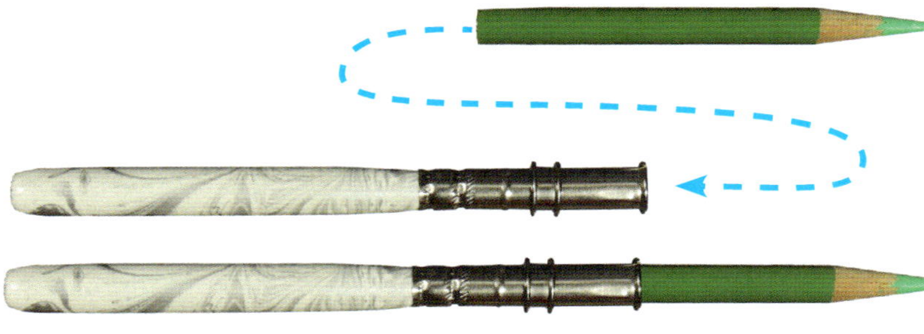

Regular wood graphite pencils and colored pencils will eventually become so short they will be hard to handle. You can "lengthen" them and get more life out of them (i.e., save money) with pencil extenders.

Electric Eraser

I had thought that owning an electric eraser would be an unnecessary luxury … until I bought one! Now I consider it an essential tool. It does a wonderful job of erasing colors laid down by colored pencils easily, precisely, and quickly — an almost impossible task with ordinary erasers.

It works on regular graphite drawings as well.

Moderately priced ($10+) electric erasers may be found at Hobby Lobby, Michaels, and similar stores, but they are likely of dubious quality. Higher quality, more expensive ($30+) models are available at art supply stores and online. I use the Sakura brand — shown here, purchased from www.dickblick.com for about $30 — and highly recommend it.

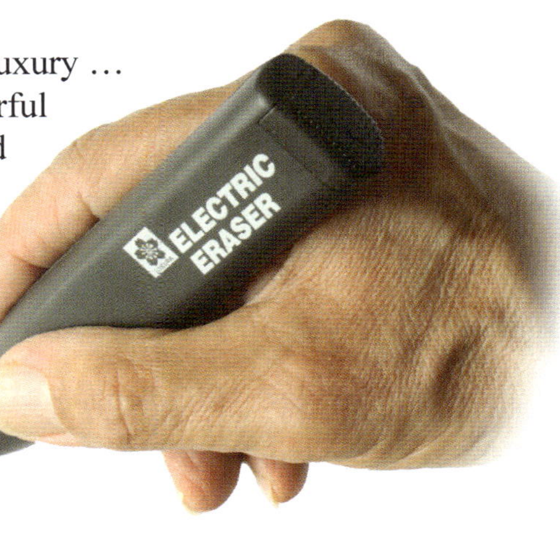

About Lightfast Colors

Some colors change or fade in several weeks when exposed to light; others change very little or not at all after many years of exposure. These latter are said to be *lightfast*. Just how lightfast depends largely on the minerals and chemicals that give colored pencils and other media their color.

In the example below, colors produced by an inexpensive Crayola® brand fluid marker, a colored pencil rated "poor" for lightfastness, and a colored pencil labeled rated "excellent" were exposed to different kinds of light for several months:

- The **blue marker** did not fare well at all: its color changed when exposed in a sunlit room, and faded completely away when exposed to direct sunlight!
- The **orange colored pencil** with a "poor" lightfast rating did OK in the sunlit room but not direct sunlight. Note: a color that fades in direct sunlight will eventually fade, over a longer period of time, in *indirect* sunlight.
- The **red colored pencil** with an "excellent" lightfast rating did well in all three conditions.

Conclusion

As long as you **do not expose your artwork to direct sunlight**, you probably do not have to worry about color changes or fading with most, but not all, Prismacolor pencils.

If you need to be assured your artwork will last a very long time, here's how to learn more about lightfastness and acquire ratings for Prismacolor pencils:

- Search the internet for "lightfast color chart - Prismacolor" and click on the entry that lists **www.prismacolor.com**. The company offers a printable PDF chart similar to this one with lightfast ratings from I (excellent) to V (poor). If you can't find the chart, click "contact" on their website and request it.
- Visit the Colored Pencil Society of America's website, **www.cspa.org** to learn more about lightfastness and colored pencils in general.

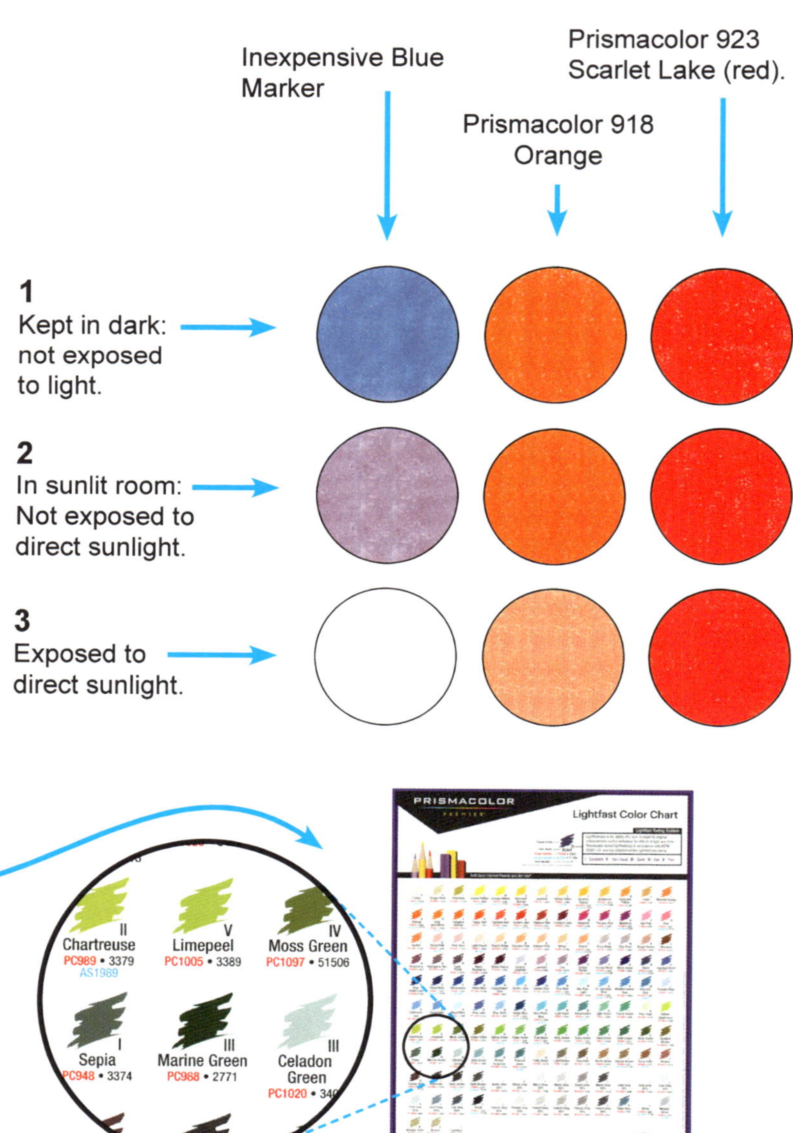

Fixative

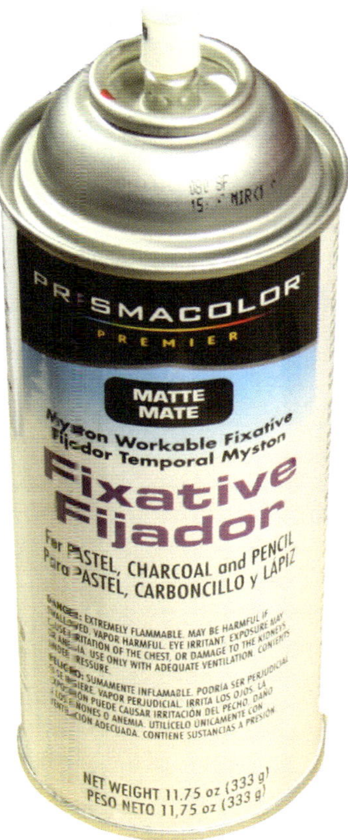

To keep graphite artwork from smudging, you (or an adult if you are young) will need to spray it with a fixative, which permanently "fixes" all the graphite particles onto the paper.

Fixative must also be applied to drawings made with Prismacolor colored pencils in order to keep them from developing a waxy "bloom" on the surface. This should be done just after completion; if, however, the drawing has sat for several days unfixed, the surface of the drawing may need to be wiped with a soft cloth — then fixed.

CAUTION!

Breathing fumes from fixatives can be

DANGEROUS TO YOUR HEALTH!

You'll learn more on pages 77 & 78.

Pencil Sharpeners

It is usually necessary to keep both graphite and colored pencils sharp: the use of a good quality pencil sharpener is required. The inexpensive Prismacolor hand-held sharpener would be a good choice. With a KUM® hand-held sharpener (also affordable), you can remove the wood around the lead in the first hole, then bring the lead to a very sharp point in the second hole. The moderately priced Dahle hand-cranked rotary sharpener automatically disengages when the desired pre-set sharpness is reached. A spring clamp grips and automatically feeds the pencil, allowing you to steady the sharpener with one hand and crank the handle with the other. It disassembles for easily removing broken lead parts (which sometimes happens). Visit www.dahle.com for more info. Multipoint is a similar brand for about the same price. Search online for "multipoint pencil sharpener".

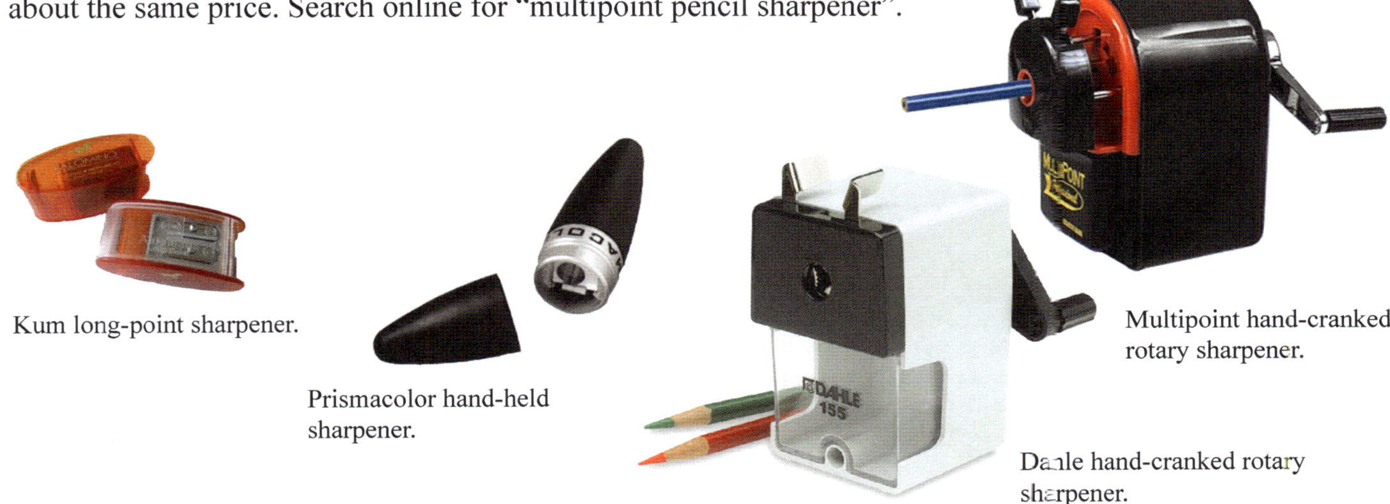

Kum long-point sharpener.

Prismacolor hand-held sharpener.

Multipoint hand-cranked rotary sharpener.

Dahle hand-cranked rotary sharpener.

Colored pencils need frequent sharpening — as often as once a minute. For those who prefer to spend more time drawing than sharpening pencils, an electric sharpener is strongly advised. They may be more costly than hand-held and hand-cranked models, but worth their cost to the serious artist.

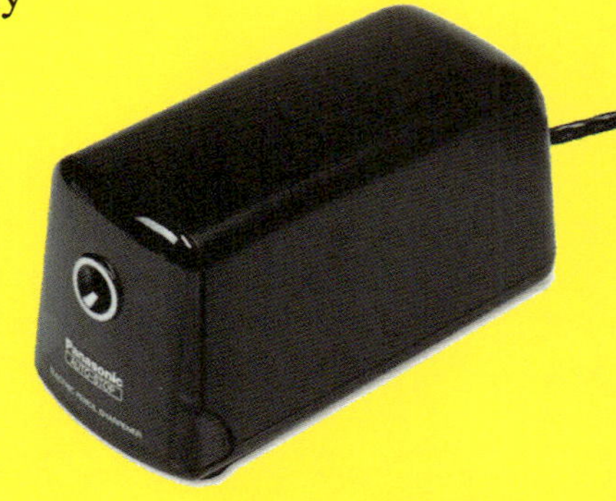

If you visit www.amazon.com and search "electric pencil sharpeners", you'll find reviews of sharpeners such as the Panasonic KP380-BK, which has been recommended by colored pencil artists.

A plug-in type will likely perform better than a battery-operated model.

TIPS

- **You'll have better luck if you hold a colored pencil vertically when sharpening with a hand-held sharpener.**
- **When using a hand-cranked or electric rotary sharpener, first sharpen a graphite pencil each day before using colored pencils. This lubricates the sharpening blades and reduces chances of damage.**

Other Media

The term *media*, as used in this book, refers to materials used to create art on paper: Pencils, colored pencils, markers, watercolors, acrylics, and oil paints are all media (also called *mediums*).

For this book I have favored mostly graphite and colored pencils. There are, however, many other kinds of media that can be used to create great pictures of monsters and aliens. Some deserve brief consideration:

Ball Point Pens

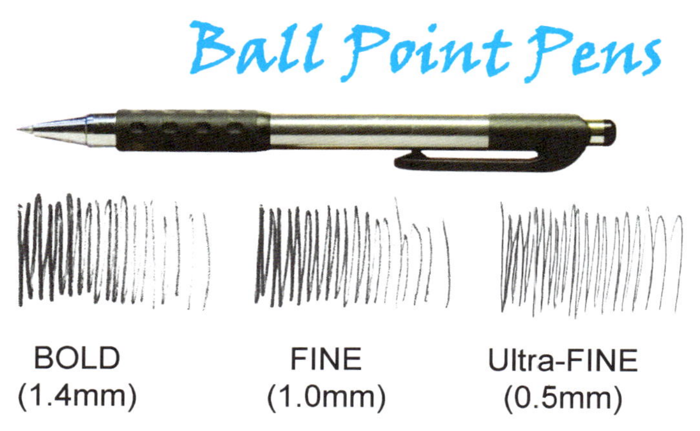

Ball point pens deserve respect in the art world.

- Decent quality pens are moderately priced, such as the Foray™ brand 0.5 and 1.0 "Precision Point" pens used for the drawing on page 8.
- They can, depending on the force you apply, be used to create lines of varying density and are easy to control.
- They are available in different sizes.

Markers

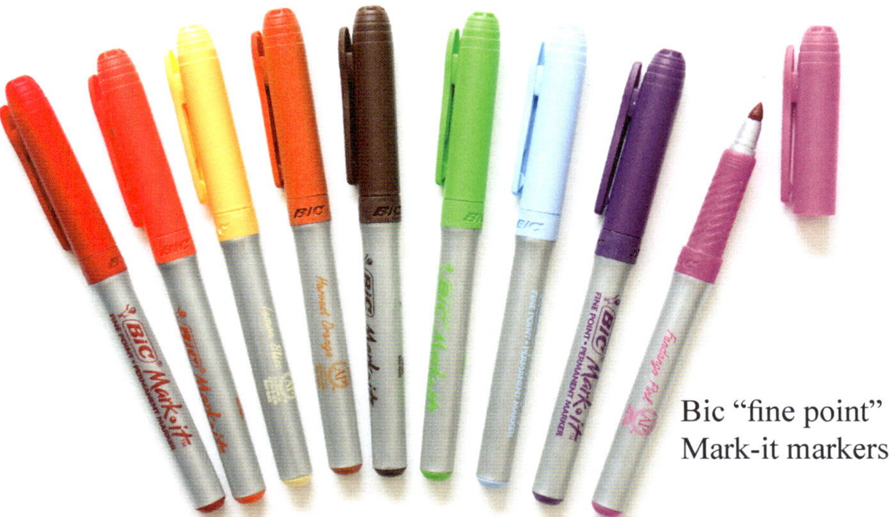

Bic "fine point" Mark-it markers

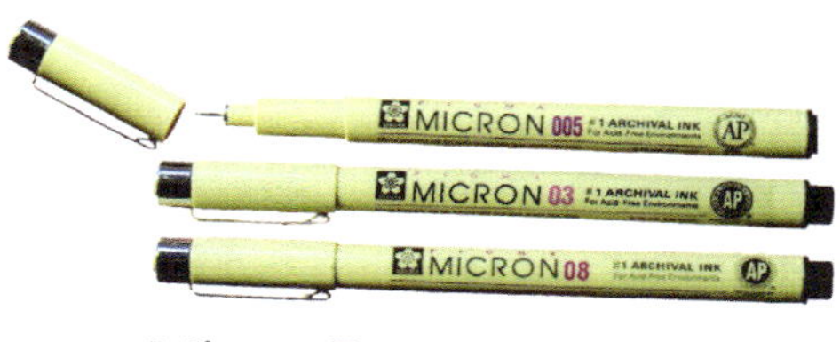

Micron Pens

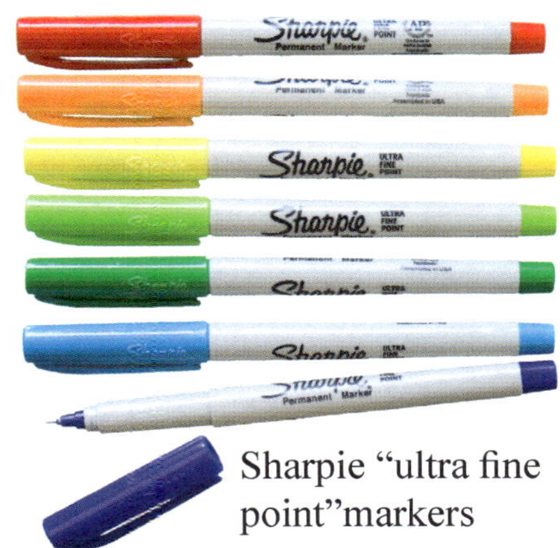

Sharpie "ultra fine point"markers

Micron®, Bic®, and Sharpie® brand markers and pens are good for outlining and shading by themselves or in combination with colored pencils. Their ink is said to be fade resistant.

Micron brand pens are available in six different line thicknesses and up to 14 different colors.

Sharpie and Bic Mark-it™ markers are available in two thicknesses, "fine" and "ultra fine". Sharpie is available in up to 25 colors, Bic up to 36 colors. They are both very good for the price. Their lines, though labeled "fine" and "ultra fine" are in fact not very thin:

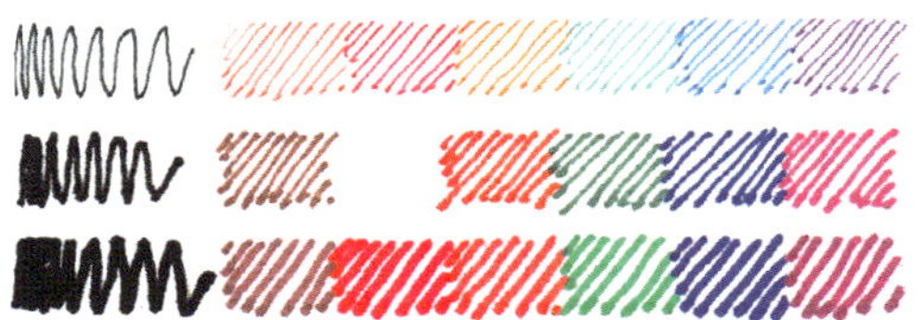

Micron size 01 point

Sharpie "ultra fine" point

Sharpie"fine" point

If your budget allows, I suggest you acquire a Sharpie 25-marker pack. When you run out of a color you may be able to replace it: Stores such as Target, Hobby Lobby and Michael's often carry a variety of individual Sharpie markers. (Personally, I favor Bic Mark-it packages of 36 markers — so many colors to choose from — but individual replacements are hard to come by.)

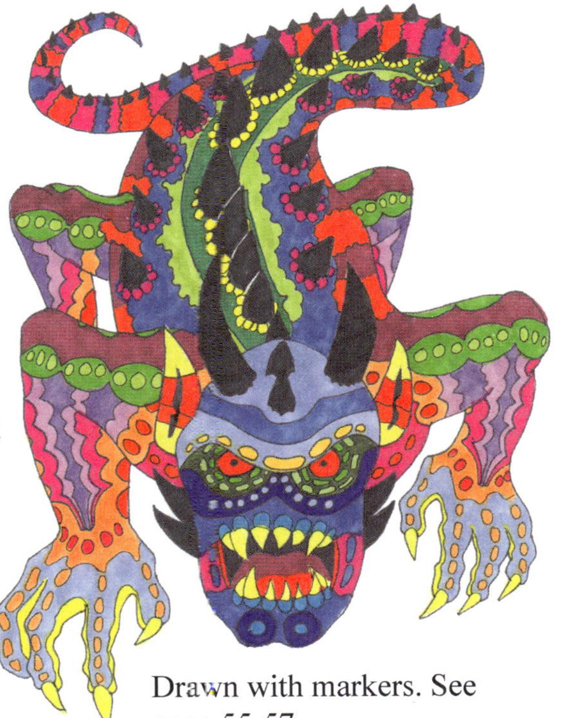

Drawn with markers. See page 55-57.

Professional Grade Broad-tipped Art Markers

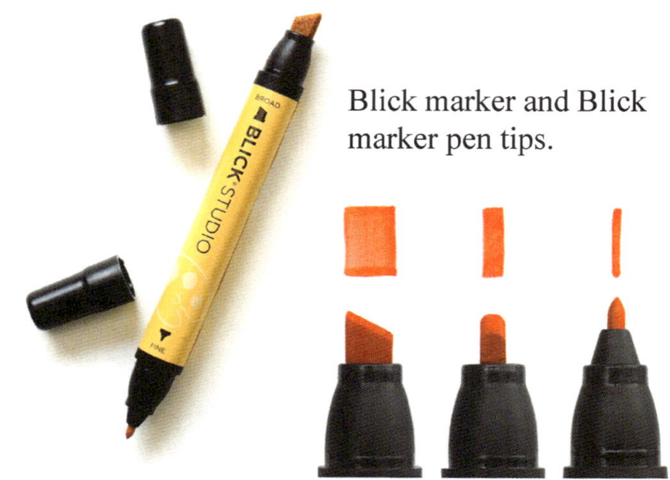

Blick marker and Blick marker pen tips.

Professional grade (i.e., expensive) broad tipped markers can lay down bright colors very quickly. I suggest you use alcohol-based markers such as Prismacolor and less-expensive Blick Studio Markers that do not contain xylene.

Though xylene-based Chartpak® Ad Markers® and similar markers may be certified nontoxic, breathing their fumes tells my nose to be wary — that plus research into the effects of xylene. Besides, their colors tend to "bleed" when not using special marker paper, making it difficult to create lines with sharp edges.

A big advantage of professional grade markers is that they can be purchased one-at-a-time from as many as 96 different colors. If you run out of a color you don't have to buy a whole new set.

CAUTION

Some artists materials contain toxic substances that can be dangerous, especially to younger artists. Some markers, for example, contain xylene — a chemical that can damage the skin and lungs. Some paints have cancer-causing pigments such as cadmium. Handle such materials with care or, better yet, use alternative materials that do not contain dangerous substances.

TIP

NOTE: Markers tend to seep through some papers. Use throw-away paper underneath!

When using pens by themselves, use a paper whose label states that it accepts "pen and ink".

When using pens with water color and/ or colored pencils, look for paper clearly designated for use with mixed media, such as **Strathmore Mixed Media** or **Canson XL Mix Media** paper. Tablet covers will indicate use for "wet and dry media" or "Acrylic / Watercolor / Pen and Pencil" or similar phrasing. Consider 140lb paper or thicker if possible.

TIP

Marker lines on colored pencil drawings will appear sharper if they are applied *after* the drawing is sprayed with fixative.

Transparent Watercolors and Gouache

You can usually see through transparent watercolors. Gouache ("gwash") is a thicker watercolor that tends to hide what's underneath, depending on the pigment (color) used. Each can be used with colored pencils and other media. They vary greatly in price, depending on quality.

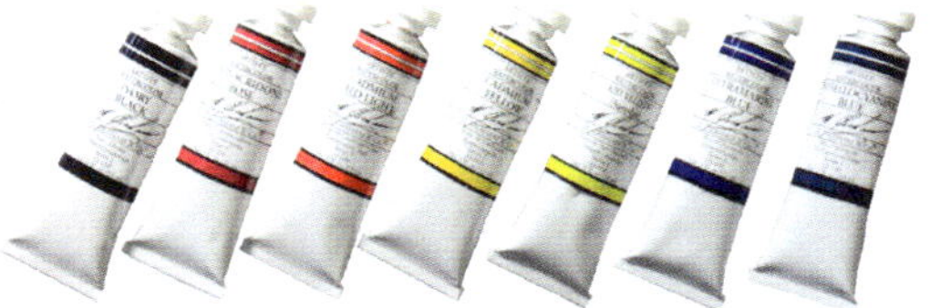

M. Graham produces high quality transparent watercolors and gouache, available in individual tubes. Create most any color from these seven: Hansa Yellow, Azo Yellow, Naphithol Red, Quinacridone Violet, Anthraquinone Blue, Phthalo Green and titanium white.

Savoir Faire® and Art Advantage® produce moderately priced watercolors and gouaches of lesser, but probably adequate quality. You'll need to purchase a whole new set if you run out of one color.

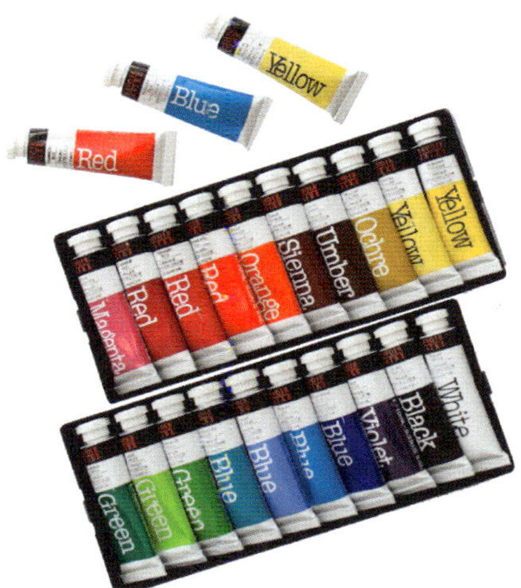

On pages 57-59 you'll learn a cool way to use watercolors and colored pencils together to make large painting/drawings quickly and easily.

Acrylics

Regular **Acrylics** (ak-kril-iks) are water based colors that dry very quickly and, once dry, cannot be changed. GOLDEN OPEN ACRYLICS dry more slowly, making it easier to make smooth blends and such before drying. Heavy body acrylics are as thick as toothpaste; fluid acrylics flow like cream.

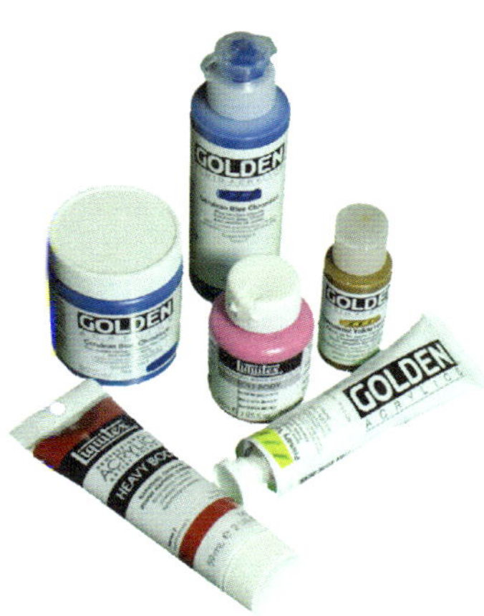

www.goldenpaints.com

Oil Paints

Although **oil paints** have been used for centuries by the world's most accomplished artists, and are still in wide use, many artists are turning to other media due to oil's toxicity. Many solvents used in oil painting have obnoxious and possibly dangerous fumes and can be a danger to one's skin. Oils are also expensive, messy, and difficult to clean up. They are definitely NOT recommended for young artists. (For art outside this book I use M. Graham's oils, which are walnut oil based and can be thinned with walnut oil rather than a solvent. They are much safer.)

Crayons, Water-based Markers, Poster paints & Tempera

Although crayons do not lend themselves to making the sort of precise, detailed drawings illustrated in this book, they may be suitable for beginners on a *very* limited budget.

I DO NOT recommend very cheap markers, tempera, and poster paints whose quality is poor and whose color will likely fade over time.

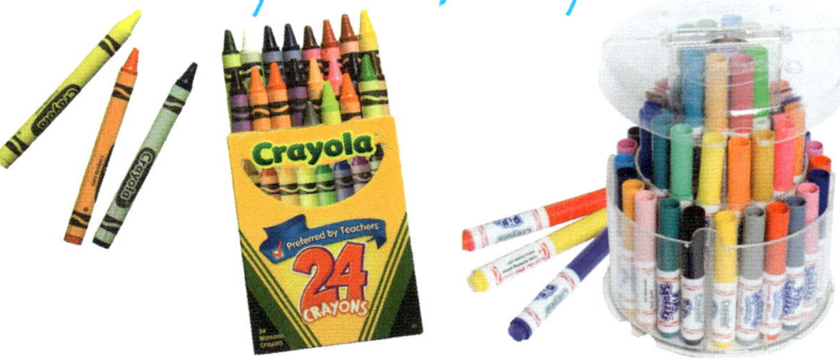

Draw a MONSTER! as a LINE DRAWING

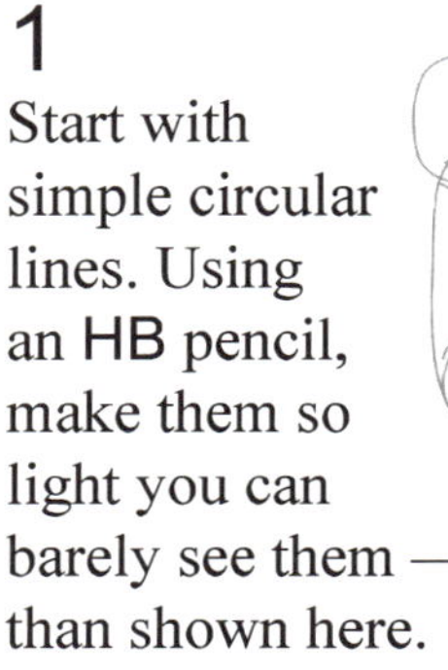

1

Start with simple circular lines. Using an HB pencil, make them so light you can barely see them — lighter than shown here.

DO NOT be tempted to use a harder H lead because it will be more difficult to erase.

These lines will be your *guide lines.* They will help you establish the overall size of the monster and help you make sure that one part is not too big or too small compared to another part.

2

Erase some of the lines that might get in your way when you make more lines. Use a kneaded eraser, described on page 11.

3

Although it is not necessary, you can draw a *center line*, perhaps with a ruler, to help keep your drawing balanced, so that stuff on the left looks pretty much like stuff on the right.

4

Add more circular lines if necessary, then start drawing *feature lines* — the monster's outline, muscles, eyes, etc. These do not have to be precise, since you are likely to partially erase and redraw them.

Refer to monster anatomy drawings starting on page 82 to get the muscles right.

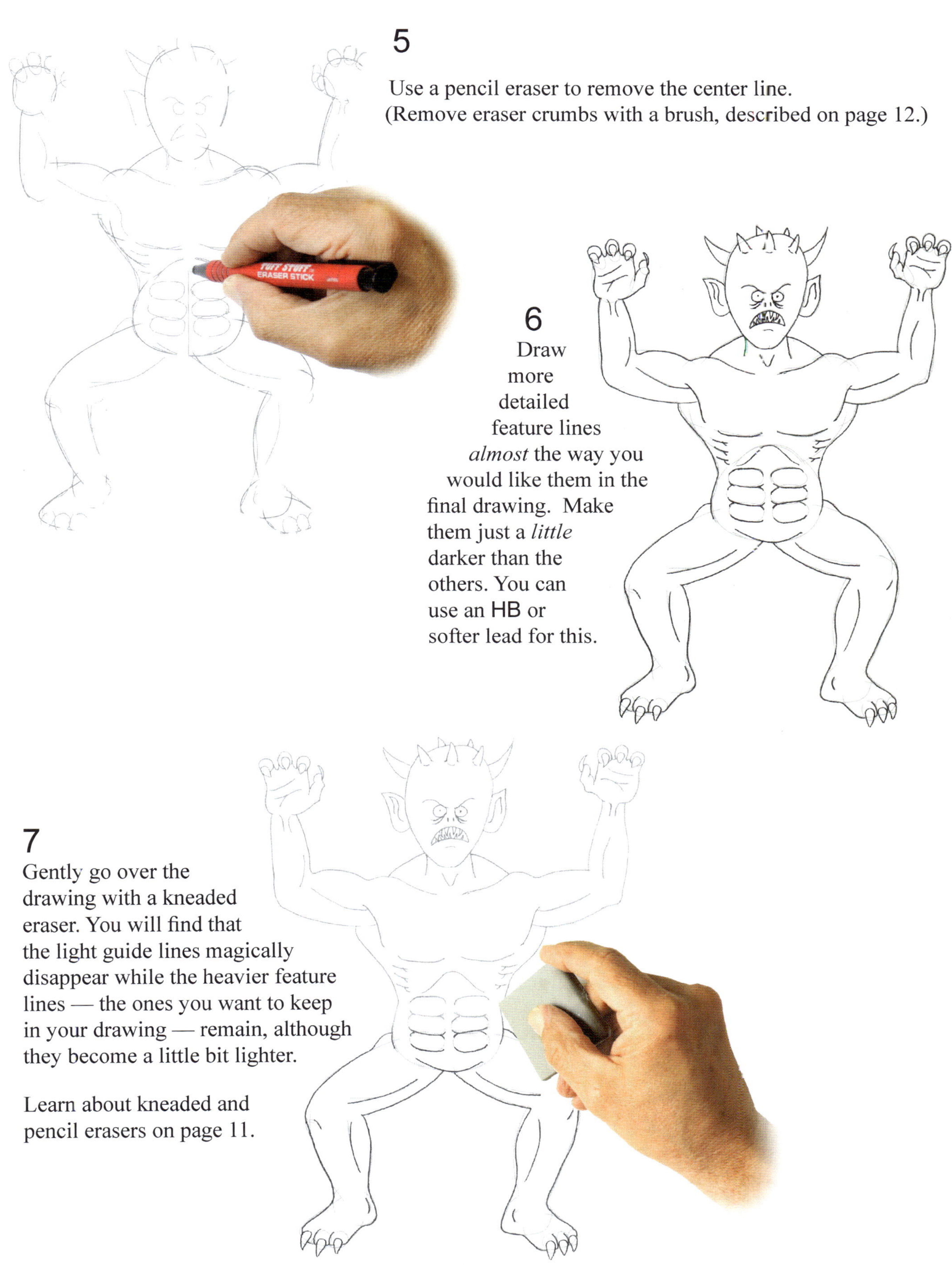

5

Use a pencil eraser to remove the center line.
(Remove eraser crumbs with a brush, described on page 12.)

6

Draw more detailed feature lines *almost* the way you would like them in the final drawing. Make them just a *little* darker than the others. You can use an HB or softer lead for this.

7

Gently go over the drawing with a kneaded eraser. You will find that the light guide lines magically disappear while the heavier feature lines — the ones you want to keep in your drawing — remain, although they become a little bit lighter.

Learn about kneaded and pencil erasers on page 11.

8
Darken the feature lines. You can make them more interesting by varying their thickness.

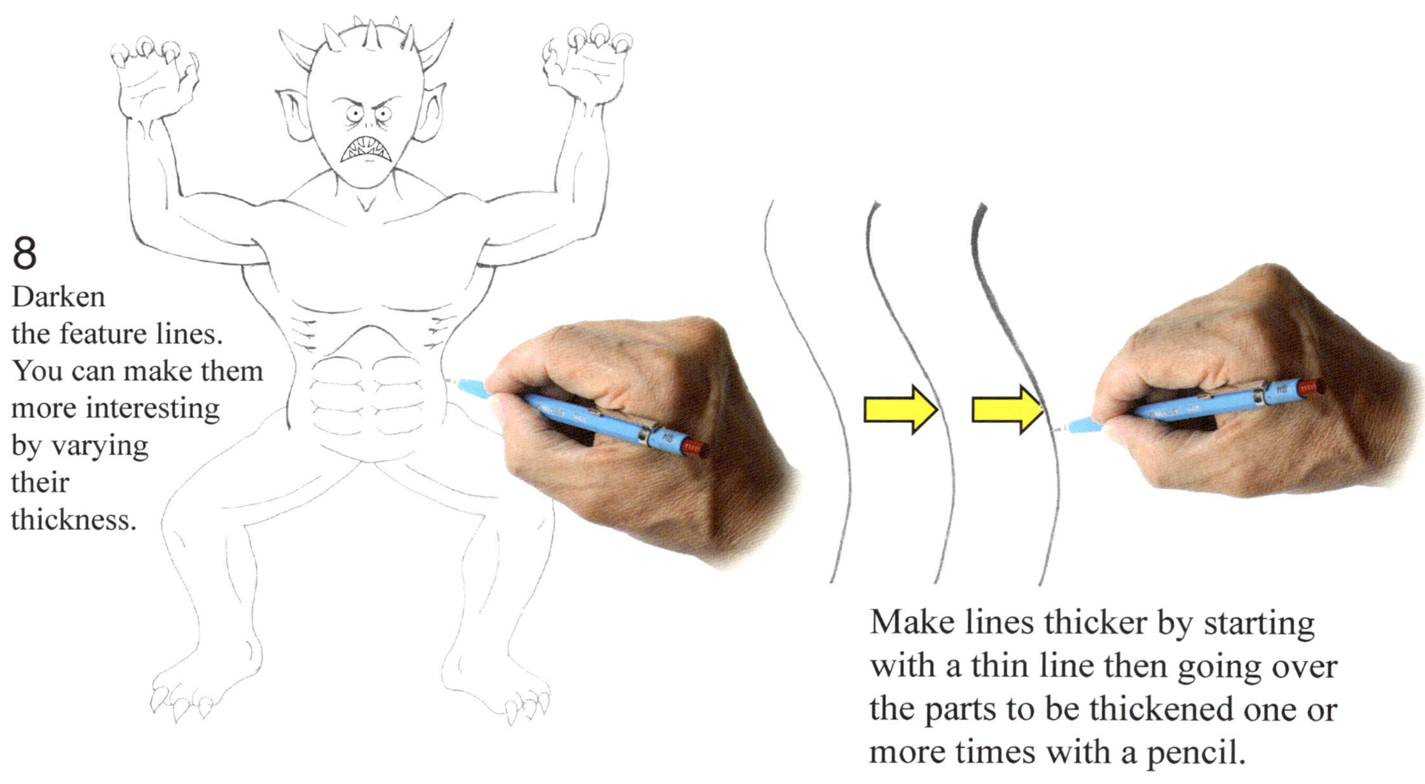

Make lines thicker by starting with a thin line then going over the parts to be thickened one or more times with a pencil.

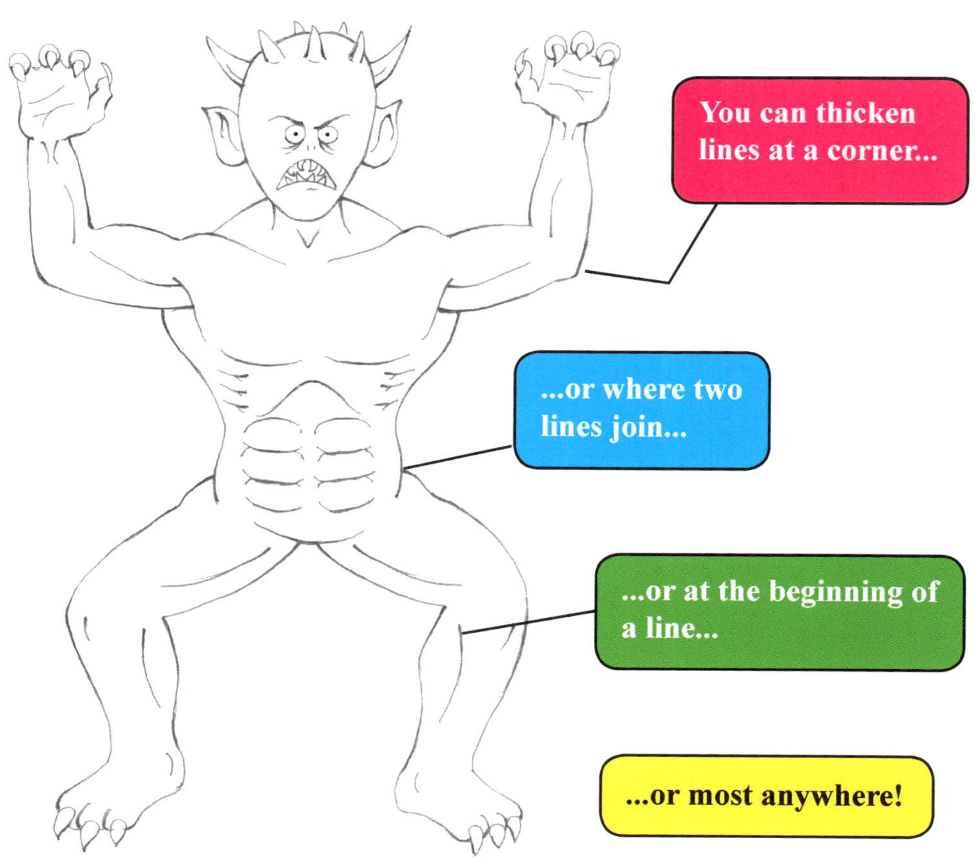

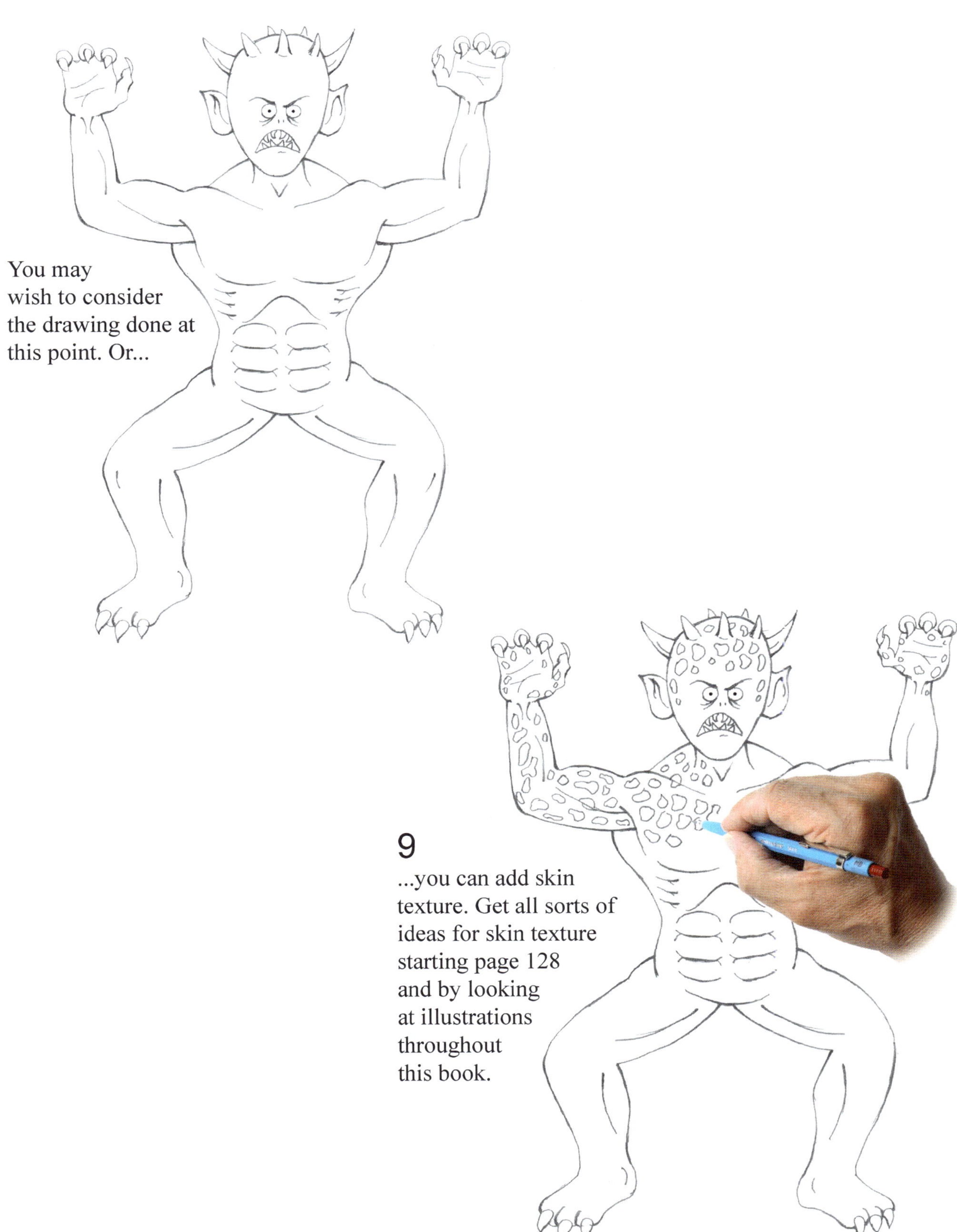

You may wish to consider the drawing done at this point. Or...

9

...you can add skin texture. Get all sorts of ideas for skin texture starting page 128 and by looking at illustrations throughout this book.

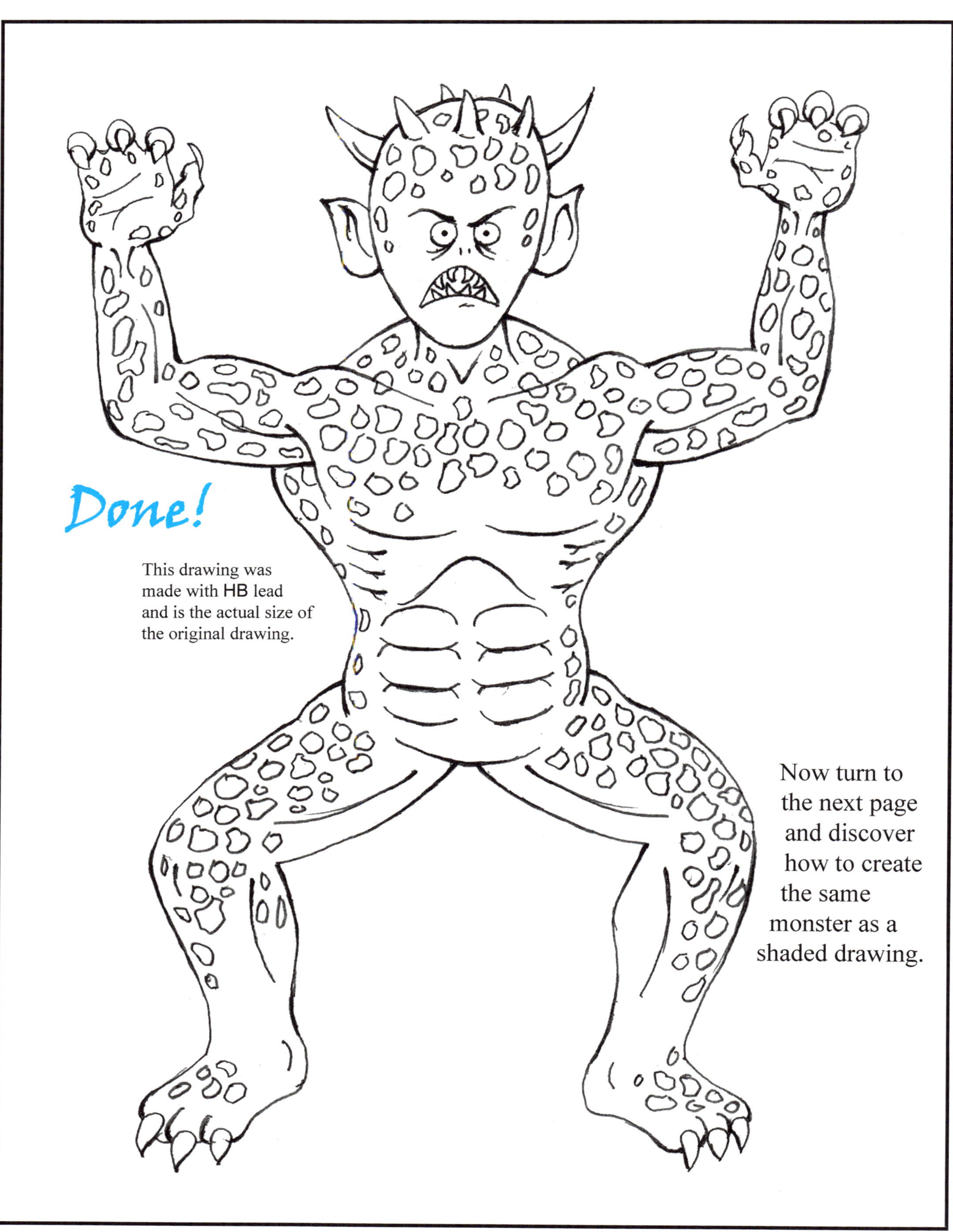
Done!
This drawing was made with HB lead and is the actual size of the original drawing.
Now turn to the next page and discover how to create the same monster as a shaded drawing.

Draw a MONSTER! as a 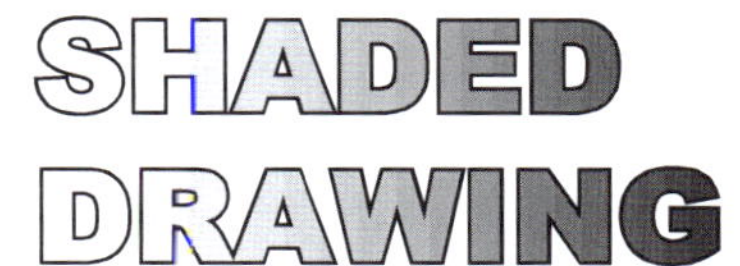

Before you start your drawing, study steps 1 through 10 to get an over-all view of what you'll do. Then create the drawing, first following steps 1 through 4 in a way *similar* to the method illustrated on pages 22 and 23, but note that *soft feature lines* will be kept light, as explained in steps 5, 6, and 7.

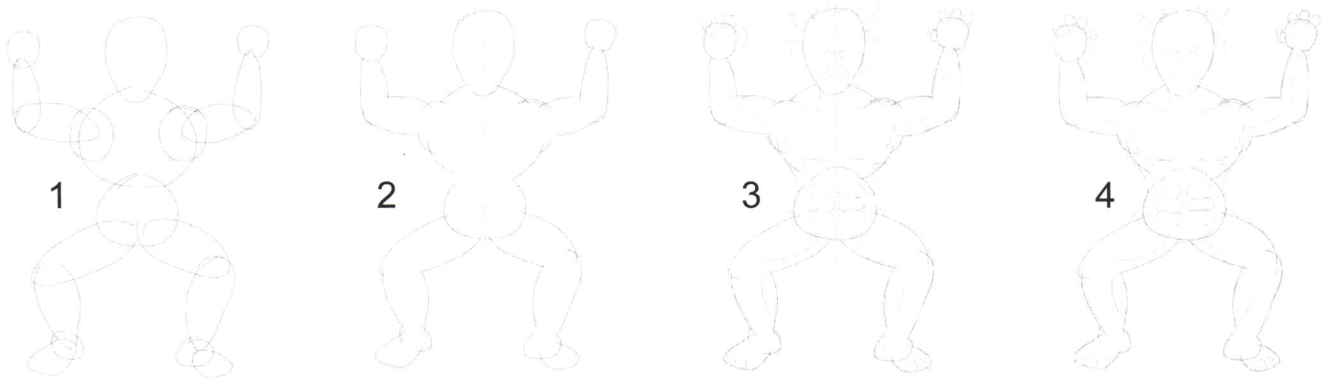

1

Rough guide lines

2

Some guide lines erased. Center line drawn — if you wish.

3

Hard and soft feature lines drawn.

4

Center line erased.

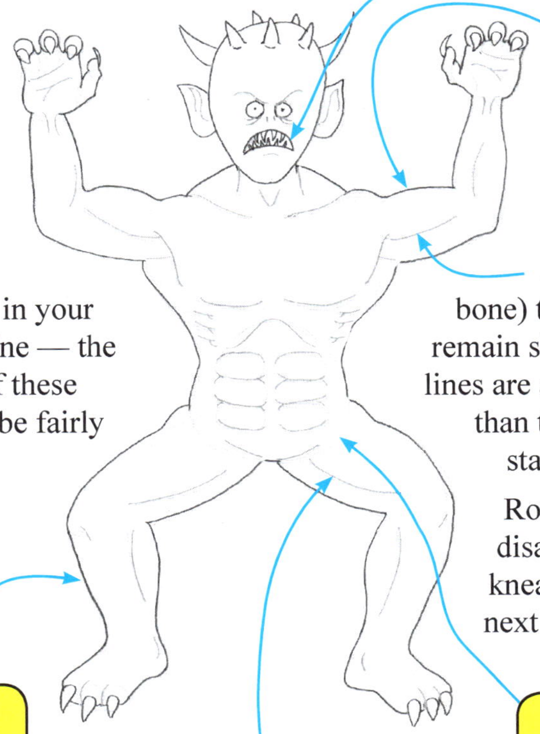

5

Hard feature lines indicate the creature's eyes, teeth, claws, and other items that are to remain *sharp* in your drawing. They also include the outline — the line on the outside of the creature. If these lines are the way you like, they can be fairly dark.

Soft feature lines indicate muscles and some bones (like the collar bone) that will be visible, but *not* remain sharp in the drawing. These lines are at first to be a little darker than the rough guide lines you started with, but not *too* dark.

Rough guide lines are to disappear...probably with your kneaded eraser as shown in the next step.

Hard feature lines

Outline

Soft feature line

Rough guide line (Barely visible)

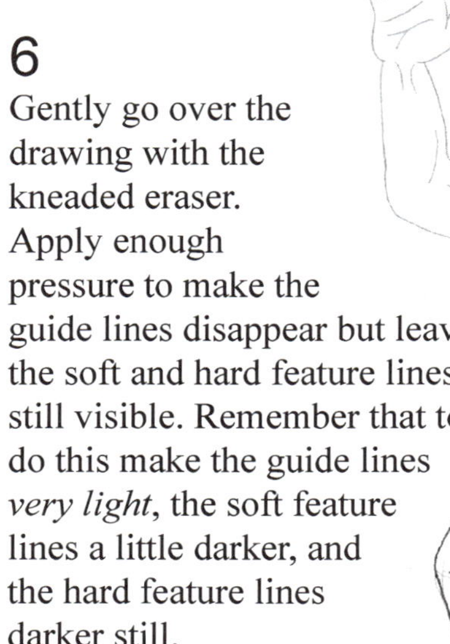

6

Gently go over the drawing with the kneaded eraser. Apply enough pressure to make the guide lines disappear but leave the soft and hard feature lines still visible. Remember that to do this make the guide lines *very light*, the soft feature lines a little darker, and the hard feature lines darker still.

The guide lines are the circular ones you first laid down. For *this* lesson, they are not to appear in the finished drawing.* The hard feature lines will clearly show. The soft feature lines will act as guides for shading and will be *barely visible*.

*Actually, you *can* leave the guide lines and all other lines in the final drawing if you wish. This may be interesting, but for shaded drawings, I recommend erasing guide lines.

Tip

If You choose to transfer your drawing to a new sheet of paper, you can copy just the feature lines without needing to erase the guide lines. Learn how to transfer drawings starting on page 65.

Hard feature line

Soft feature line

Outline

Soft feature line

7

You can complete the outline and hard feature lines at this time or you can wait until you have finished shading. If you wish, darken them and make them more interesting by varying their thickness as shown on page 24.

Do NOT darken the soft feature lines!

(When creating a shaded drawing, some very good artists prefer to have no hard feature lines at all!)

Note that the circular guide lines that were barely visible in the drawing on the previous page have been removed in this drawing.

8

Begin shading. Use a variety of pencil leads if you have them: any of the H series for light tones, HB for medium, any of the B series for dark, and 8B for *really dark* tones (see page 10).

You can get away with an HB lead by simply varying the pressure you apply, but the resulting appearance may not be satisfactory.

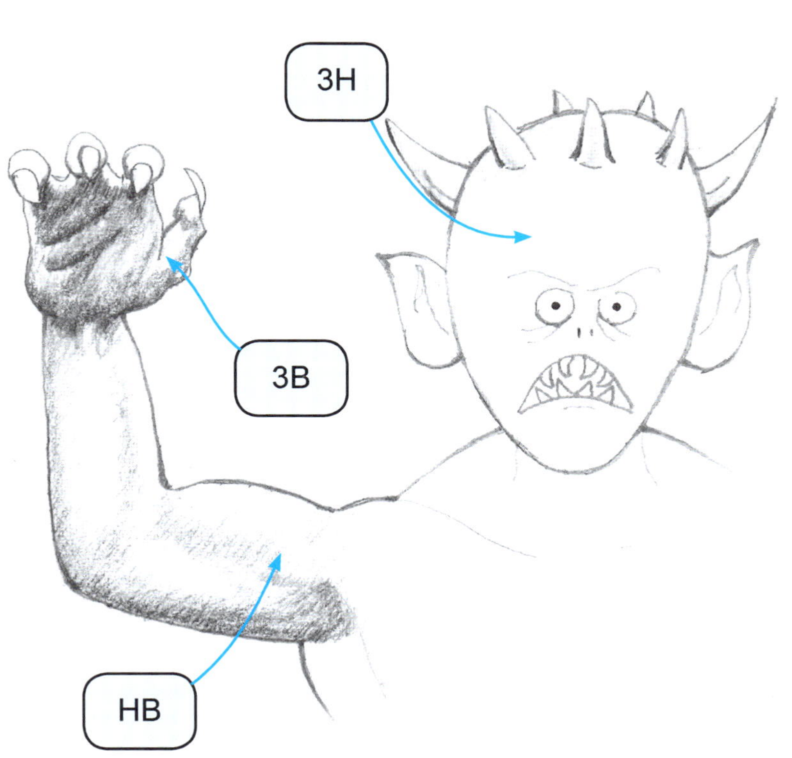

A 7B lead was used near the eyes to create a very dark shadow area. An H series lead was used to slightly shade the eyeballs.

9

Use a pencil eraser or kneaded eraser shaped to a point to "draw" white and lighter lines on an area that's already been shaded.

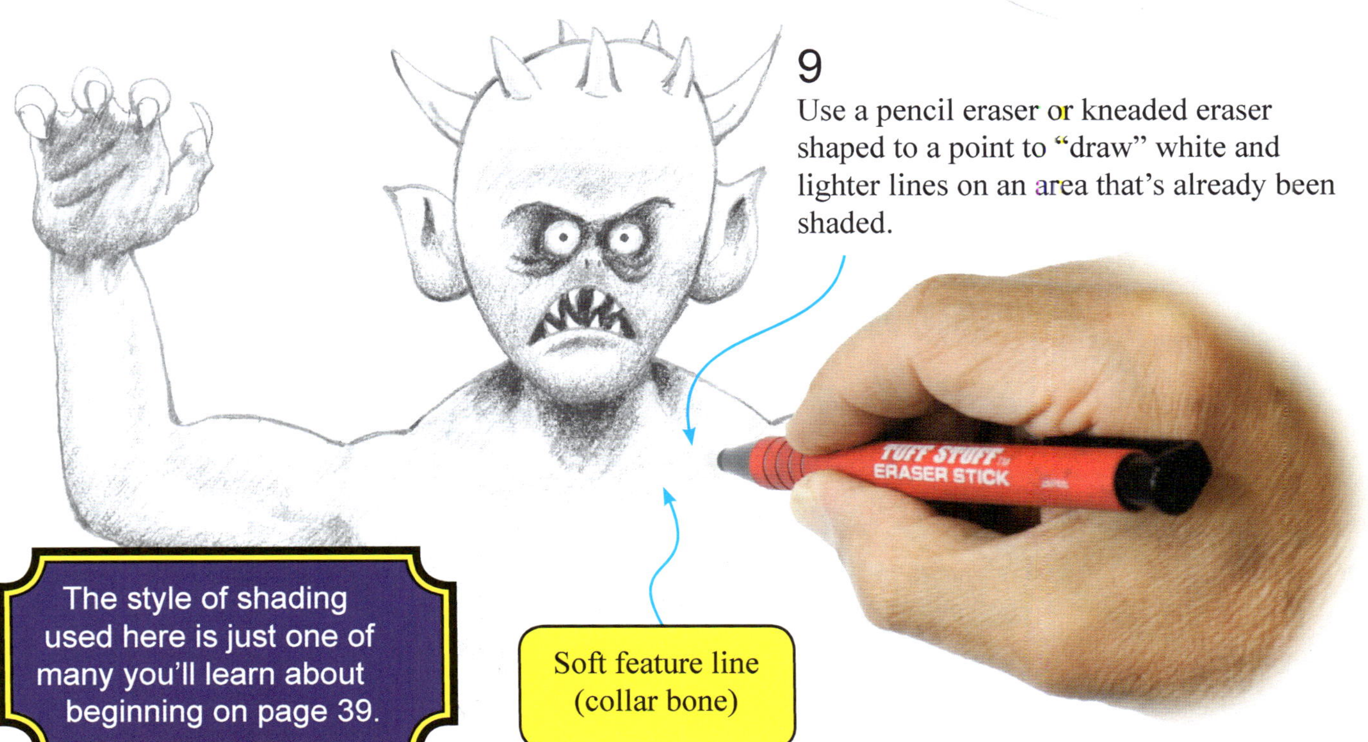

Soft feature line (collar bone)

The style of shading used here is just one of many you'll learn about beginning on page 39.

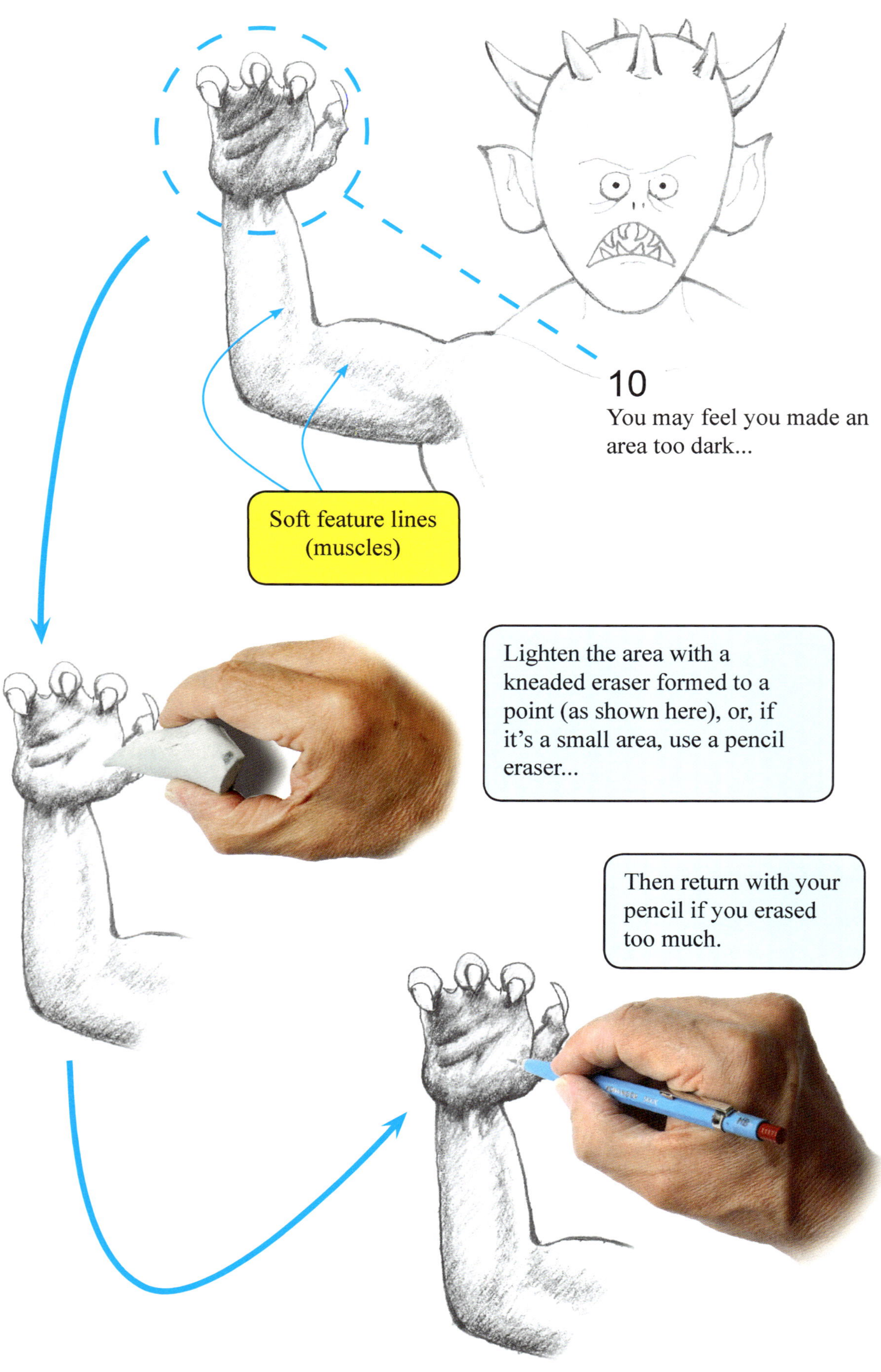

10

You may feel you made an area too dark...

Lighten the area with a kneaded eraser formed to a point (as shown here), or, if it's a small area, use a pencil eraser...

Then return with your pencil if you erased too much.

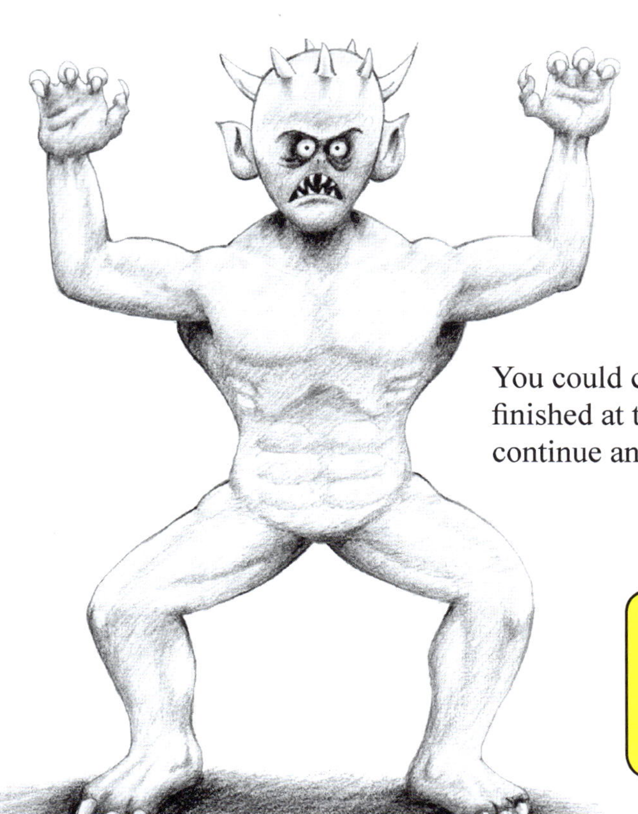

You could consider your drawing finished at this point; or you can continue and add skin texture.

Note that the thin *soft* feature lines that represented muscles in the earlier stages of this drawing are now masked by the smoother, broader shading of those muscles.

11

These spots represent scales — patches that are a bit tougher than skin and raised a little above the skin.

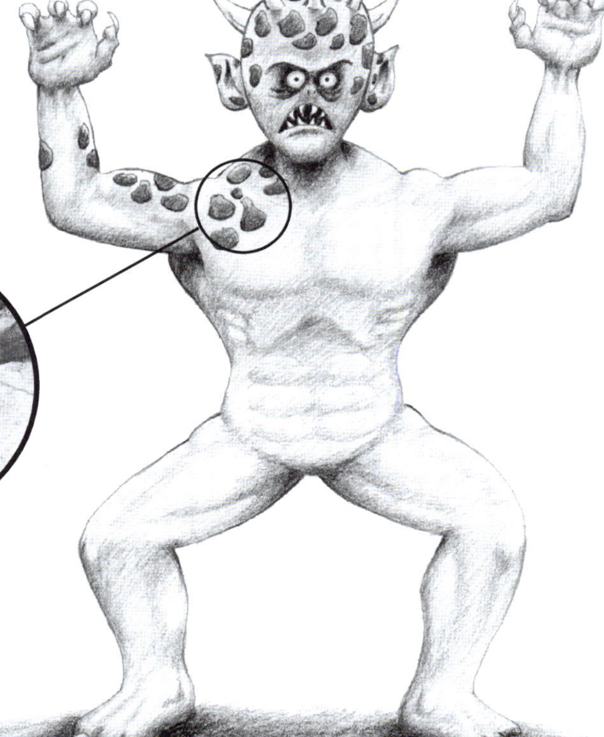

To make the scales stand out from the skin, draw the top parts lighter than the main part...

...make the lower part darker...

...and put a thick dark line at the bottom of each scale.

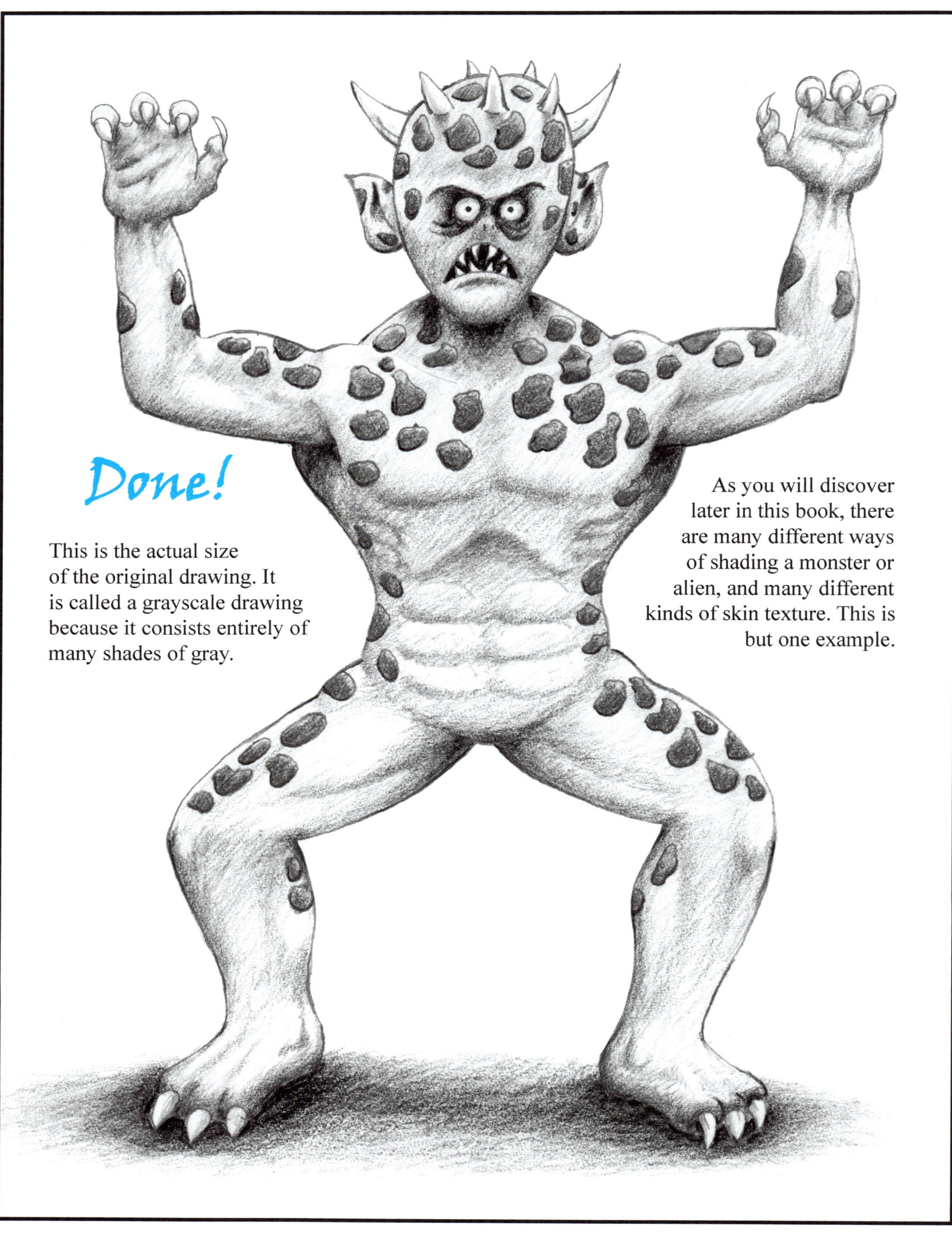

Done!

This is the actual size of the original drawing. It is called a grayscale drawing because it consists entirely of many shades of gray.

As you will discover later in this book, there are many different ways of shading a monster or alien, and many different kinds of skin texture. This is but one example.

Two Great Tips

Tip 1: Practice!

Athletes practice hours for each minute of competition. Actors rehearse weeks before opening night. Flawless performances by musicians are preceded by not-so-flawless attempts to perfect their performance. Follow their lead and ***practice*** drawing your monster or alien on throw-away scratch paper. Make changes. Toss out stuff that doesn't work. Focus on stuff that does work. Commit to good paper only when you are satisfied and ready. (But even then, with the aid of an eraser, you can still make improvements!) I followed this advice in preparing this book: many rough sketches were made and "almost good enough" drawings were discarded *before* the illustrations you see were completed.

Tip 2: Let Your Creature Evolve!

Start a drawing *without* an idea of what you actually want your creature to look like! Begin with some simple shapes (circles, lines, etc.) and/or very rough sketches. Constantly force yourself to follow a different path than you might normally take. You'll likely find that the drawing takes on a life of its own: an addition here, a change there, and it may very well ***evolve*** into something you didn't expect — a monster or alien that is very original that reflects creative abilities in you that you didn't know existed.

In the next few pages you'll see how I let rough, amateurish sketches change and grow into a rather appealing creature — a creation I didn't even slightly expect to see when I started.

Evolve a MONSTER!

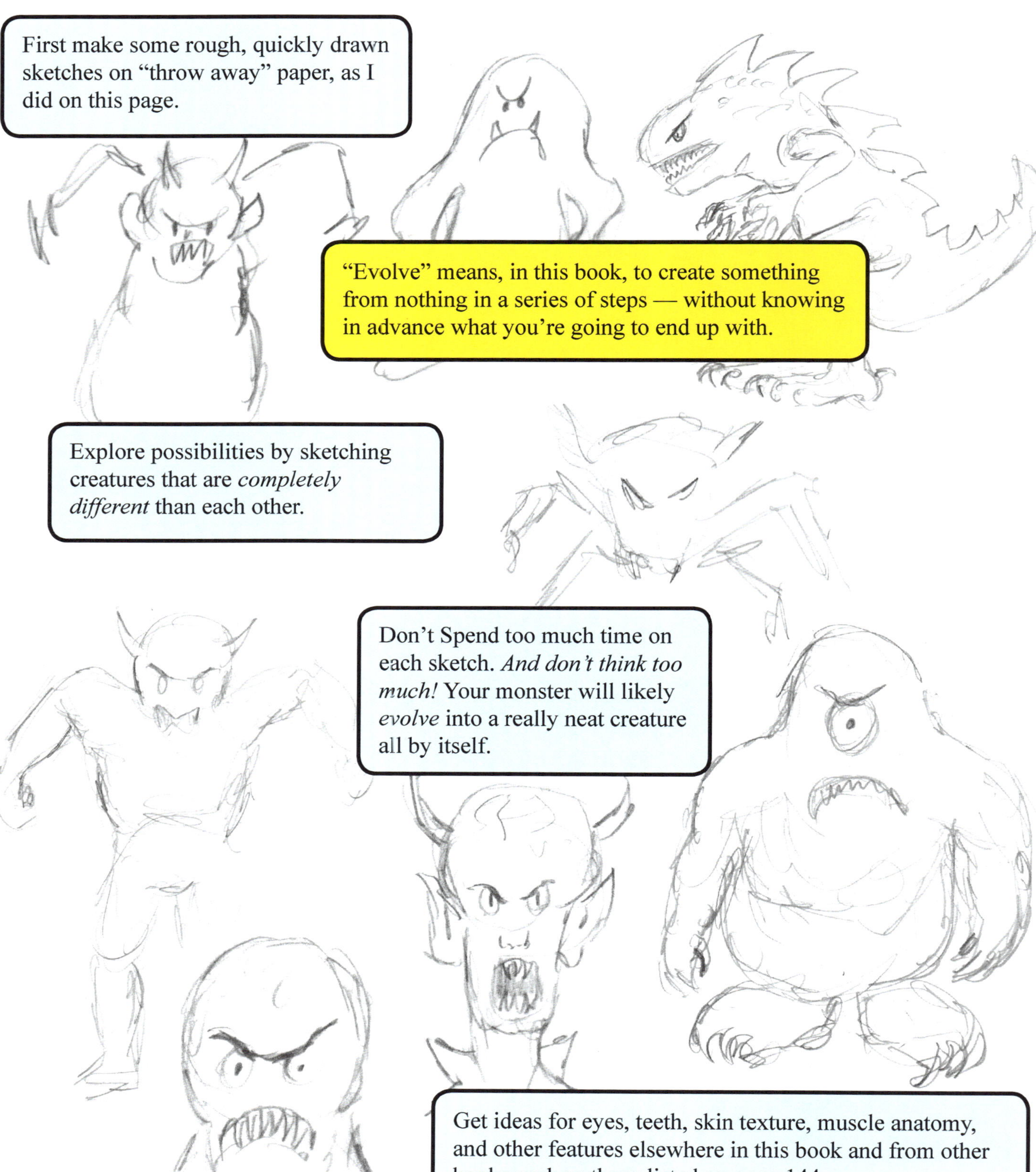

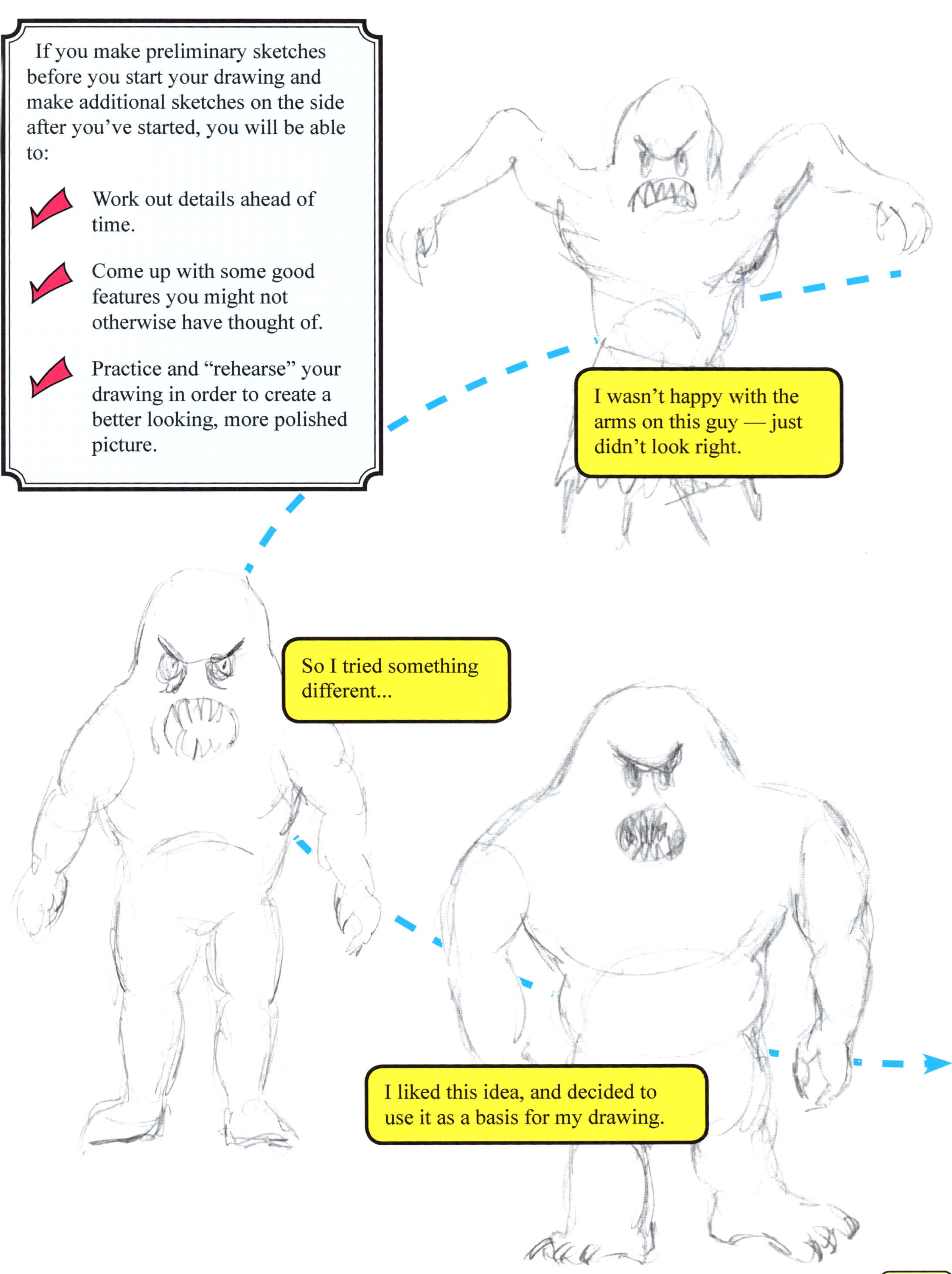
If you make preliminary sketches before you start your drawing and make additional sketches on the side after you've started, you will be able to:
Work out details ahead of time.
Come up with some good features you might not otherwise have thought of.
Practice and "rehearse" your drawing in order to create a better looking, more polished picture.
I wasn't happy with the arms on this guy — just didn't look right.
So I tried something different...
I liked this idea, and decided to use it as a basis for my drawing.

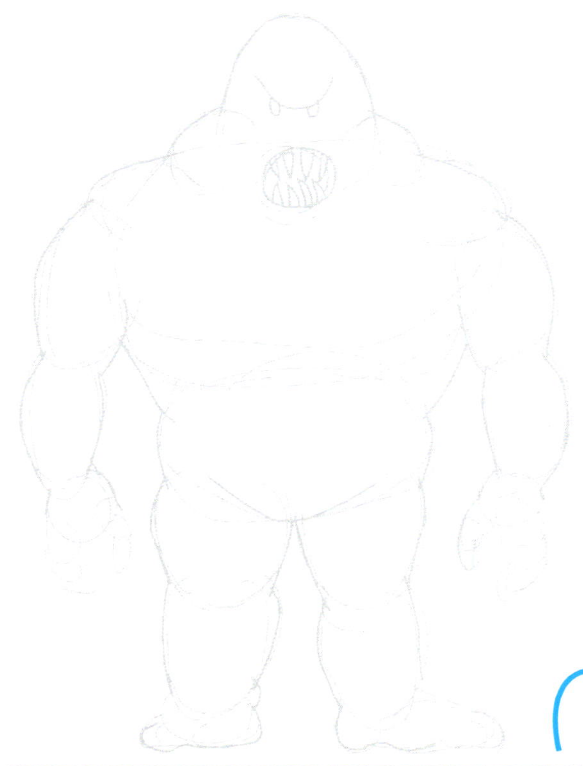

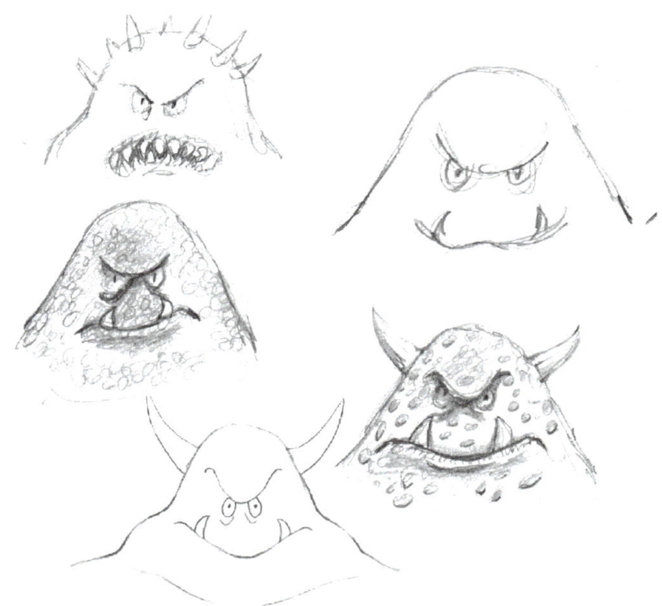

I wasn't happy with the creature's head, especially his mouth, so I tried different ideas with side drawings — sketches made to the side of the main drawing or on a separate sheet of paper. While I was at it, I experimented with skin texture.

I usually start my "almost final" drawings by making very light circular lines on inexpensive "throw away" paper.

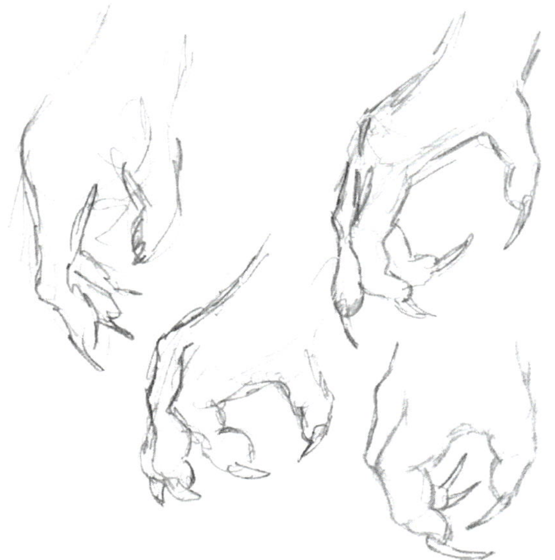

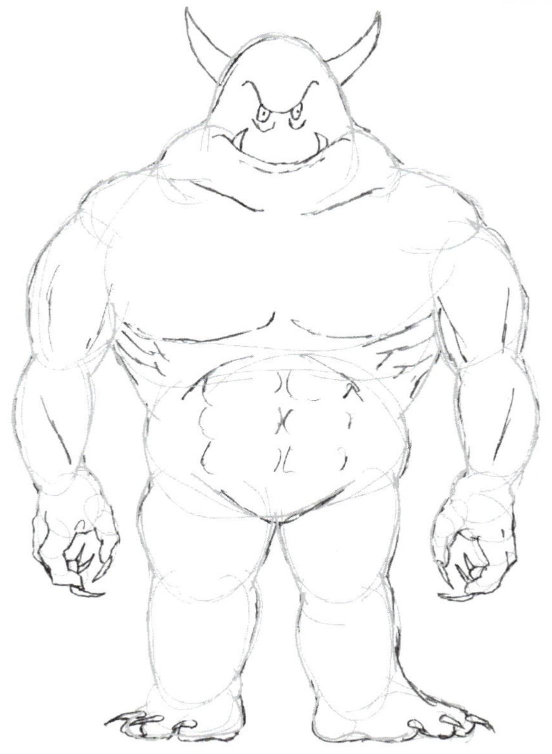

The hands were a challenge. I practiced drawing hands until I was satisfied. I referred to my own hand as a model.

The mouth and eyes were erased and new ones drawn, along with more detailed hands, toes, and other stuff. Notice how completely different the mouth has become!

At this point there were at least two possibilities:

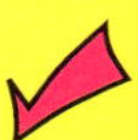

If the monster was first drawn on good paper, the lighter, unimportant lines could be erased.

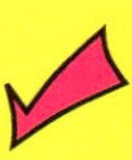

If drawn on throw-away paper, the heavier lines — the ones I wanted to keep in the drawing — could be transferred to good paper then perfected by making them darker, varying their widths, etc.

You'll learn more about transferring drawings starting on page 65.

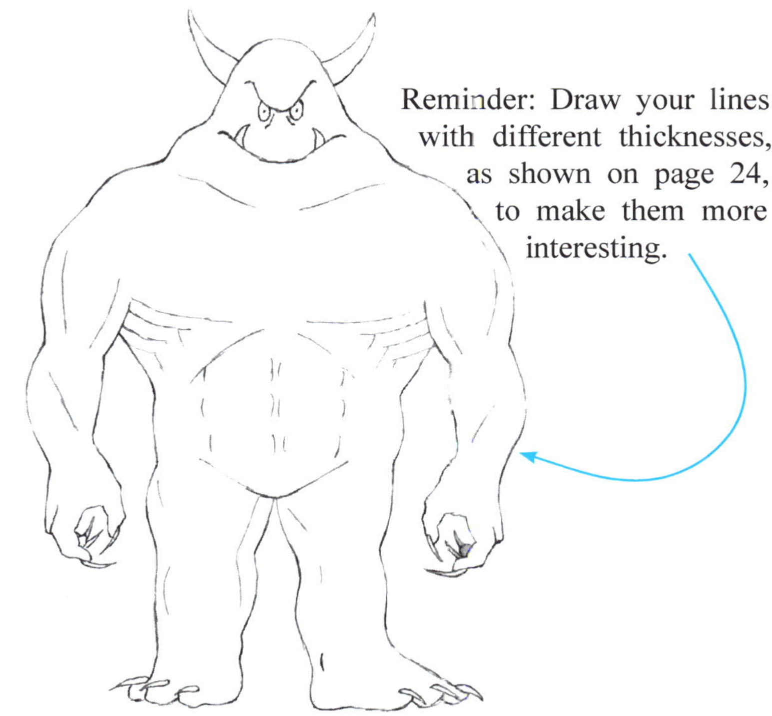

Reminder: Draw your lines with different thicknesses, as shown on page 24, to make them more interesting.

To get the muscles right, I relied on the "Human Connection" illustrations on pages 82 - 85, as well as several books on human anatomy for artists. The latter can be found at hobby and art supply stores.

I used the "smoothed" technique to create his skin. You'll learn about this technique in pages 41 - 46.

It would have been OK to leave this drawing as is, but I chose to add scales to his skin, as you'll see on the next page...

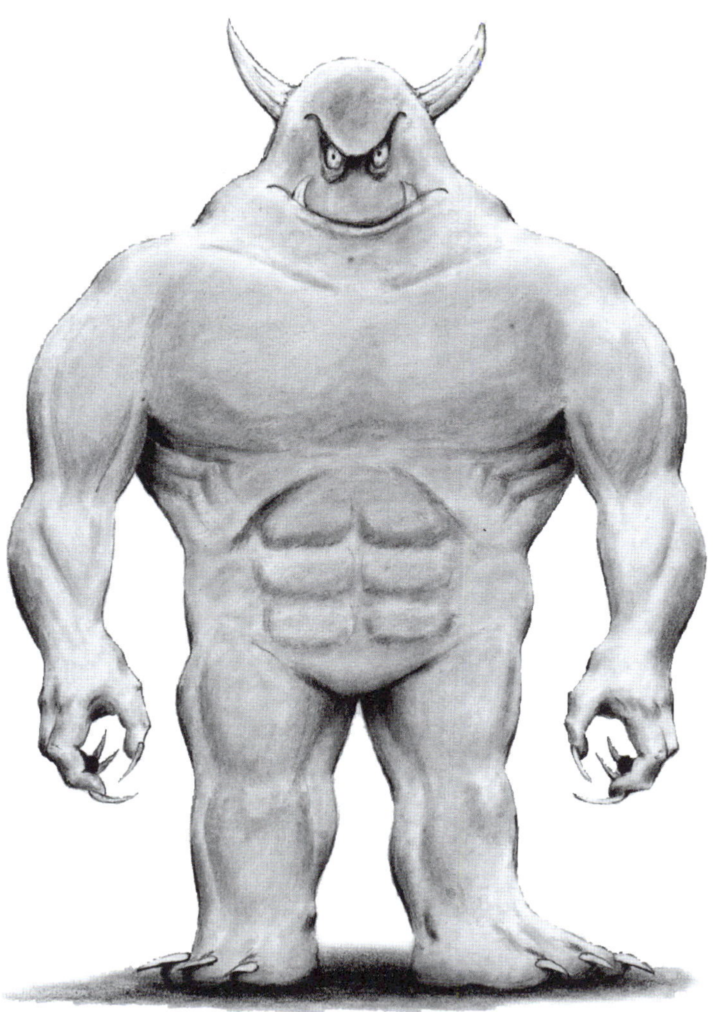

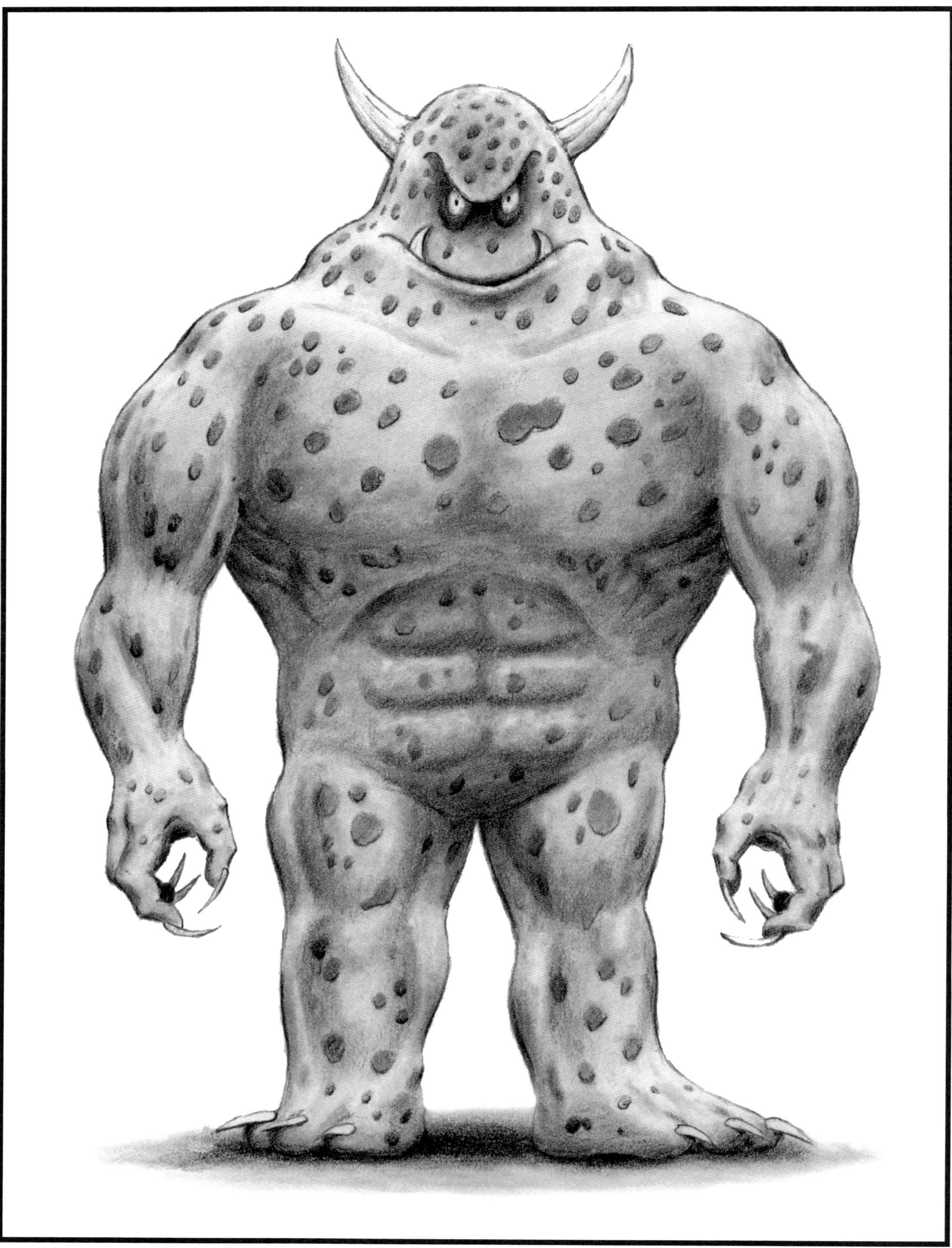

SHADING Grayscale Drawings

Grayscale drawings consist of black and many shades of gray but no color. Methods you can use to shade your drawings are unlimited. This section of the book illustrates a few of those methods. The pencil leads used for many of the drawings were H series for light thin lines, HB for middle tone lines, B series for darker lines, and 7B or 8B for very dark or black lines. Step-by-step directions are not given for every example — you'll be able to figure how most were done just by looking at them.

Fast and Loose

This drawing was shaded in just a few minutes. Rough, fairly thick lines were quickly laid down with HB and 7B pencils. I did not care about precise details — and in fact avoided them. Multiple outlines around the head, eyes, and elsewhere help give the drawing a spontaneous "unrehearsed" feel.

The lesson of this sketch is that you do not need to use the sort of precise, highly controlled techniques illustrated in the next few pages to create drawings that are fun to look at!

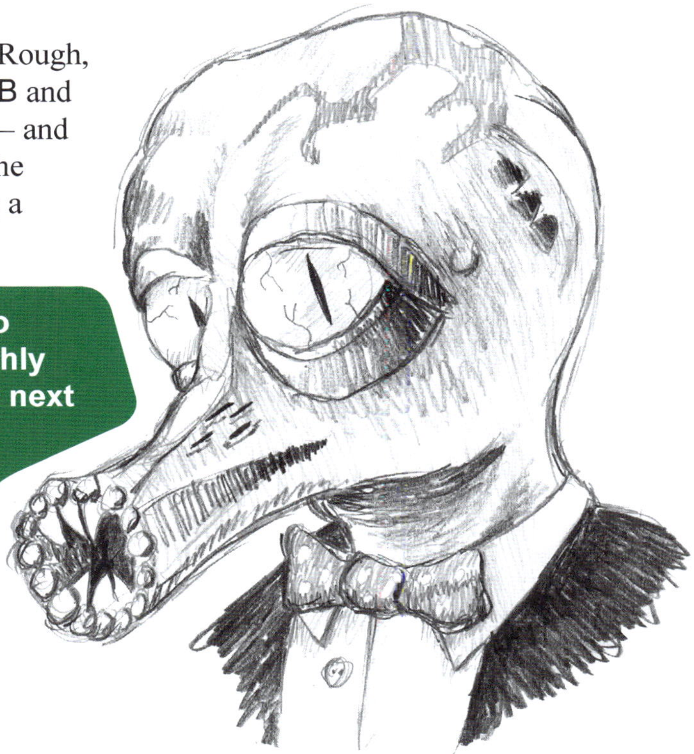

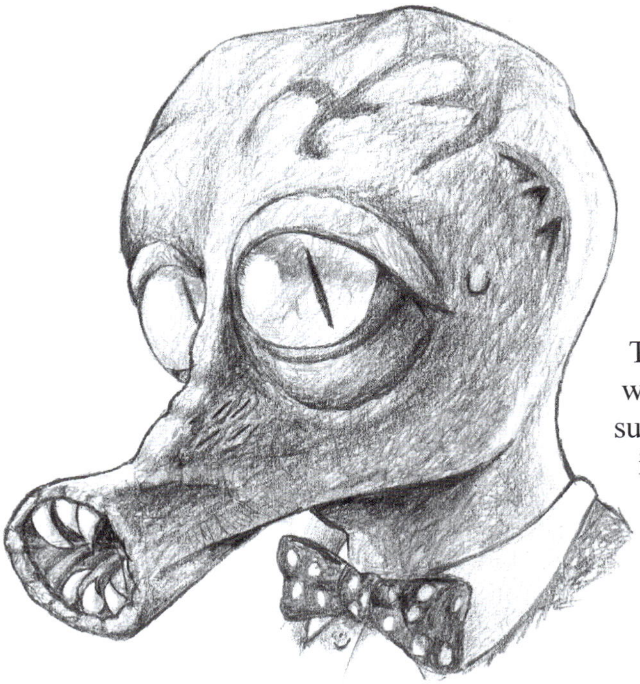

Hodgepodge

The shading lines go every which way. This will do, I suppose, but there are more interesting styles.

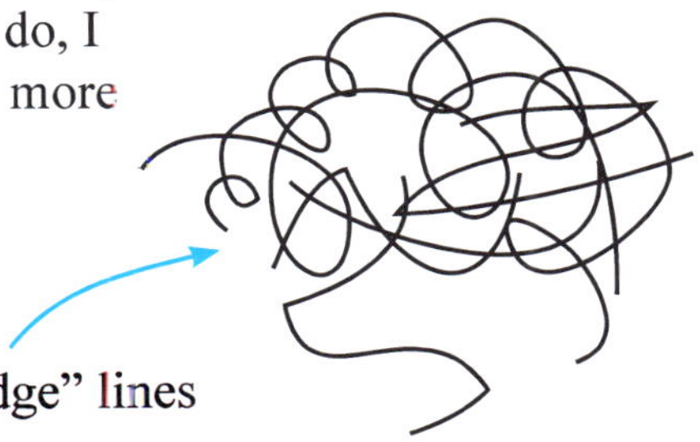

"Hodgepodge" lines

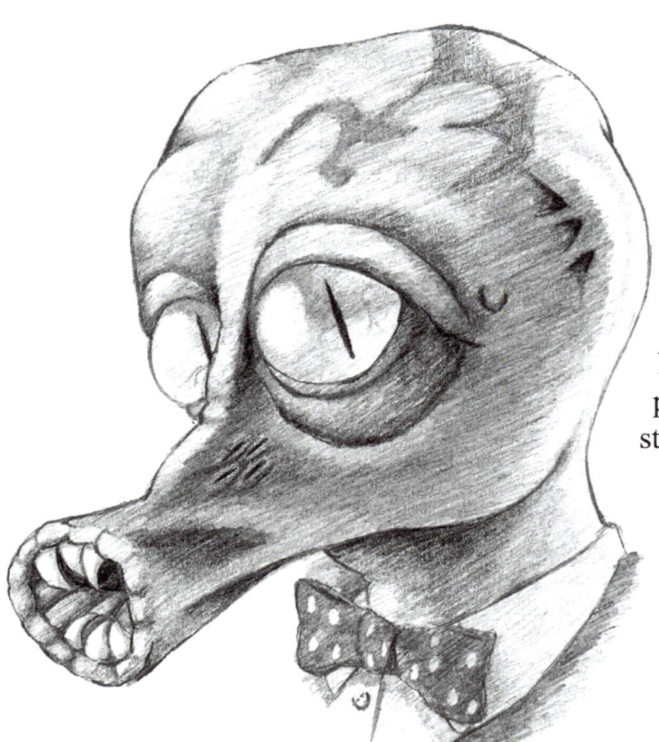

Parallel

Nearly all the shading lines go one direction, parallel to each other. Would you agree that this style is more appealing than "hodgepodge"?

Cross-Hatch

This technique is similar to the parallel method, except that while there are parallel lines, they go in different directions and cross each other.

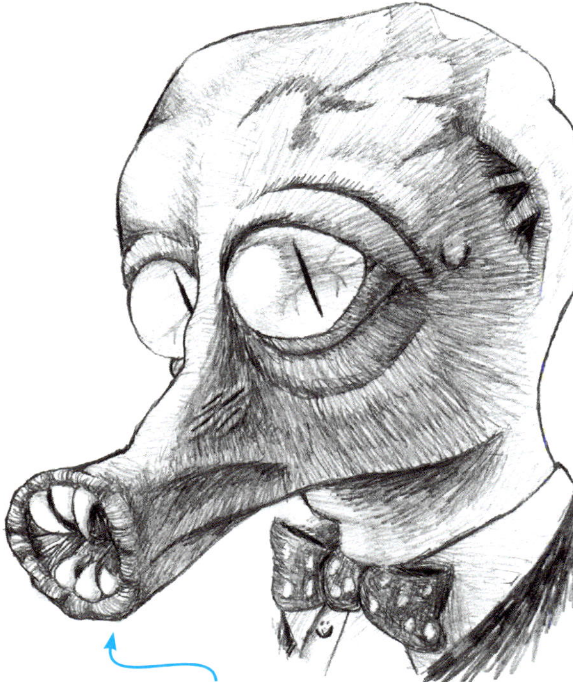

Note that the lines around the lip go with the "grain" of the lip.

Focused

Here many of the lines come together, guiding the viewer's focus to the creature's eye. They are interesting and pleasing; they make the drawing more *artistic*. Most of the drawing was made with an HB pencil. Bristol smooth surface paper was used to make the lines appear sharp and distinct. The technique was championed by an artist named Paul Calle (Kal-ay).

Smooth Textured Grayscale Drawings

In such drawings, shades of gray are blended smoothly, from white through shades of gray to black.

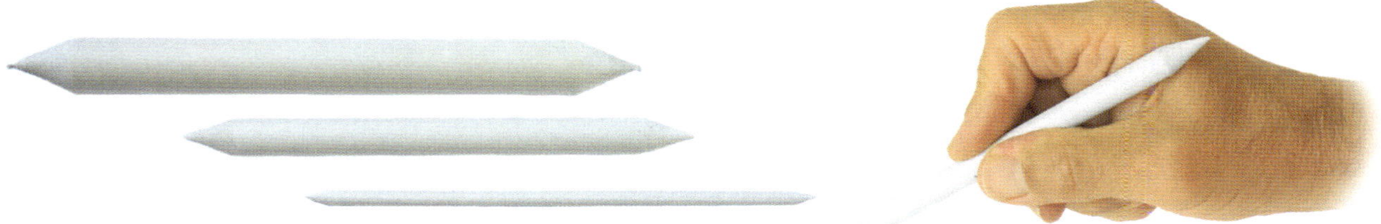

Blending stumps (also called tortillions) are simple and effective tools for applying and blending graphite on drawings. They come in a variety of sizes and can be found in hobby and art supply stores. I frequently use stumps for blending.

1

Use an HB lead to make your initial drawing, applying slight, gentle pressure to make *very light lines*. Do not be tempted to use a light H lead that will likely leave a dent in the paper that may show through the darker areas of your final drawing.

2

Apply patches of graphite (pencil lead) onto a piece of rough-surfaced "throw away" drawing paper or fine grain sandpaper. (I use a sanding block — a small wooden paddle with layers of sandpaper as shown here.) Sandpaper will hold more graphite, which is good when you want to shade dark areas, but will make it more difficult to get a light coating of lead on your stump, which is not so good when you want to shade light areas. So, use both paper *and* sandpaper!

I suggest medium, dark, and very dark leads, such as HB, 3B, and 6B, though others will do.

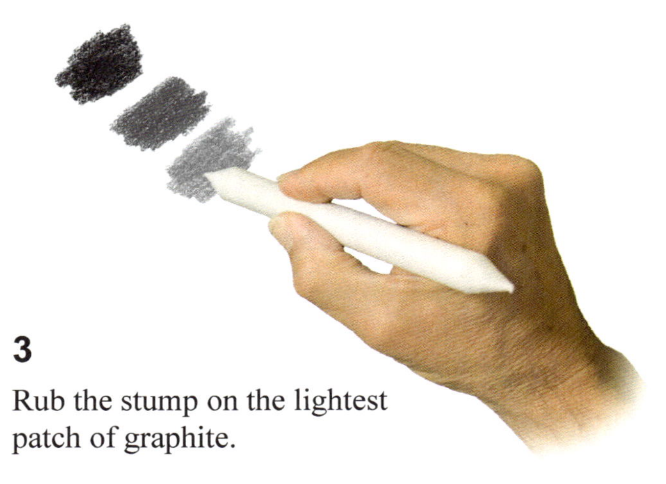

3

Rub the stump on the lightest patch of graphite.

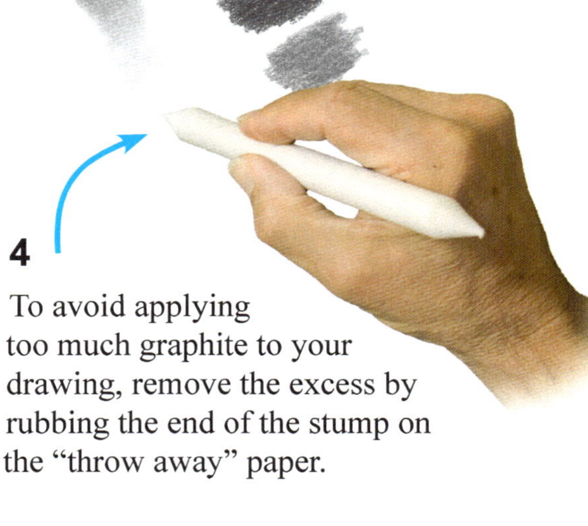

4

To avoid applying too much graphite to your drawing, remove the excess by rubbing the end of the stump on the "throw away" paper.

5

You will usually want to fill in lightest areas first — it will be easy to darken them later if you wish.

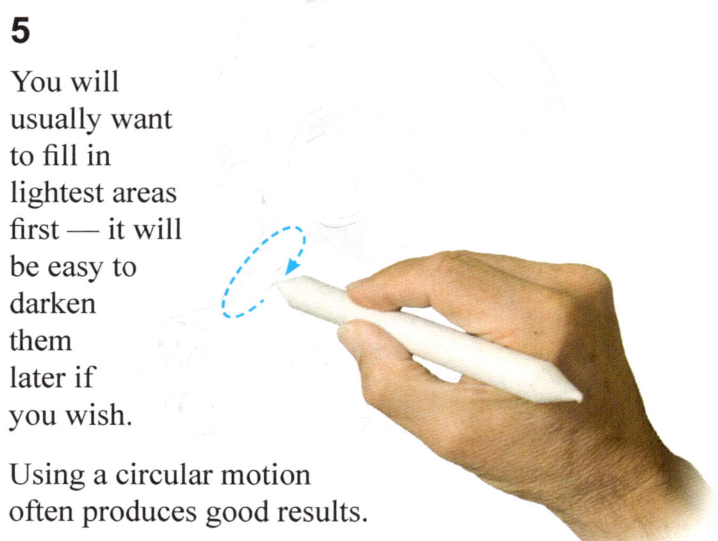

Using a circular motion often produces good results.

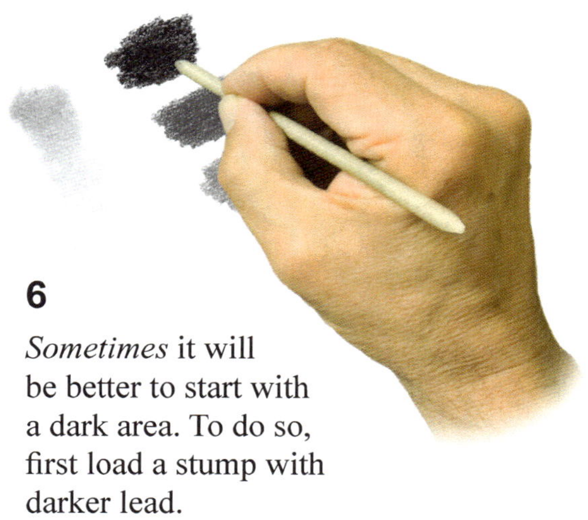

6

Sometimes it will be better to start with a dark area. To do so, first load a stump with darker lead.

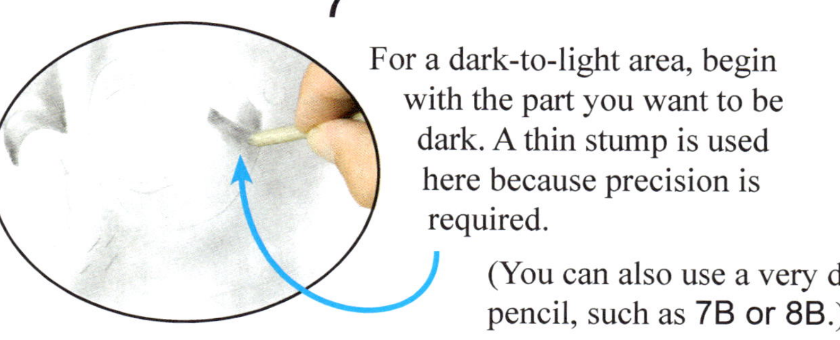

7

For a dark-to-light area, begin with the part you want to be dark. A thin stump is used here because precision is required.

(You can also use a very dark pencil, such as 7B or 8B.)

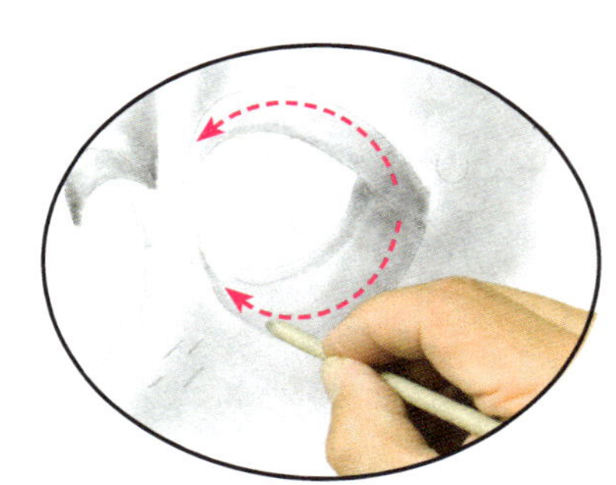

8

Move toward the lighter area and reduce pressure on the stump as you do so.

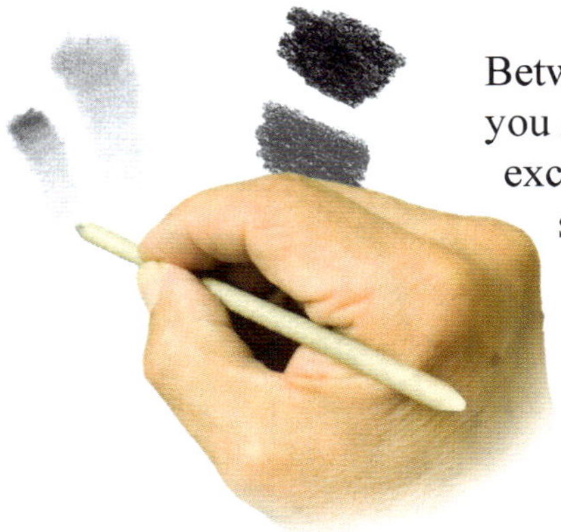

Between steps 7 and 8 above you *may* want to remove excess graphite from your stump by rubbing it on your "throw-away" paper.

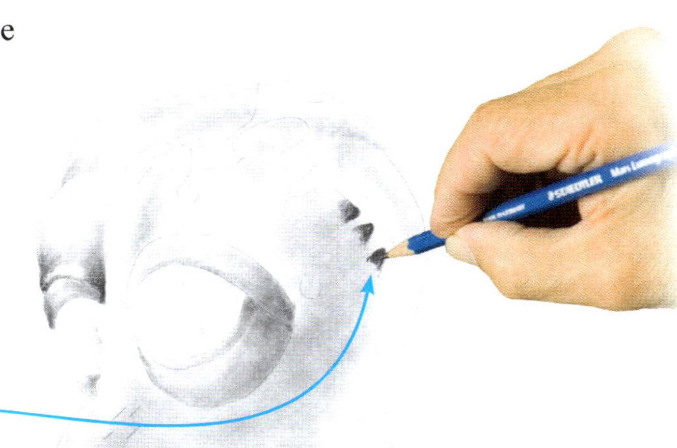

9

Use a pencil when the target area is too small for a stump, or when the stump cannot make the area dark enough.

NOTE: If you press too hard with a 6B or harder lead (5B, 4B, Etc.) in an effort to create black or nearly black areas, the area will have an unwanted glossy look when viewed at an angle to the light. Instead, use a 7B, 8B, or carbon lead.

Smooth the area with a stump afterword if possible.

Another cool way to produce a smooth area is to first apply graphite directly on the drawing with a soft lead pencil, one of the B series. Apply several light "coats", one over the other, until the area is as dark as you want. Move the pencil in all directions, making both circular and straight lines and, if possible, use the side of the pencil. Try to make lines that are NOT easily seen!

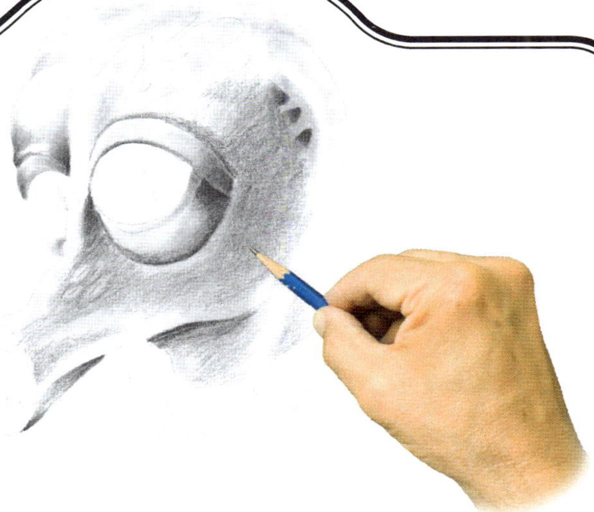

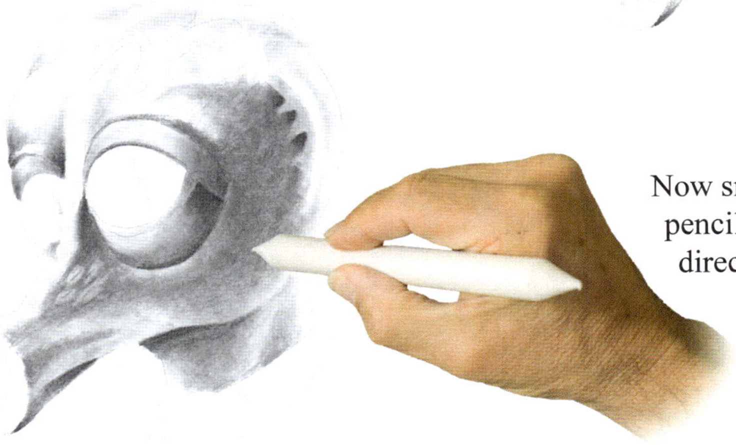

Now smooth the area. As with the pencil, move the stump in all directions — circular and straight.

10

Apply light shades with the stump, not with a pencil, except when the area is too small for the stump.

Notice that the dark lines of the eyes' irises have NOT been drawn. That will be done after the light shading in the eyes is complete...

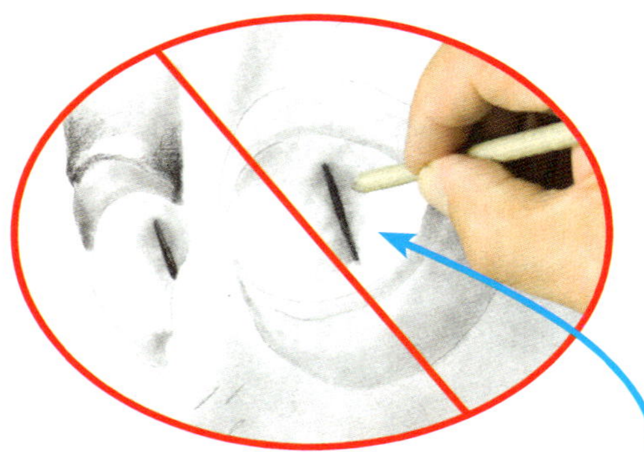

CAUTION! Unwanted smudges like this may occur around a dark shade when an attempt is made to apply a light shade next to it. When a dark shade is to appear on or next to a lighter shade, **apply the dark shade last!**

11

Now that the light part of the eyes is shaded, the dark irises can be drawn without fear of smudging.

An 8B pencil was used to make the irises black.

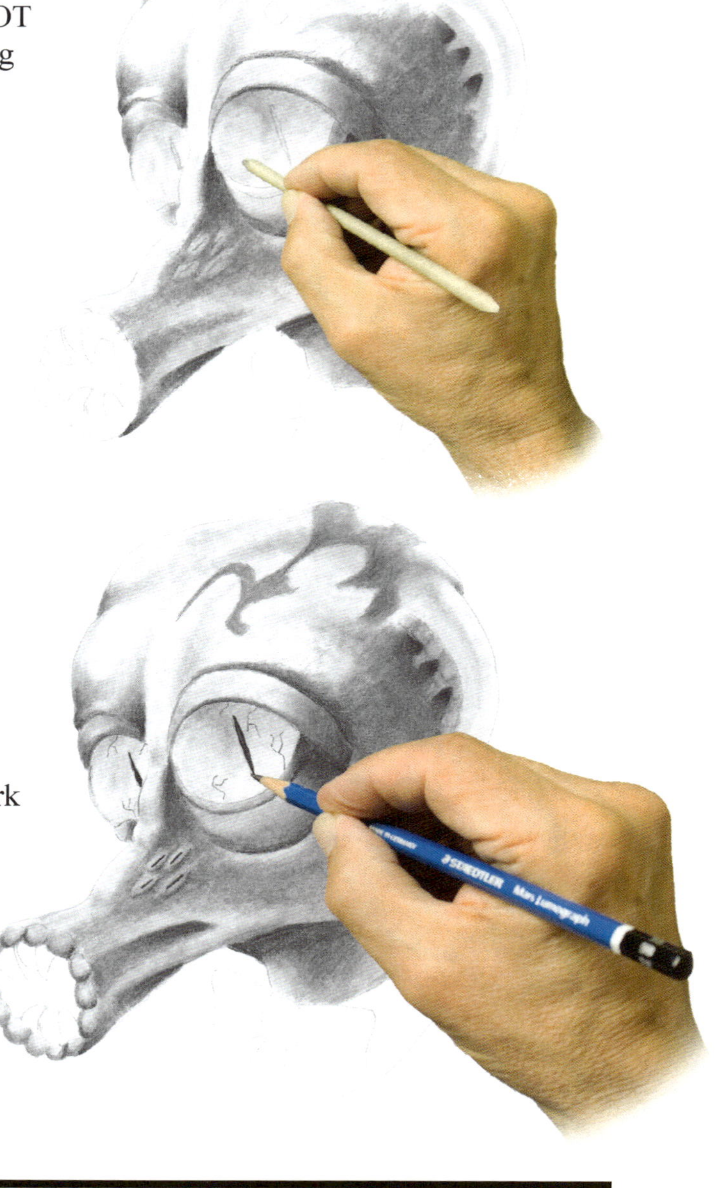

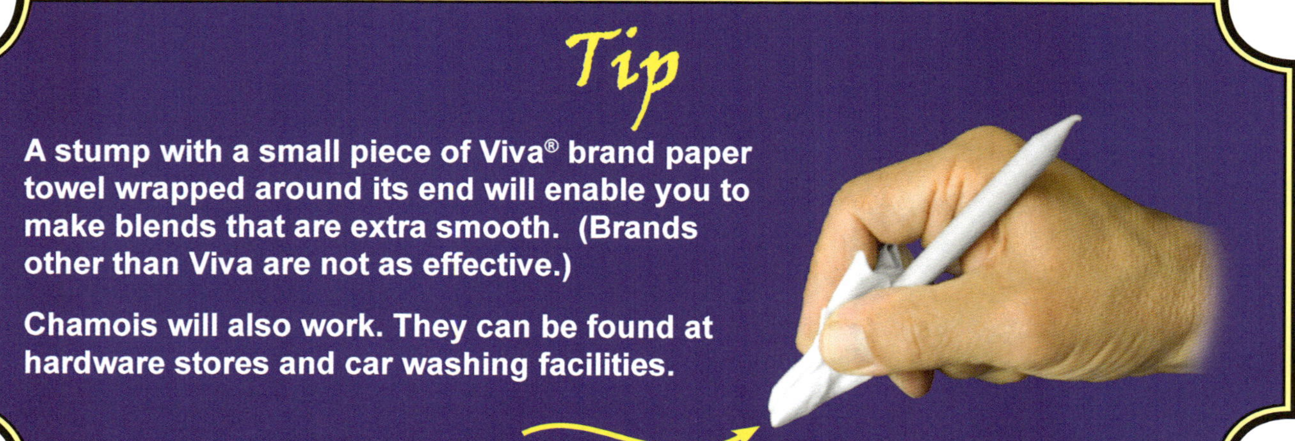

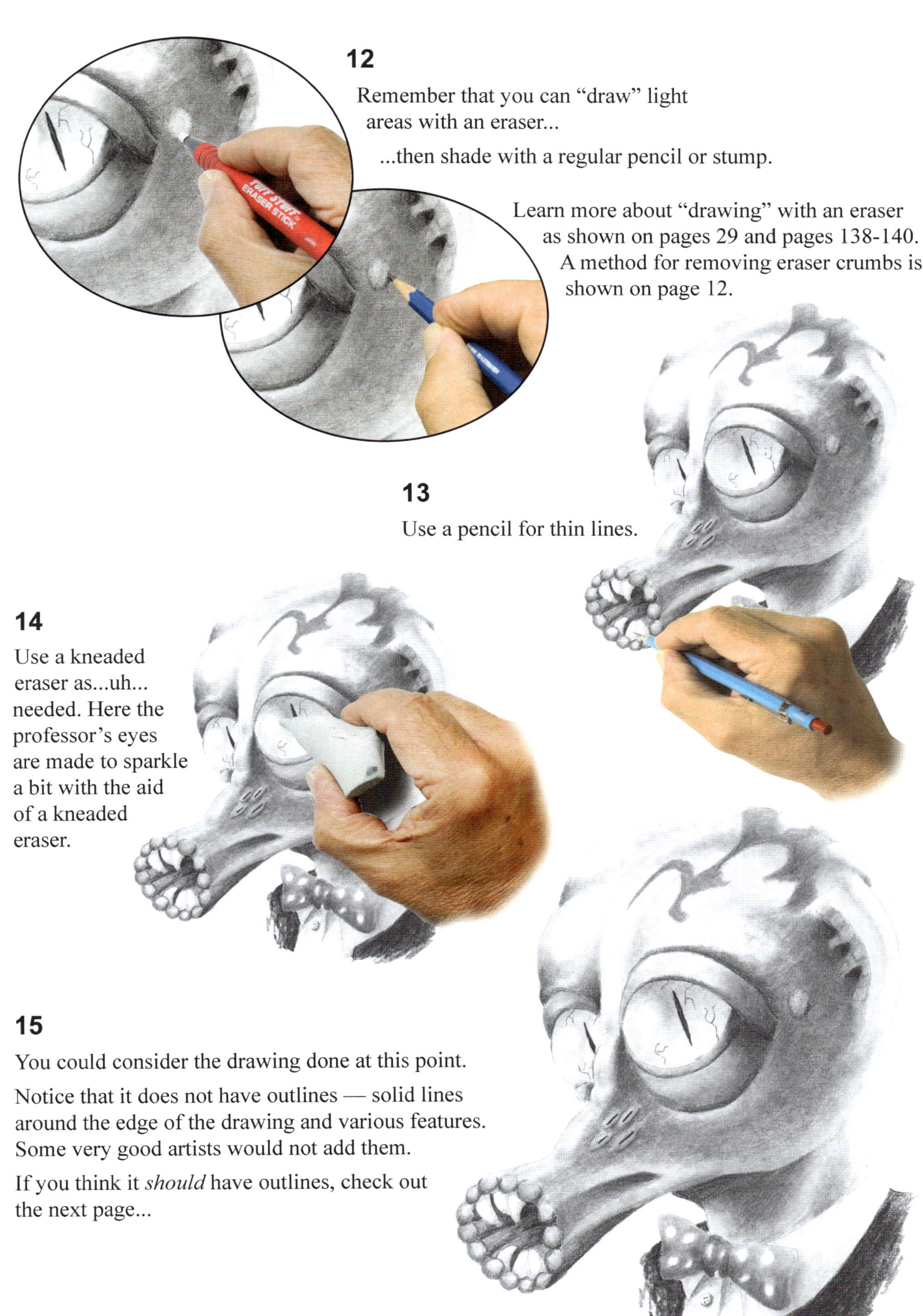

12

Remember that you can "draw" light areas with an eraser...

...then shade with a regular pencil or stump.

Learn more about "drawing" with an eraser as shown on pages 29 and pages 138-140. A method for removing eraser crumbs is shown on page 12.

13

Use a pencil for thin lines.

14

Use a kneaded eraser as...uh... needed. Here the professor's eyes are made to sparkle a bit with the aid of a kneaded eraser.

15

You could consider the drawing done at this point.

Notice that it does not have outlines — solid lines around the edge of the drawing and various features. Some very good artists would not add them.

If you think it *should* have outlines, check out the next page...

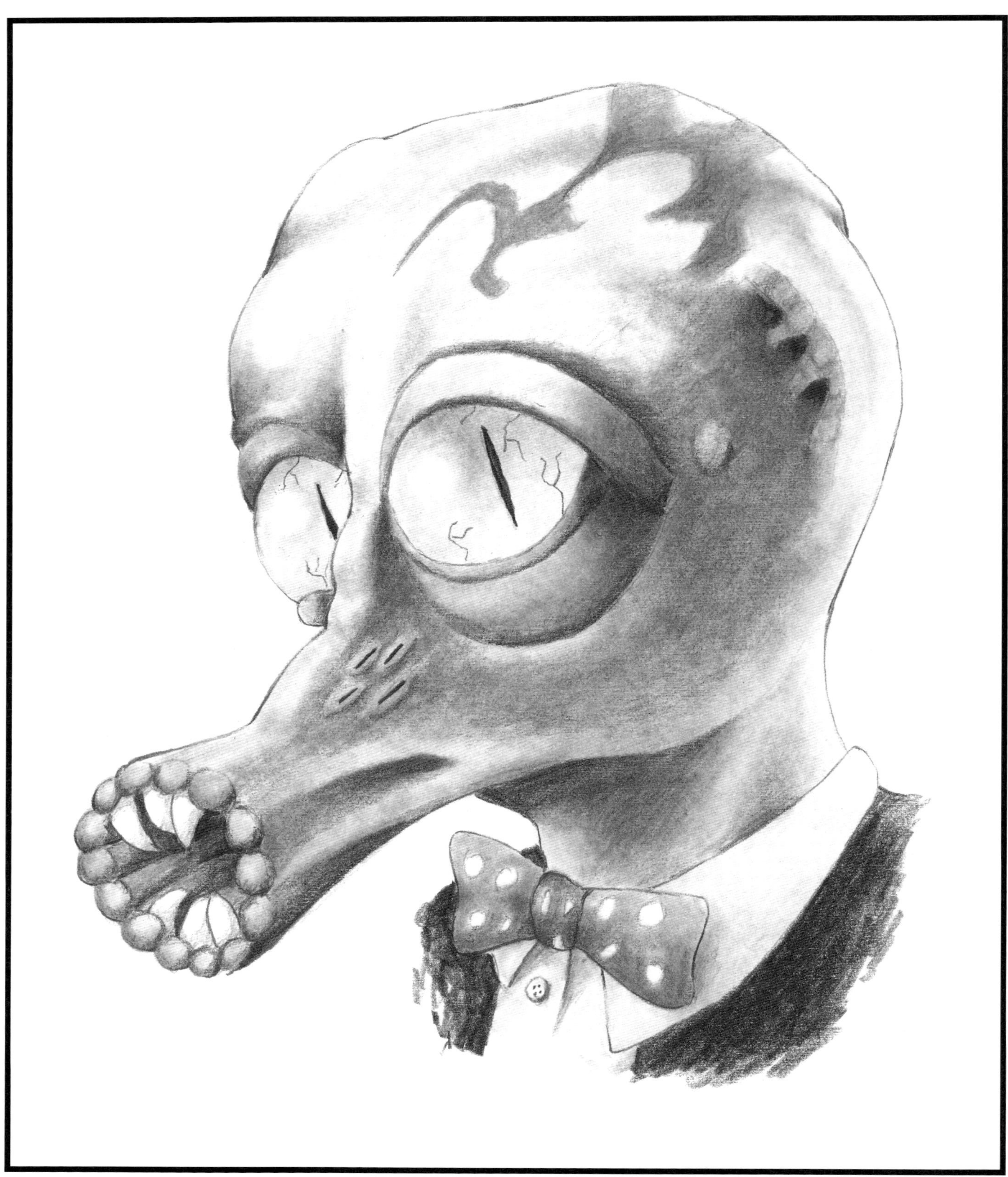

I preferred to add outlines to the drawing. Compare this version to the one without outlines on the previous page. What do you think?

This drawing is the same size as the original.

SHADING *in Color*

Before you learn how to shade your drawings in color, it will help to understand the nature of color…

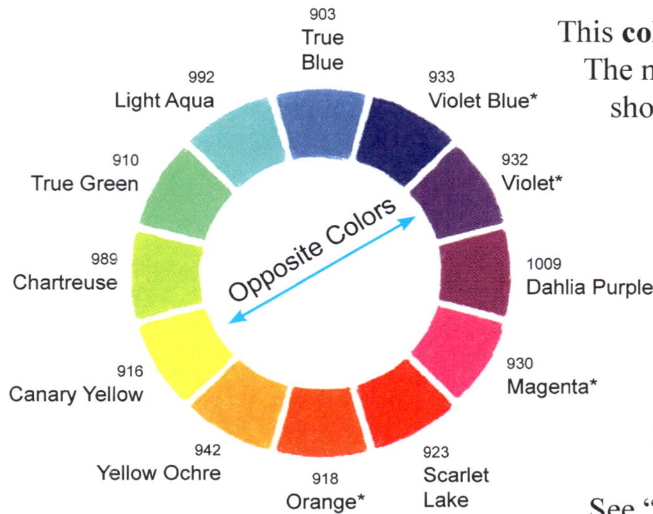

This **color wheel** was made with Prismacolor® colored pencils. The name of each color and its Prismacolor number are shown.

If you purchase pencils one-at-a-time, these would be a good choice for your basic "palette" in addition to white, black, a middle gray, and brown.

*As of this writing, the colors with an asterisk (*) are not considered lightfast, meaning they will likely fade over a very long period of time when exposed to strong light.

See "About Lightfast Colors" on page 16.

This strip was made with the same Prismacolor colored pencils used to make the color wheel. The colors next to each other on the color wheel are also next to each other on the strip. The colors blend smoothly where they overlap and are easy on the eye!

Here the colors next to each other can be found on opposite sides of the color wheel. The colors do not blend together smoothly; dark bands are created where they overlap and the colors contrast with each other. The colors may be appealing, but in a much different way.

Tip

Similar colors can overlap and blend together without much of a problem. When colors overlap that are *not* similar to each other, another, darker color may result.

There are many excellent books available that describe in detail how to draw with colored pencils. An excellent choice would be ***Masterful Color: vibrant colored pencil paintings layer by layer*** by Arlene Steinberg, available from Amazon.com. (The paperback version will save you money.)

Shading Techniques with Colored Pencils

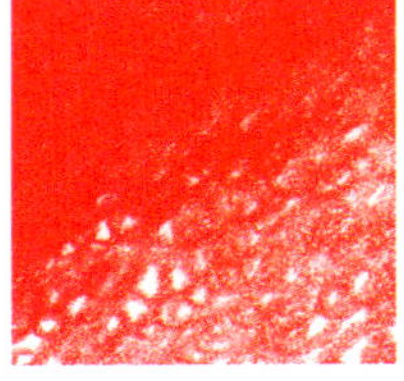
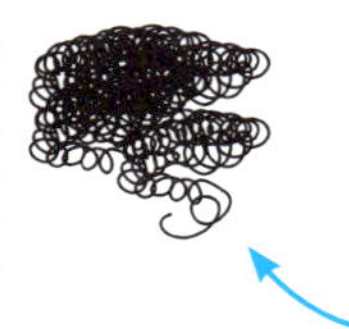

When using colored pencils, you'll achieve the smoothest look by applying small circular strokes with a sharp point, going over the area until it is saturated.

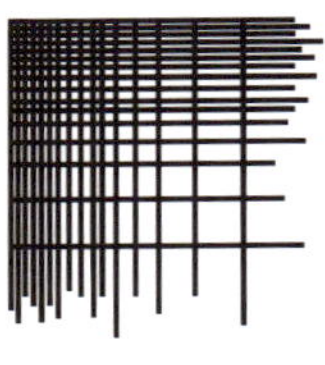

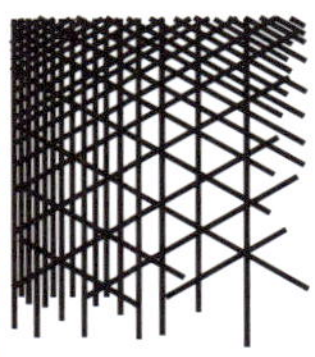

Another method is to cross hatch, making more or less straight lines in two or three directions. This can produce an appealing effect if you allow the lines to show.

1 When you shade with colored pencils, start with a light application, then build up, one layer at a time.

2 Lighten a color by adding a lighter color or white. Darken by adding black or an opposite color as shown on the color wheel on the previous page.

3 More white, violet blue and black were added, little by little, until they saturated this sample.

4 The colors were smoothed out with a colorless blender. (More about colorless blenders page 15.)

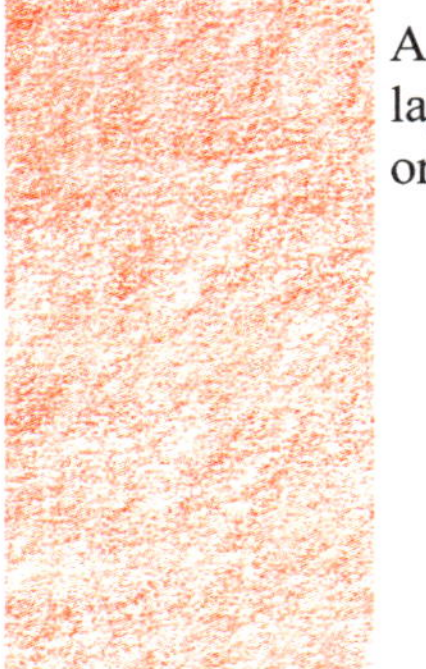

A light layer of orange.

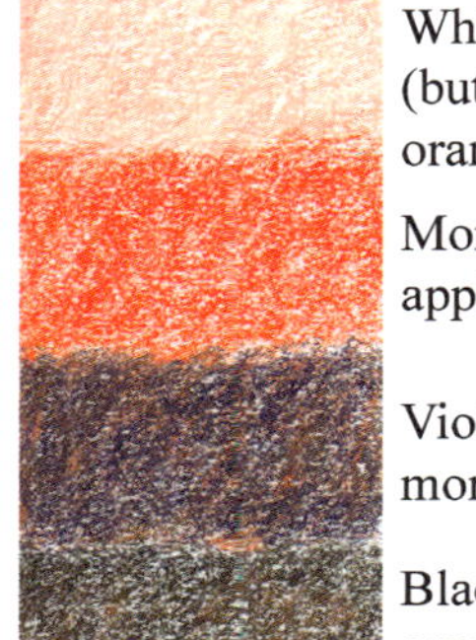

White added (but no more orange).

More orange applied.

Violet blue and more orange.

Black and more orange.

Note that the violet blue, *opposite orange on the color wheel*, darkened the orange to a grayish-purple color that you may find more appealing than the very dark gray created by adding black.

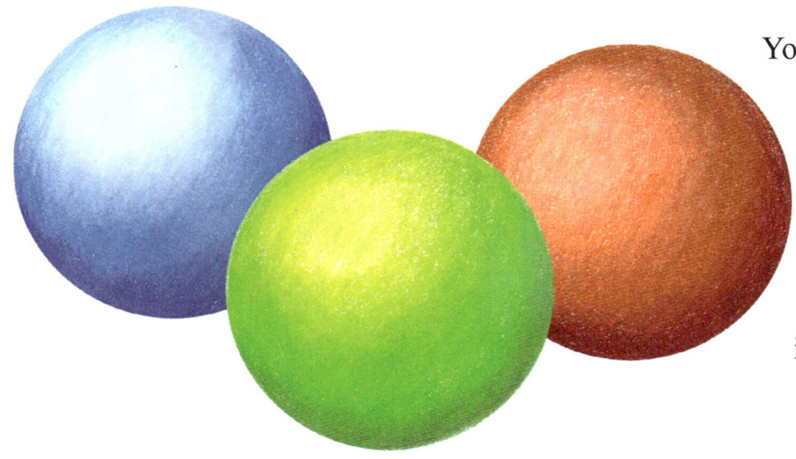

You can also create different values of a color, from light to dark, by simply applying different shades of that color. Light, medium, and dark shades of blue, green, and brown Prismacolor pencils were used to render these three balls. A colorless blender was NOT used; instead, a lighter shade was rubbed over a darker shade. This is often better way to blend a color.

Shade a MONSTER with Colored Pencils

The "multiple layer" technique described on this and the next page involves applying several layers of color, one at a time, until the drawing is saturated with color.

1
As always, begin with a sketch. Keep the lines very light so the pencil's graphite does not corrupt, or leak into, the colors. You don't need to show every detail. If possible, use a good quality drawing paper (see "paper" pages 12&13).

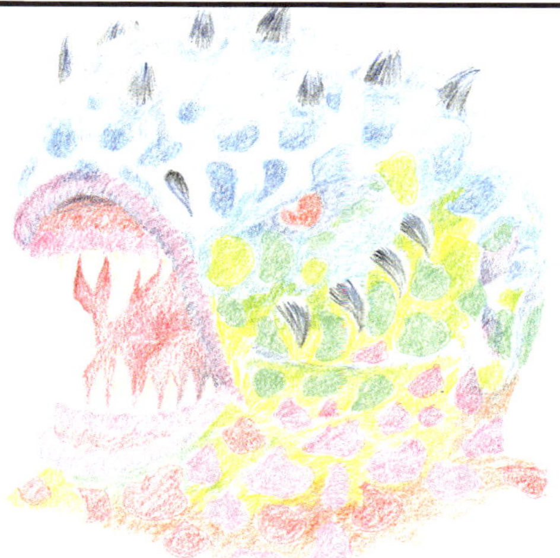

2
First apply a light layer of colors. This helps establish how the colors relate to each other, allows you to think about how you'd like the finished drawing to look, and, leaves room for changes down the road.

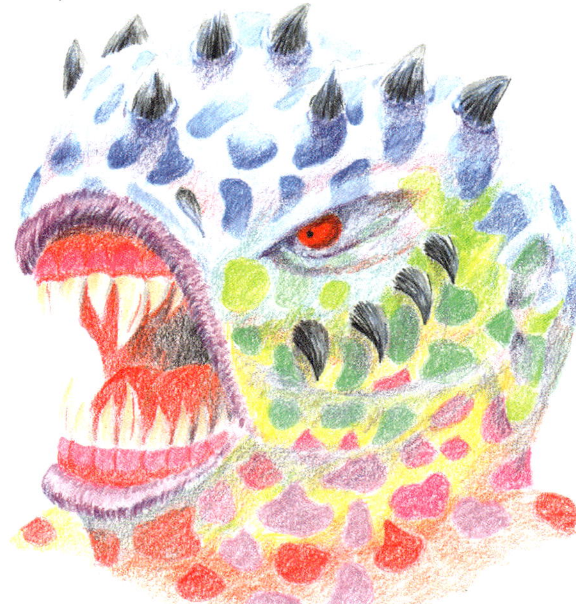

3
Apply more color, including darker shades for the shadow areas. Rather than using black, you may wish to use colors opposite each other per the color wheel illustrated on page 47.

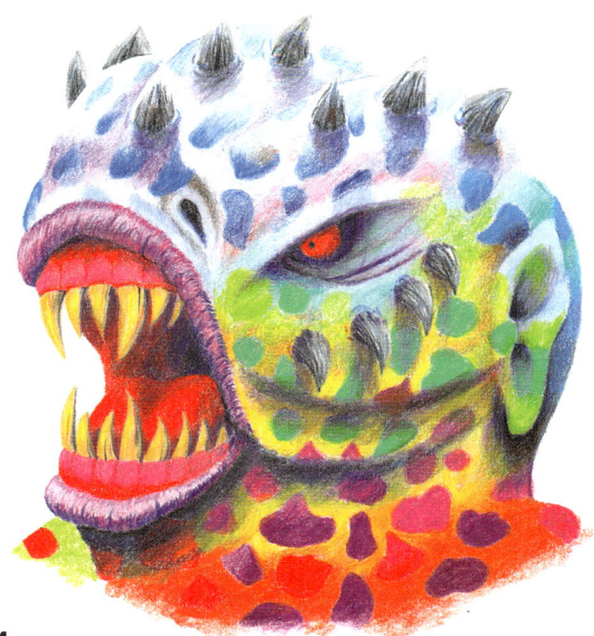

4
Continue applying color, a little at a time, one layer upon another. At some point you can consider the drawing finished. Or, you may prefer to add more color and detail…

5

Refinements are added, then…

Finished!

It is usually (but not always) recommended to apply different colors to a base color to make the base color more visually interesting and realistic. For example, the base color at the top of this fellow's head consists mostly of shades of blue, but look closely and you'll see touches violet, red, and brown as well.

Although the horns are predominantly black, they are created from light and dark gray, blue, light yellow, *and* black.

Dark purple was applied around his eye — more appealing, I think, than gray or black.

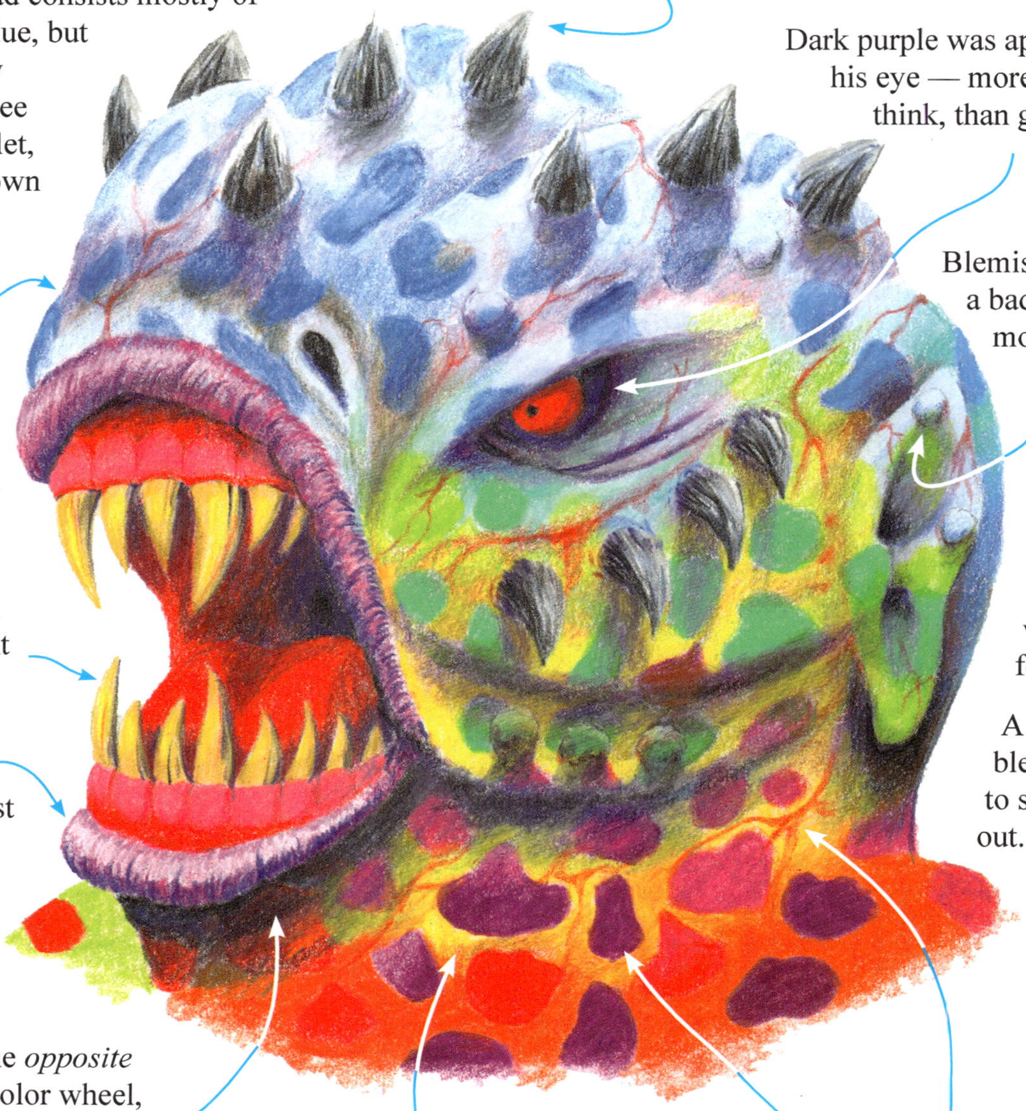

Blemishes are never a bad idea on monsters.

Note that the teeth are NOT white. They are a kind of yellow-orange with hints of light brown, red, and gray.

About sixteen different colored pencils were employed for this drawing.

A colorless blender was used to smooth them out. (See page 15.)

Lips: not just violet, but violet, dark blue, red, and white.

Colors on the *opposite* side of the color wheel, in addition to black, were used to produce shadow areas. For example, indigo blue, other dark blues, *and* black were used against yellows and orange to make dark grays.

I wanted colors on *some* parts of the skin to blend together fairly smoothly and look nice (even on this scary creature), so I used colors *near each other* on the color wheel.

But *opposite* colors were used to contrast some of the scales against the skin.

Veins were added at the last minute to make him look extra gruesome — good move, don't you think?

Taking Advantage of Colored Paper

When colored pencils are used on colored paper, the paper itself can provide color for a drawing. For example, the blue paper in the drawing below and on the next page provided color for most of the creature's body. This saved considerable time that would have been spent applying a similar color with colored pencil. Another advantage to colored paper: The "tooth" of the paper can show through the applied colors and be less annoying than might be the case with white paper. This saves time that might otherwise be spent laying down thick layers of color to cover white paper's grainy surface.

Additionally, colored paper sometimes makes for a much more appealing drawing than white paper.

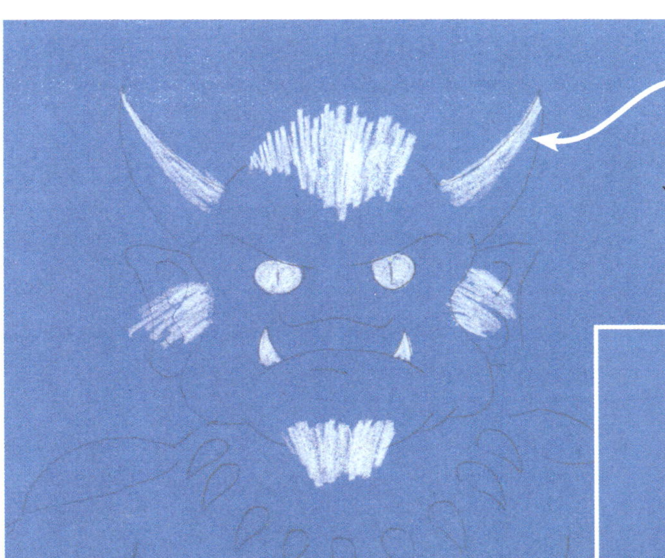

In this drawing, white was first applied so that the red and yellows applied over the white would be brighter than the red and yellows would be if applied alone, without white.

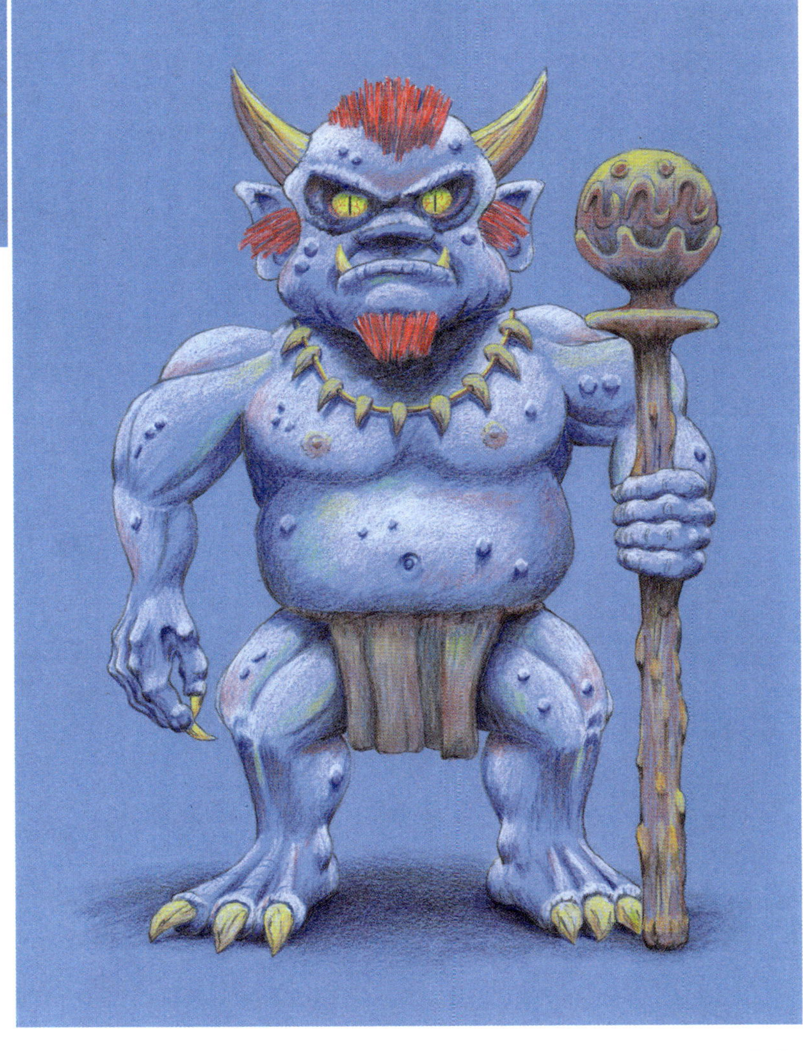

Light blue was used on the creature's body for the highlights (the brightest parts of the drawing). Darker blues and blacks for the shadows. Yellowish-brown and browns were used elsewhere.

Light touches of green, red and yellow were added for interest. Do you think they add to, or detract from, the drawing?

Notice how dark shading around the eyes accents the eyes and makes them more sinister.

The drawing at this point could be considered finished; however, it was felt that this mostly blue "Tribal Chief" may not stand out adequately from the blue background. Turn to the next page to see how this possible problem was solved.

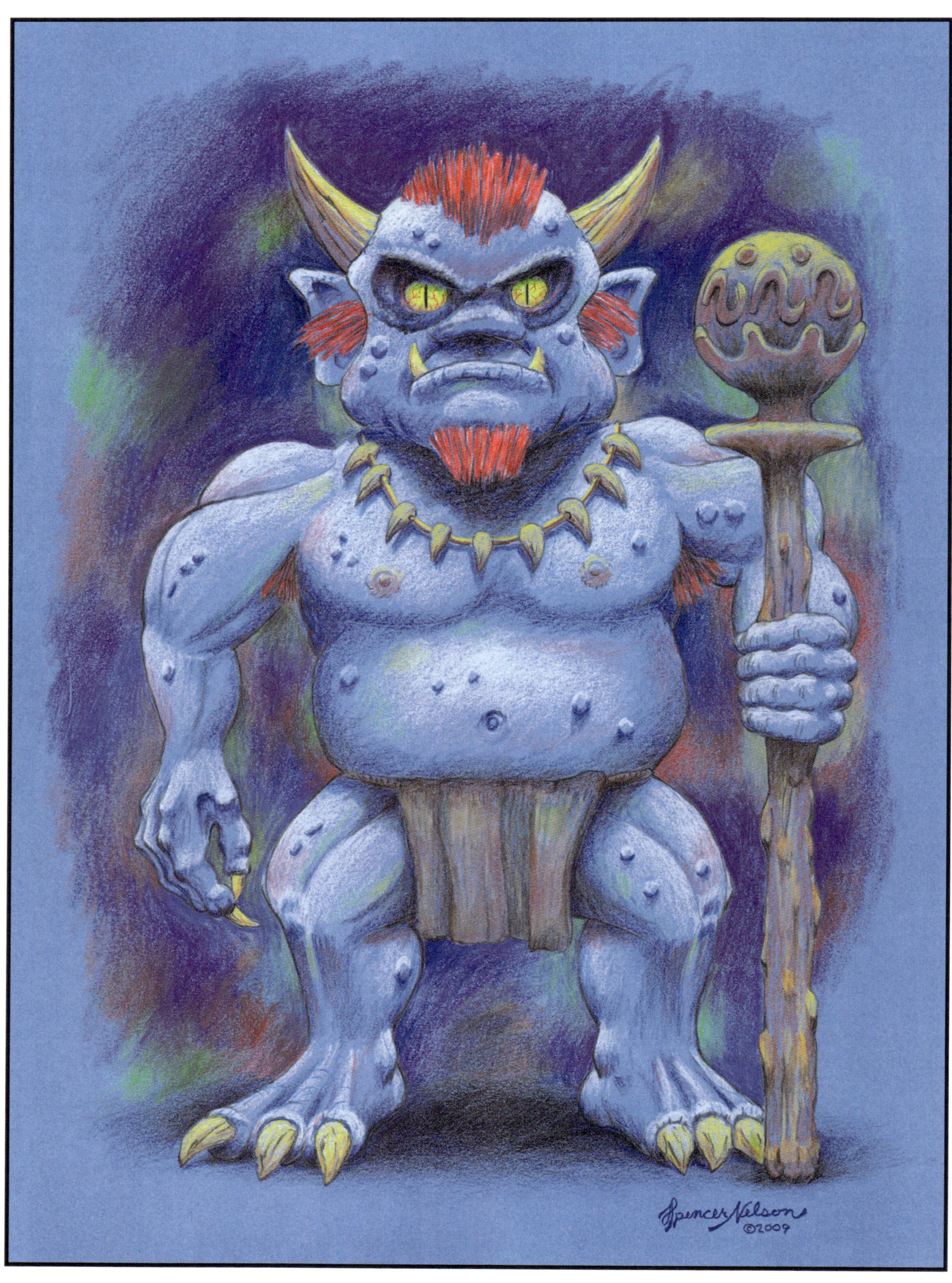

To further help make the chief stand out, darker colors were applied next to highlights on his body and lighter colors were applied next to shadow areas. Pencils were NOT kept sharp for much of this drawing, especially the background.

Drawn on Canson Colorline "blue lagoon" pastel paper with Prismacolor colored pencils. Original size 11" x 15".

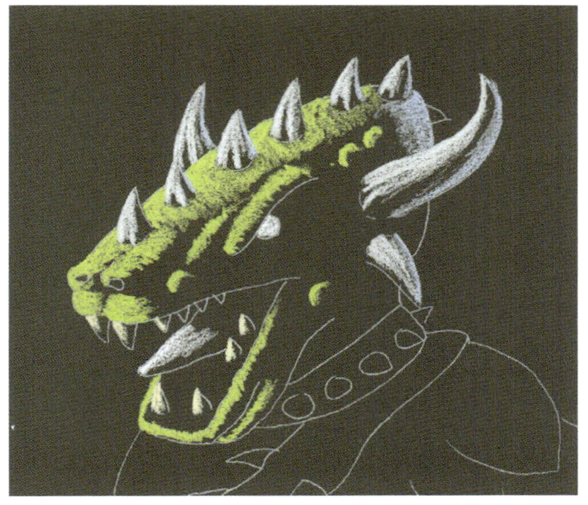

Single Layer Technique

On Pages 49 & 50 you learned that starting with a light layer of color, then building up, one layer over another, is a good way to control your drawing as it progresses. A faster but still acceptable method is to lay down heavy layers of color right from the beginning, using firm pressure on your pencils so that you don't need to return to that same area of the drawing to build more color. This works especially well on colored paper.

"Single layer" does not mean using only one color for the entire drawing; rather, it means putting down a *heavy* layer of a color in a specific area. For example, this drawing began with a single thick layer of color for each area of the drawing — parts of the monster's forehead, horns, and back of his head. There was no need to go back and add more of the *same* colors to those areas.

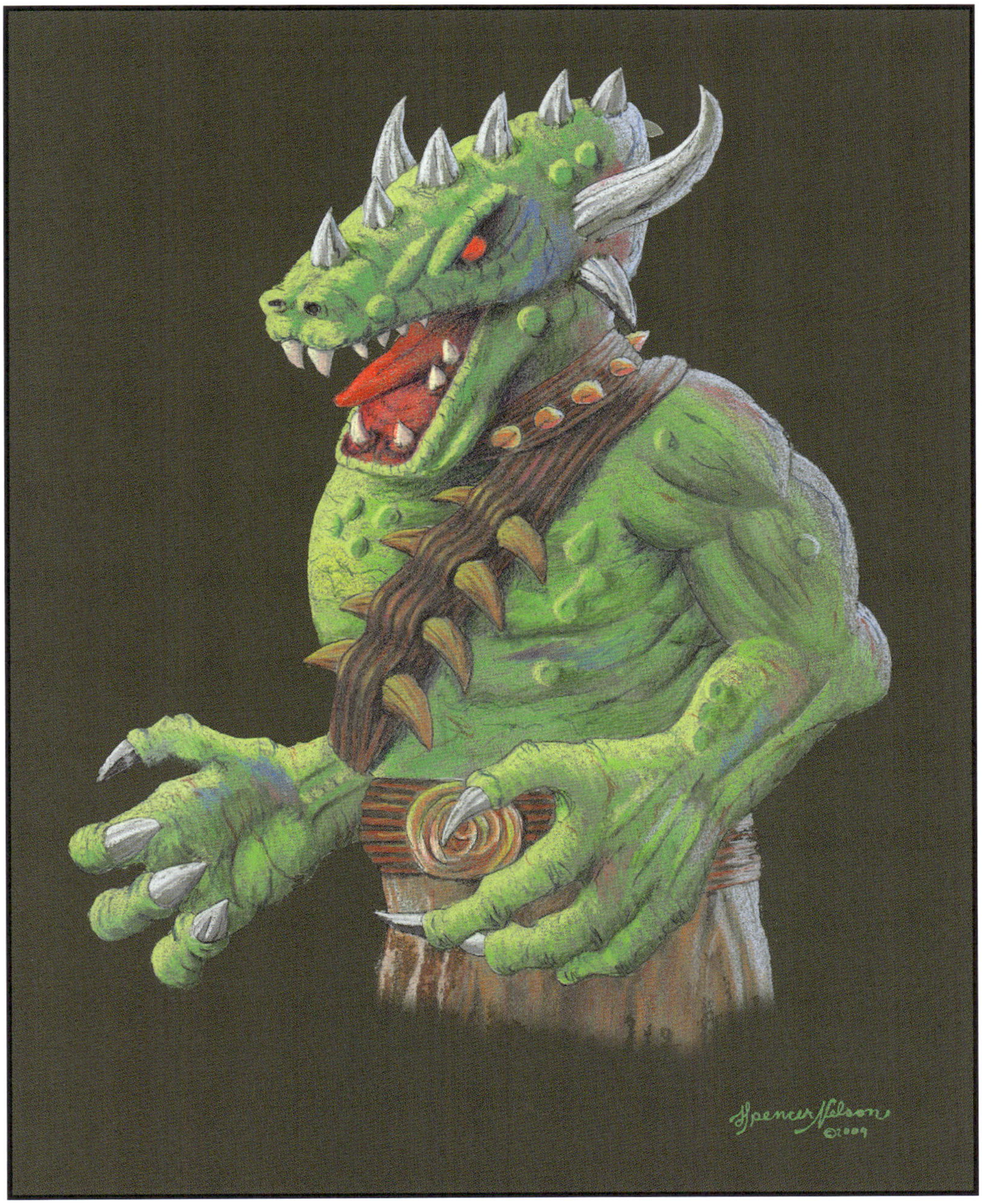

Similarly, dense colors were applied to the rest of the drawing.

Still, *different* colors were applied over the already-thick base colors to make them more interesting. You can see spots of red, blue, and violet on top of the greens, for example, but no more greens were applied.

Because the drawing is on colored paper, I did not feel a need to saturate the paper with color to mask the paper's texture — the paper's "teeth" appear through the colors and that, for me, is OK.

Drawn on pastel paper with Prismacolor colored pencils. Original size 11" x 14.75".

About STYLE and TOSSING OUT the RULES

For most (but not all) of the illustrations in this book, I used techniques that produce monsters and aliens that appear to be somewhat realistic. This has been my *style*. To draw creatures using similar techniques, you are advised to follow the "rules" that have been described.

…but ONLY IF you want to do as I have done.

To create very appealing art, however, it is NOT mandatory that you follow my rules! You can think of those rules as merely *suggestions* and, if you wish, disregard them altogether and emulate (copy) the styles of other artists or, better yet, create rules of your own and thus set your own style.

On the next two pages you will see how I abandoned my own rules and used a technique inspired by Boulder artist Phil Lewis (phillewisart.com). In the drawing on the next page, there are no highlights and shadows — all the suggestions I have made previously for shading and line thickness are ignored. Colors are not subtle or blended together. Minimal attention was paid to anatomy. The monster is not drawn in a realistic manner. It is highly *stylized*. The technique draws attention to itself. BUT… the drawing is, hopefully, appealing and fun to look at.

It is ART!

And that's all that matters!

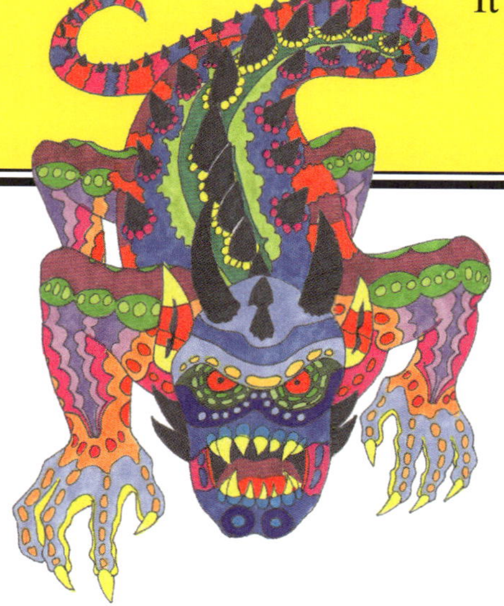

This monster was rendered on inexpensive 11" x 17" card stock paper, available from instant printing shops. Although markers were used, you could fill in color with longer lasting lightfast watercolors or acrylics.

I started with a simple drawing. Lines were made as light as possible to avoid corrupting color with graphite (pencil lead). I didn't bother to show a lot of details — they would be added later...

An "ultra fine" point marker was used for small details and to create sharp edges.

Broader tipped markers were employed to fill in colors. (The markers may be labeled "fine point", but they are fairly thick.)

I chose to make up color patterns as I went along, with little thought beforehand.

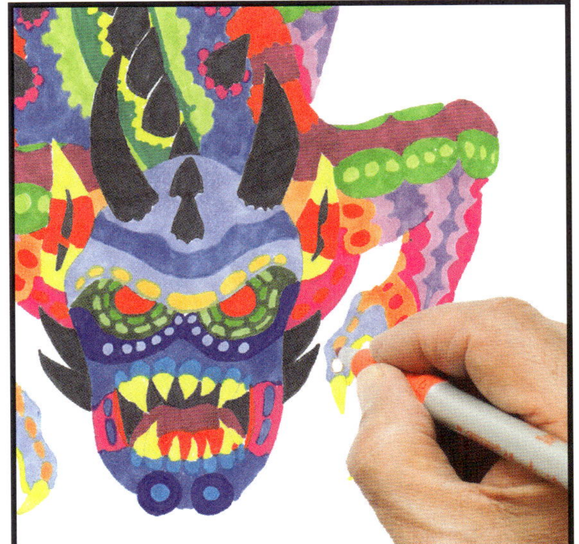

Most colors were first applied with thicker "fine" tipped markers...

Bic "Mark it / fine point" and Sharpie "ultra fine" point markers were used for this project.

(See page 19.)

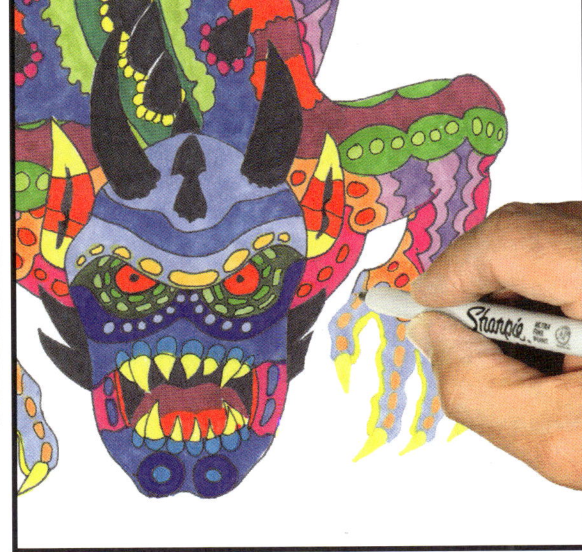

…then outlined with a black "ultra fine" tipped marker.

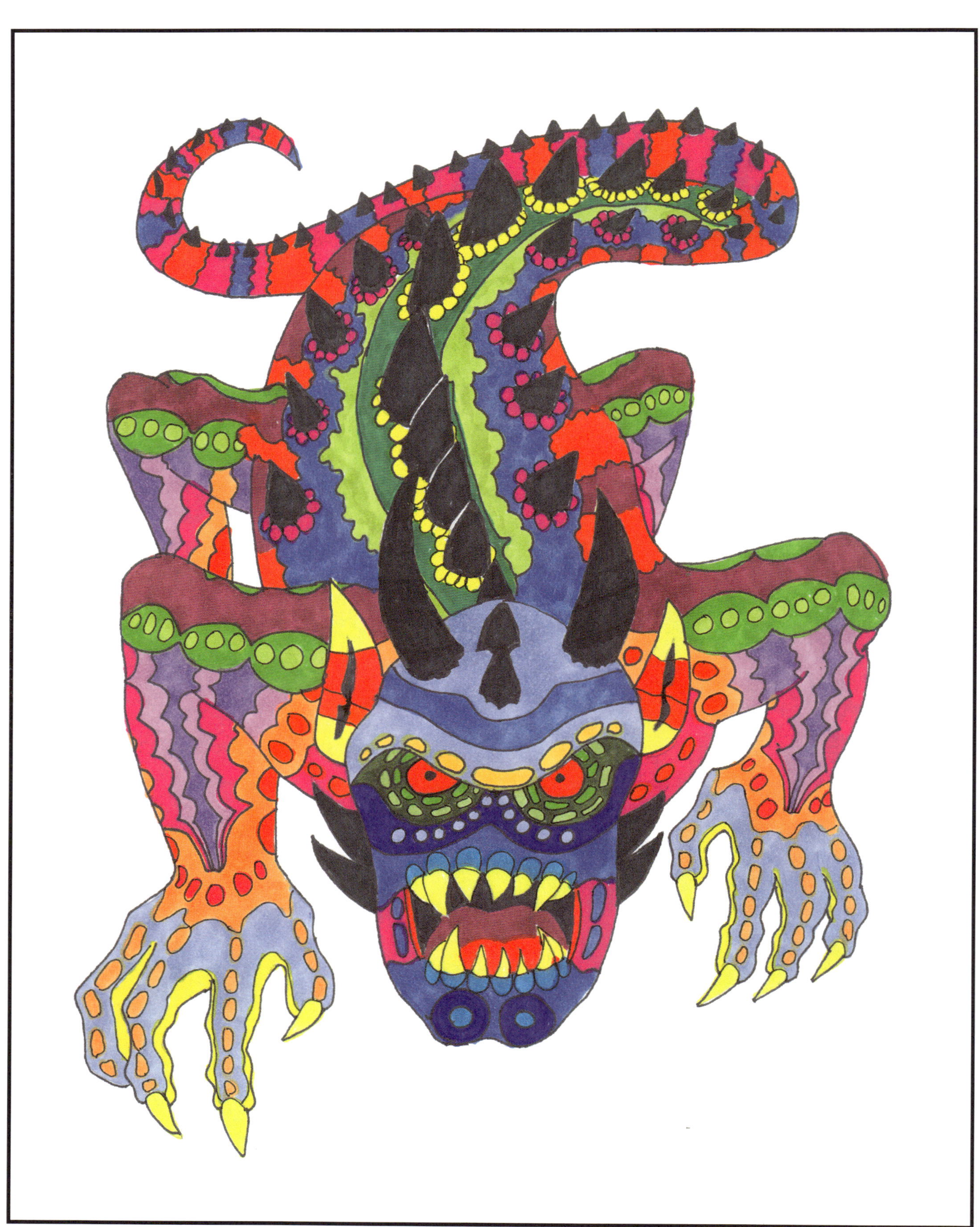

Original drawing 9" x 12", created with Sharpie and Bic Mark-it markers on 11" x 17" printers' card stock.

MIXED MEDIA

Let's face it: Using colored pencils to fill in a large area can be boring and take a lot of time, yet it's nice to have the control of colored pencils. There is a solution to this problem: Use *watercolors* to lay down sizeable areas of color fairly quickly, then use colored pencils as well as pens and markers to add shading and precise details.

Watercolors, colored pencils, pens and markers are all *media*. If you use two or more of them together you are using *mixed media*. **"Watercolors" includes both transparent watercolors and gouaches.**

Transparent watercolors and gouaches are available in tubes and as "cakes".

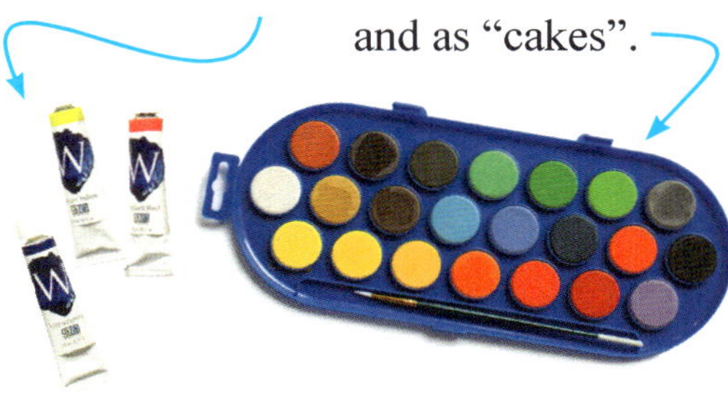

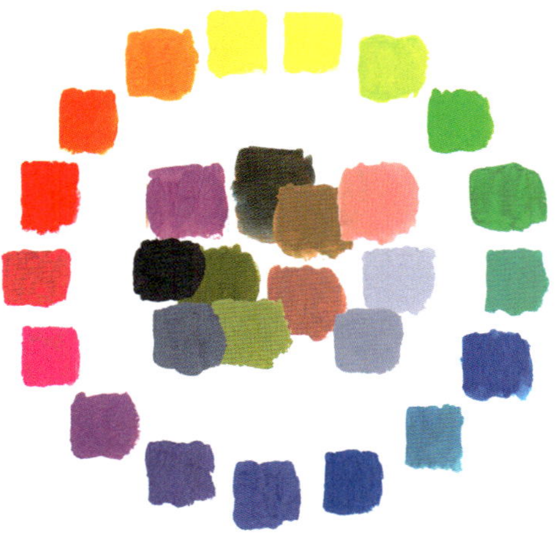

You can create *millions* of colors — including browns and shades of gray — by mixing two or three individual colors from as few as six primary colors plus white. Since experts and manufacturers have their own versions of what those primary colors are, I recommend you use basic colors from your own set and experiment.

Find out more about mixing colors and such by visiting my website — **spencerWnelson.com**

Three coats required for this Master's Touch transparent watercolor.

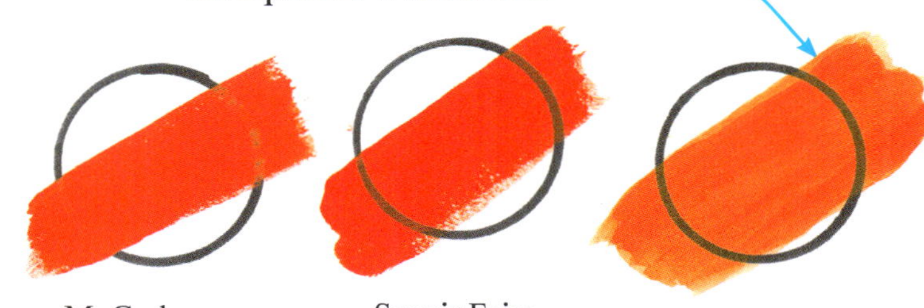

M. Graham Gouache

Savoir Faire Gouache

More about gouache and transparent watercolors on page 21. High quality gouaches such as those by M. Graham more or less mask what's underneath but are costly — a single tube of high quality watercolor can cost as much as a complete set of lower quality colors. Lower quality "gouaches" such as those by Savoir Faire obviously do a poor job of masking stuff underneath but still have reasonably good color. Transparent colors don't pretend to hide anything: affordable brands such as Master's Touch can produce OK hues but may require more than one coat to produce the desired intensity.

I favor gouaches — including lower quality gouaches — for the mixed media technique taught on these pages.

Bottom line: If you can't afford expensive watercolors, I recommend using less expensive gouaches and think of them as *transparent watercolors*, despite their being labeled "gouache" or "opaque".

A Multimedia sphere...

1
A rich basic color quickly and easily laid down with gouache.

2
Shading applied with colored pencils. (Watercolors leave a “tooth” that accepts pencils.)

3
Shading smoothed with colored pencil blender (page 15). Fixative then applied (pages 77-78). The latter helps the marker to create better, sharper lines.

4
Lines drawn with #03 Micron marker (page 19).

With a good quality gouache, you can paint over colors already laid down — provided the first color is completely dry and you limit the second color to one pass, unless it too has dried.

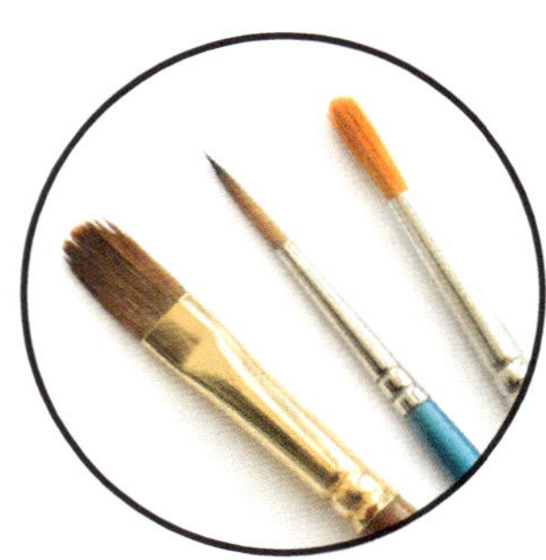

Uses brushes with soft bristles.

I suggest you do your painting / drawing on thick paper designed for both dry and wet media, such as Strathmore "Mixed Media" paper, 140lb (300g/m^2).

To reduce warping from the watercolor, you can mount the paper using blue painter's masking tape on a rigid piece of cardboard, thick foam board, particle board, or some other rigid support. (I prefer 1/2 inch thick “art board”, a dense foam core support available at art supply stores.)

Using masking tape as shown can also create a nice border.

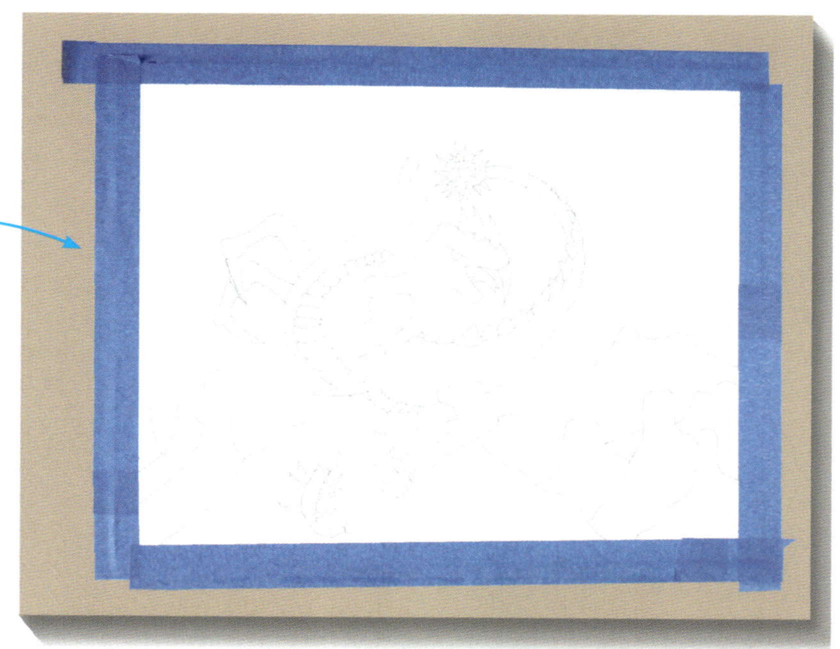

1
In the painting/drawing to follow, I started with a light drawing made with an ordinary pencil. I didn‘t want the drawing to show through the paint nor did I want the pencil’s lead to corrupt (dirty) the paint, so I made the drawing so light I could barely see it.

2

I commenced painting.

I first wet an area I intend to color — if it is fairly large — before applying paint. This will smooth out the color.

If paint overlaps an area intended for another color, I am sometimes able to cover it up using opaque paint, provided the bottom paint has dried. This is especially true if the paint is high quality.

Some unwanted paint can be removed with a small wet sponge or a piece of wet paper towel.

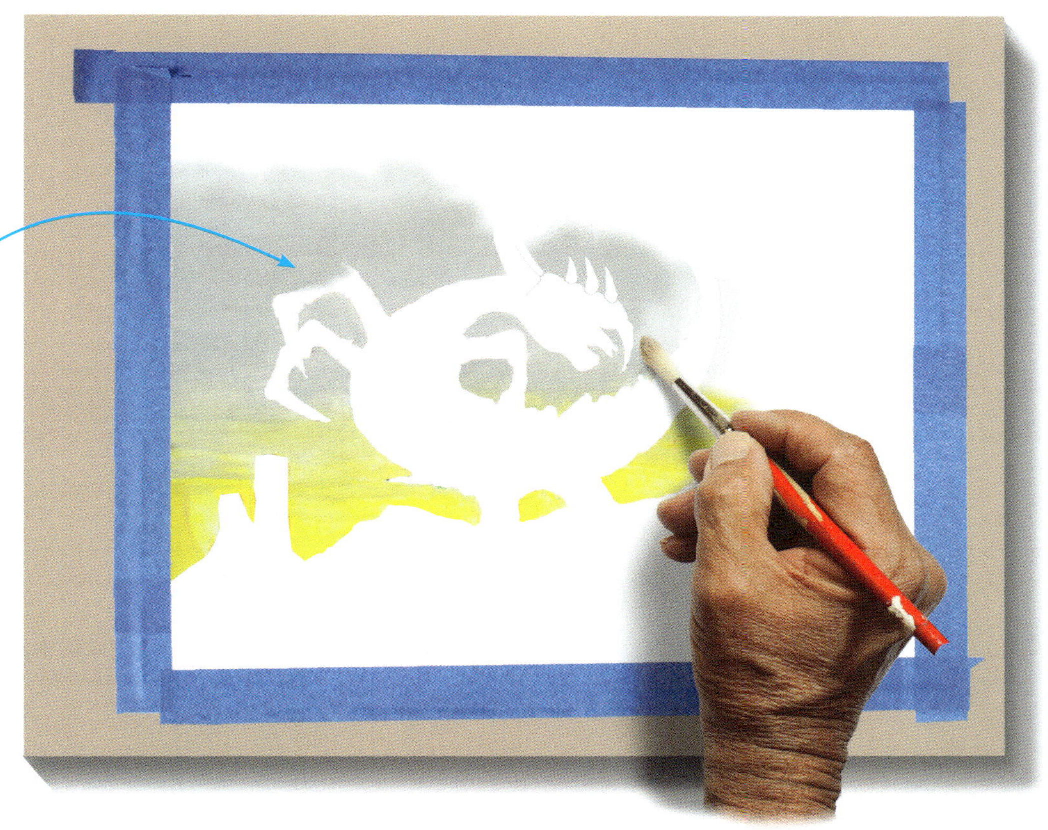

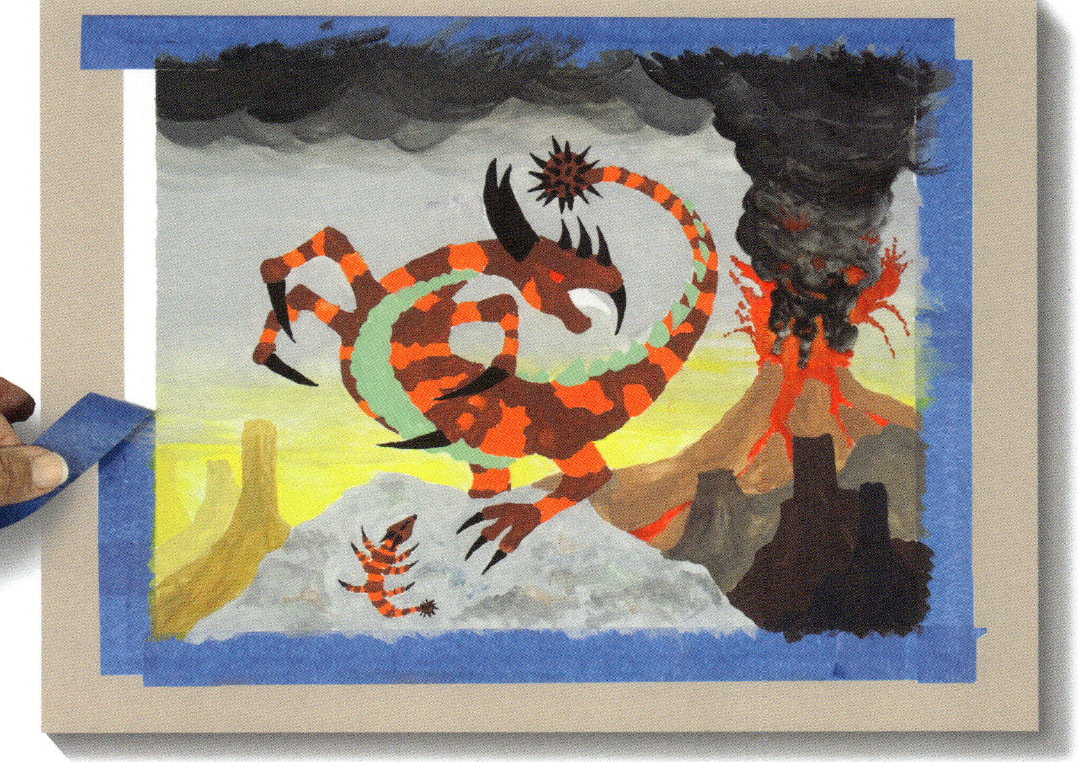

3

I removed the masking tape when the painting phase was complete, though it would have been better to wait 'till the whole painting/ drawing was finished because the border got a bit smudged in subsequent phases. (Never said I was perfect!)

4

I drew the rain and added shading and other details with colored pencils.

The lightning was painted with titanium white acrylic. (White watercolor didn't work on the waxy surface created with colored pencils.) Fixative was applied before the next phase. (See pages 77-78.)

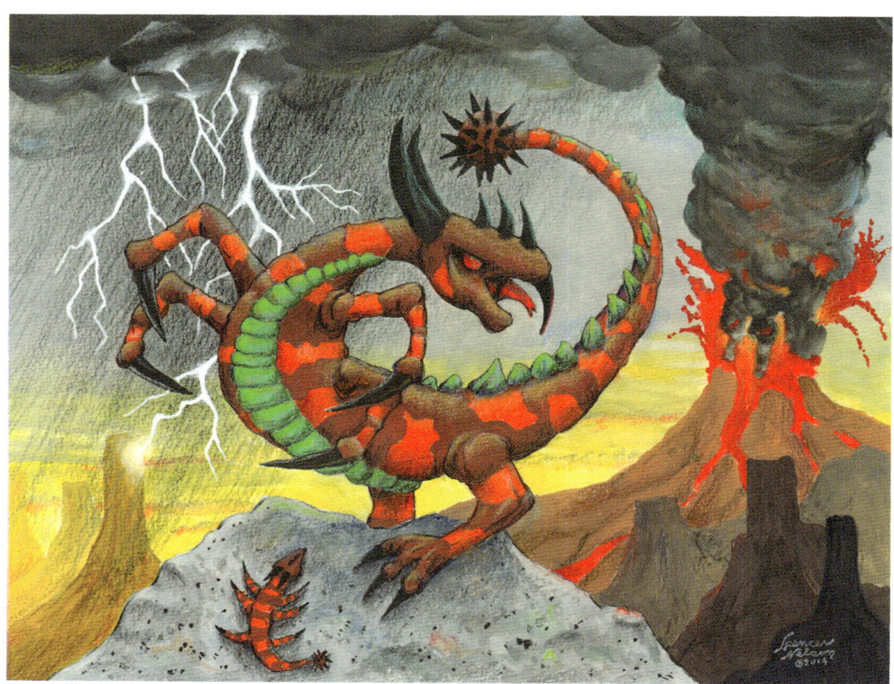

5

Finally, a Sharpie “Ultra Fine” marker was used to draw the scales.

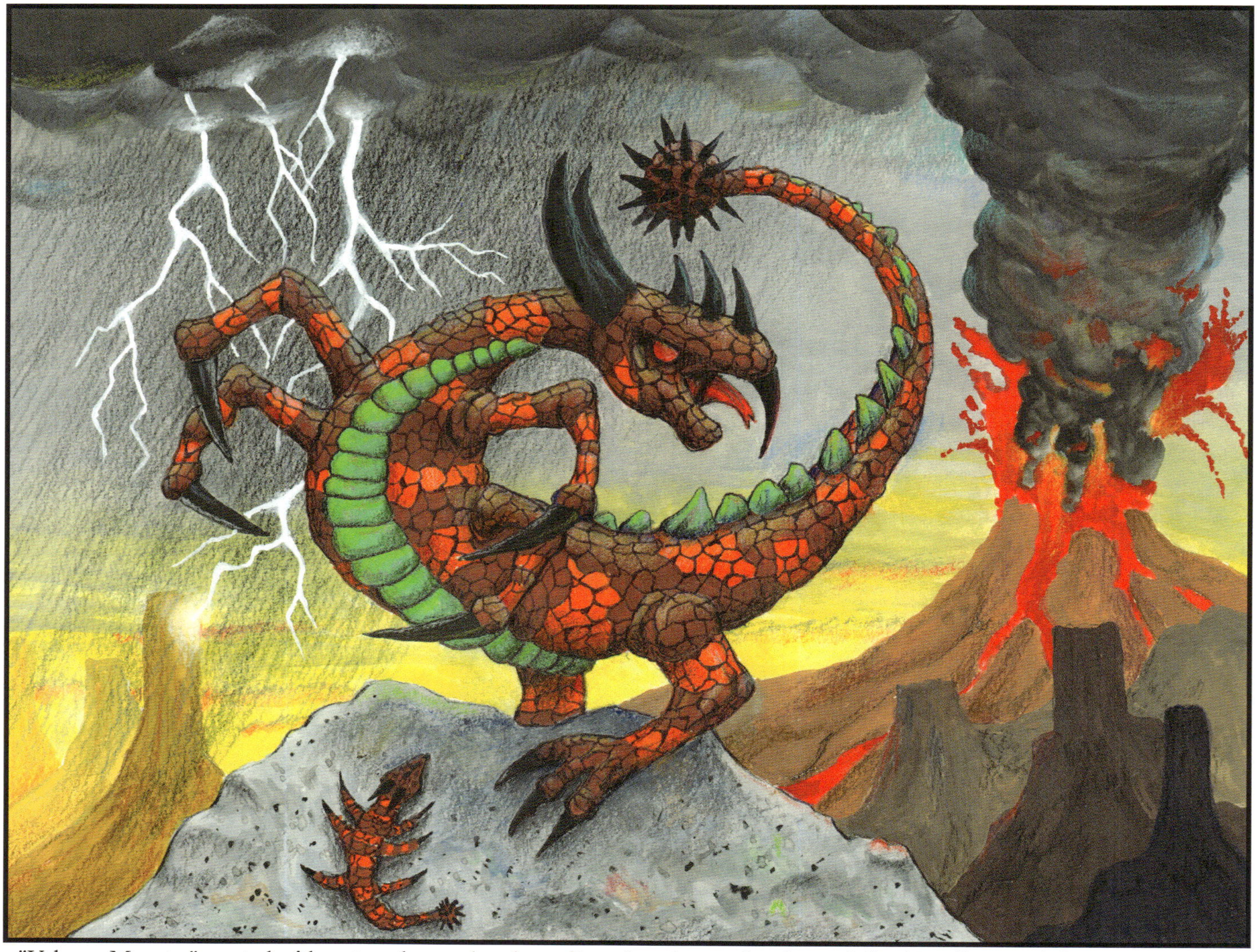

"Volcano Monster" created with watercolors, colored pencils and marker on Strathmore Mixed Media 300 g/m^2 paper, 9" x 13".

The Nature of LIGHT and SHADOW

To create monsters and aliens that look realistic, it is very important to understand how their appearance is shaped by different kinds of light and shadow.

Point Source Light

Point source light behaves as though it is coming from a single, seemingly small point, such as a bare light bulb or the sun*. It causes features to be sharp and well defined.

Because there is only one source of light shining on this monster (not counting a bit of reflected light), details in the deep shadow area cannot be seen.

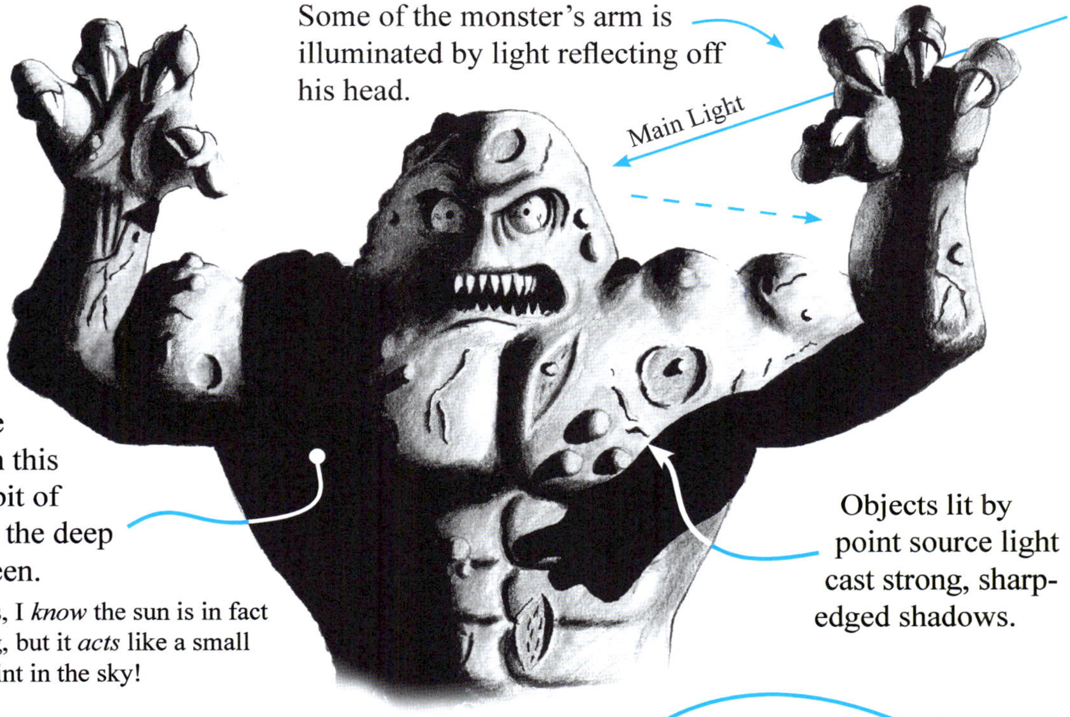

Some of the monster's arm is illuminated by light reflecting off his head.

Main Light

Objects lit by point source light cast strong, sharp-edged shadows.

* Yes, I *know* the sun is in fact big, but it *acts* like a small point in the sky!

Soft Light

This time the creature is lit by soft light, which comes from a broad source, such as a window or a big flood lamp.

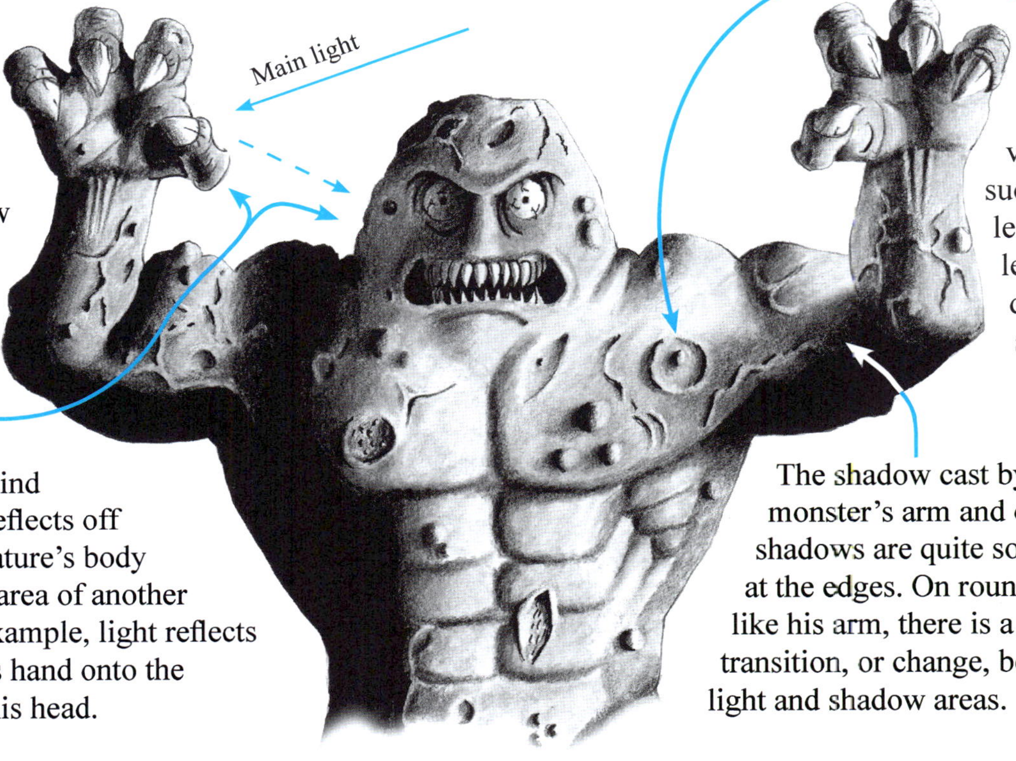

Main light

Features, like gashes, pimples, veins and such will be less sharp, less well defined with softer light.

Reflected Light

Light from any kind of source often reflects off one part of a creature's body into the shadow area of another part. Here, for example, light reflects off the monster's hand onto the shadow side of his head.

The shadow cast by the monster's arm and other shadows are quite soft and fuzzy at the edges. On rounded parts, like his arm, there is a gentle transition, or change, between the light and shadow areas.

Very Soft

Here the monster could be outside on a cloudy day or in the shadow of a building or any place where light comes from almost every direction.

Which kind of lighting do you think produces the most dramatic, scary creature?

There can still be deep shadows with very soft lighting. For example, the area just under the monster's eyebrow and inside his mouth are solid black in this drawing.

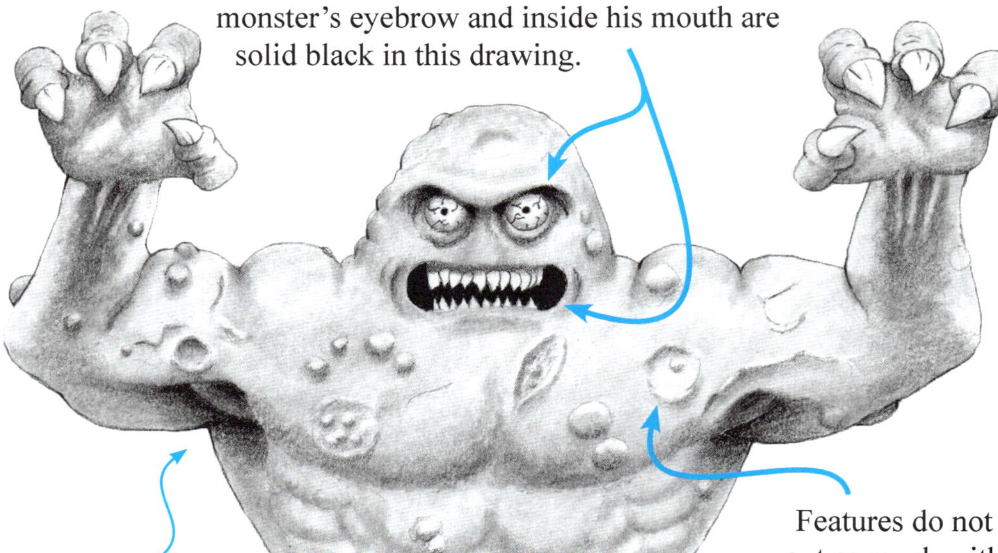

With very soft lighting, light is likely to bounce off nearby objects and into the shadow areas, revealing more detail. In this example, muscles in the creature's arm pits are illuminated by light reflected off the ground.

Features do not stand out as much with very soft lighting. Lines are less sharp. Light, coming from almost everywhere, "fills in" shadows so they are not as dark as they would otherwise be. Shadows have very soft edges and are sometimes barely visible.

Secondary Sources

I call the strongest source of light the **primary source** or **main source**. In addition to a primary source of light, there is almost always one or more additional sources. These could be another light in the room, or light reflected off nearby buildings, the ground, or anything else.

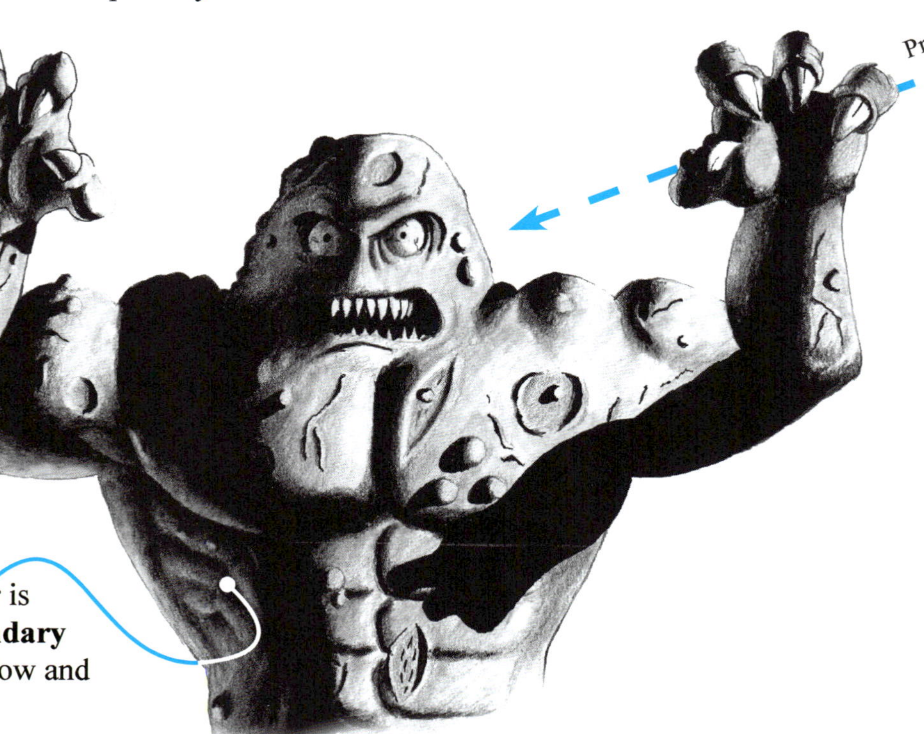

Here part of the monster is lit by a less-bright **secondary source** coming from below and to his side.

Light Combinations — grayscale

Most of the time there is a *combination* of light sources illuminating a monster (and most things in the universe).

I STRONGLY SUGGEST that you render some parts of a drawing very dark or black and some parts pure white. Here light does not reach the inside of the monster's mouth and other parts, so they are as black as I could make them. On the other hand, areas of his eye and claws that face the primary light were left white (the color of the paper).

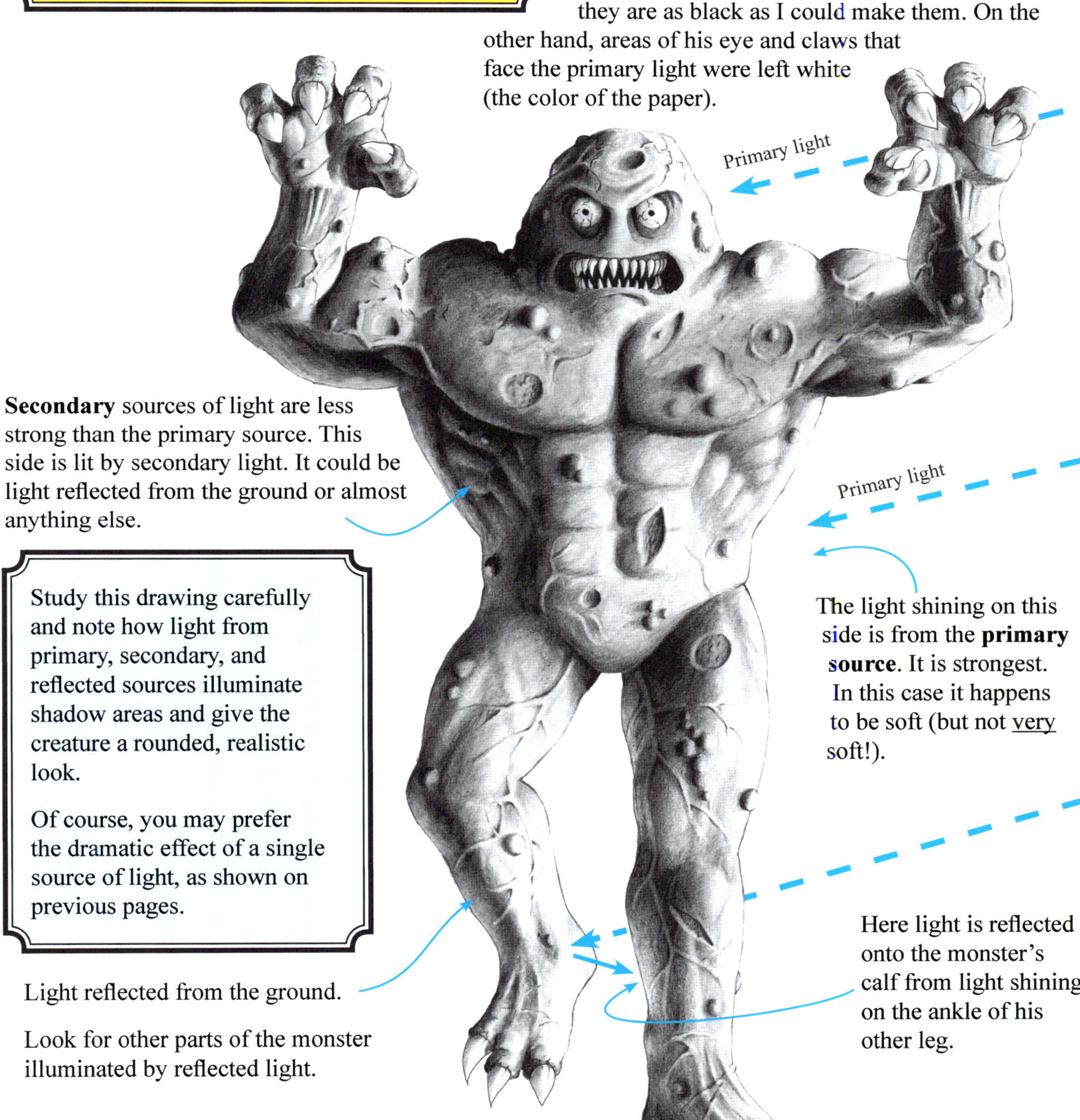

Secondary sources of light are less strong than the primary source. This side is lit by secondary light. It could be light reflected from the ground or almost anything else.

The light shining on this side is from the **primary source**. It is strongest. In this case it happens to be soft (but not <u>very</u> soft!).

Study this drawing carefully and note how light from primary, secondary, and reflected sources illuminate shadow areas and give the creature a rounded, realistic look.

Of course, you may prefer the dramatic effect of a single source of light, as shown on previous pages.

Light reflected from the ground.

Look for other parts of the monster illuminated by reflected light.

Here light is reflected onto the monster's calf from light shining on the ankle of his other leg.

Light Combinations — color

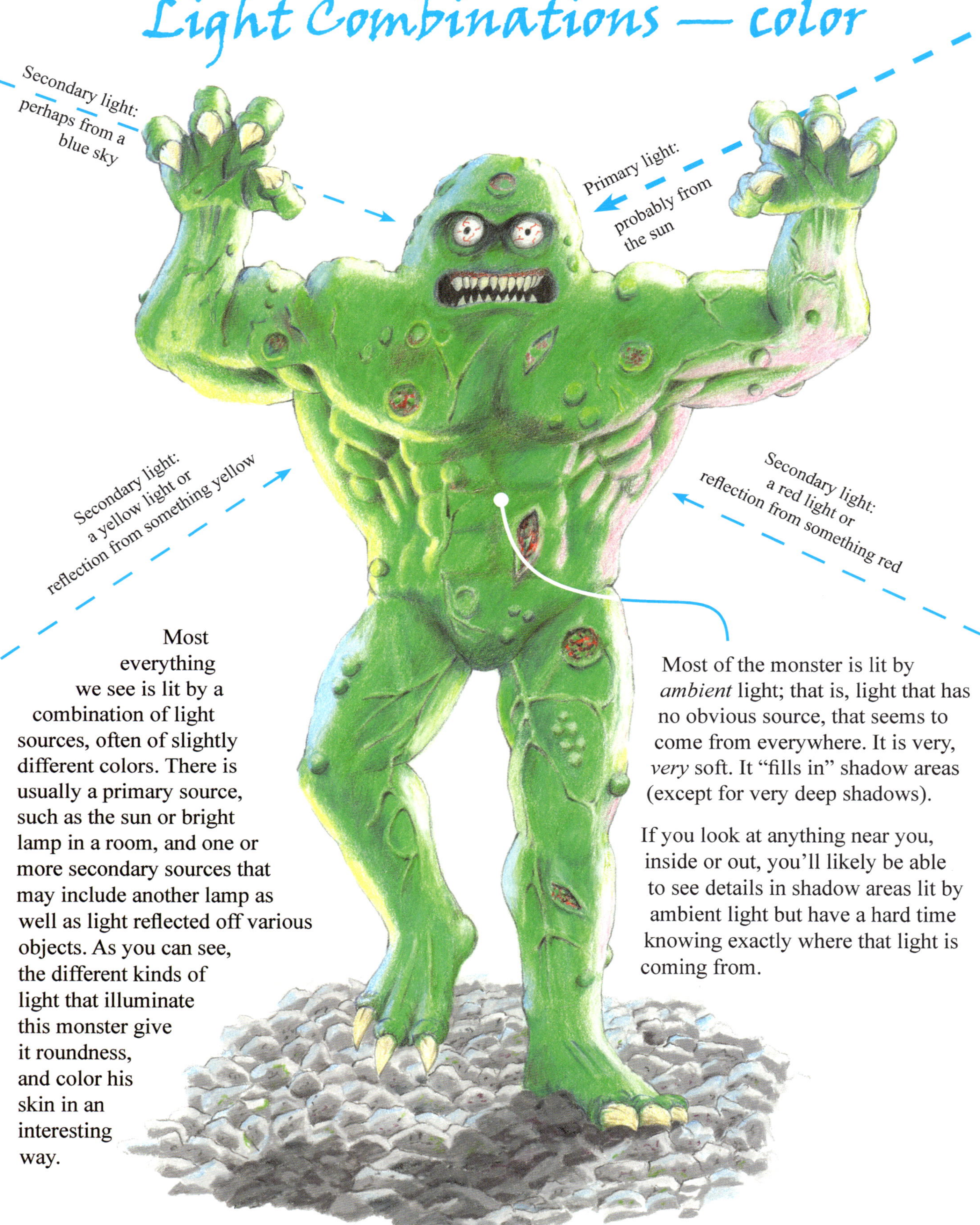

Most everything we see is lit by a combination of light sources, often of slightly different colors. There is usually a primary source, such as the sun or bright lamp in a room, and one or more secondary sources that may include another lamp as well as light reflected off various objects. As you can see, the different kinds of light that illuminate this monster give it roundness, and color his skin in an interesting way.

Most of the monster is lit by *ambient* light; that is, light that has no obvious source, that seems to come from everywhere. It is very, *very* soft. It "fills in" shadow areas (except for very deep shadows).

If you look at anything near you, inside or out, you'll likely be able to see details in shadow areas lit by ambient light but have a hard time knowing exactly where that light is coming from.

TRANSFER *Your Drawing*

Starting on page 22 of this book you learned to (1) start your drawing with simple light circles and lines, (2) create darker lines that you want to keep and, (3) remove the lighter lines with a kneaded eraser.

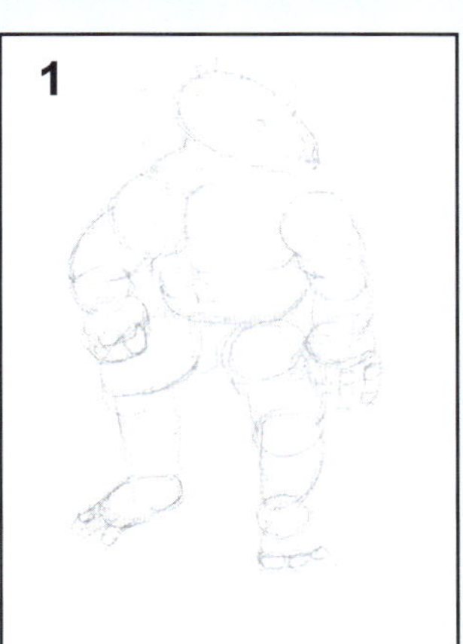

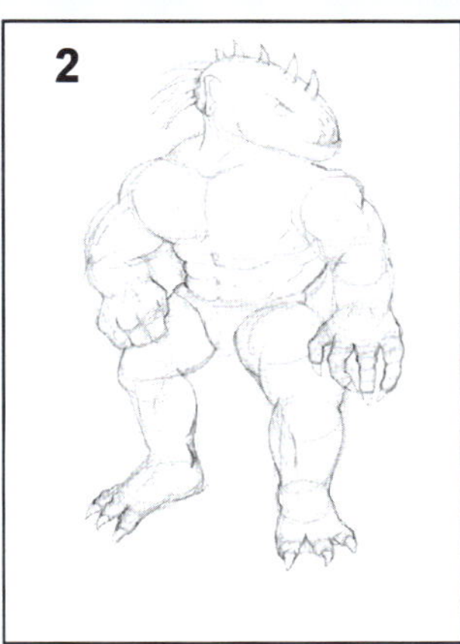

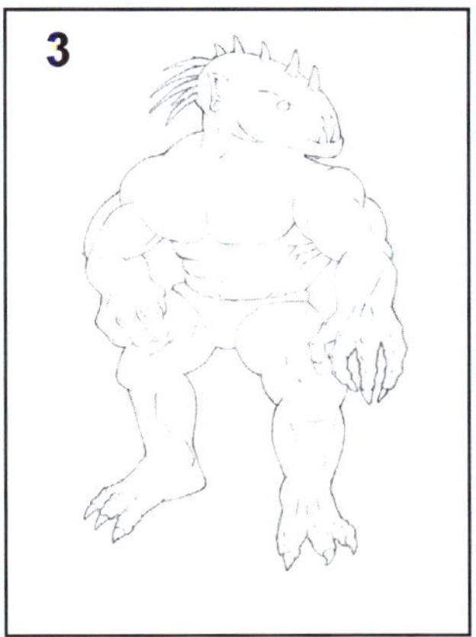

That was done on *one* sheet of paper. There may be times, however, when you wish to transfer the important lines to *another* sheet of paper. For example: the lighter lines may be too hard to erase; or you created the original on scratch paper and you want to finish it on better quality paper; or you want your final work to be on pastel paper. (See page 13.)

Following are three techniques for transferring your drawing to regular drawing paper and to opaque drawing paper.

Method A: Direct Tracing

This is a good method if you can see through both the paper containing your rough sketch *and* the paper you wish to transfer it to.

1. Place new sheet of drawing paper in front of original.

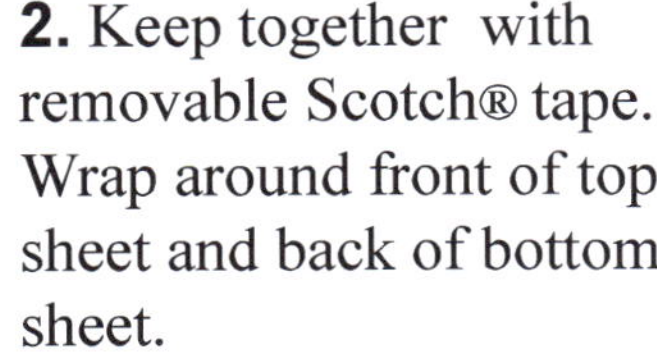

2. Keep together with removable Scotch® tape. Wrap around front of top sheet and back of bottom sheet.

3. Hold both sheets against a window and trace lines you want to keep.

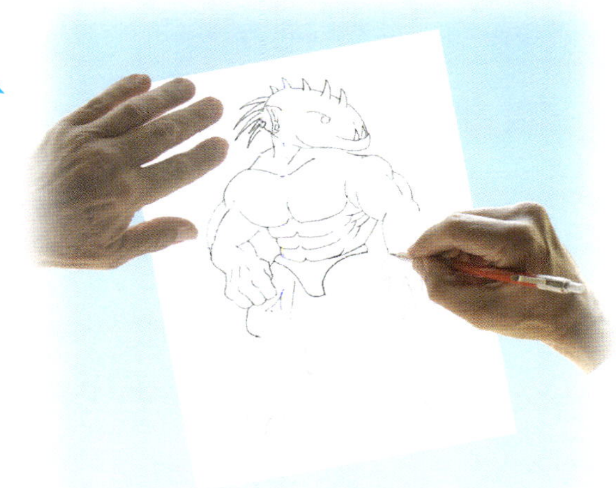

Original drawing.

New sheet of drawing paper.

Method B:

Back-Fill Method

This method works well if the paper to which you wish to transfer the drawing is too thick to see through; i.e., it is *opaque*.

1
If possible, make your rough sketch on tracing paper.

2
Place the sketch **face down o**n white paper. If you can't see the details, place it against a window.

3
Using a soft lead pencil, such as 6B, apply thick lines over the lines seen through the paper that you want to reproduce. Make thick strokes that cover the originals — don't worry about precision.

(Graphite sticks will make this process go faster. They are available from art stores.)

If you wish to create easy-to-see lines on darker pastel paper, use a white colored pencil or pastel.

3
Flip this sheet over and tape it to a sheet of good drawing paper, as shown on the next page, using Scotch® *removeable* tape.

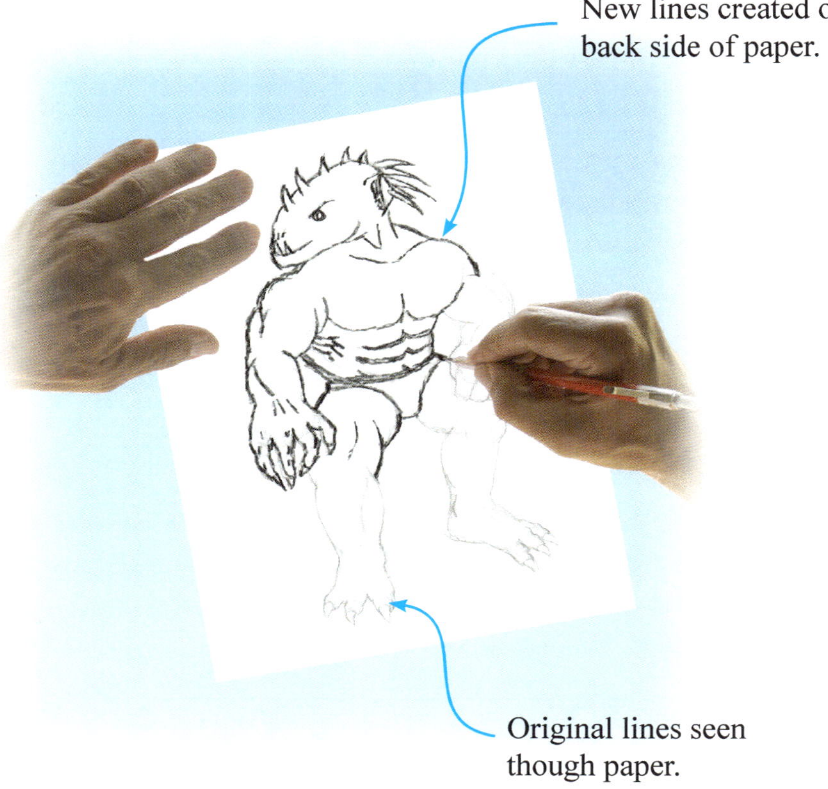

New lines created on back side of paper.

Original lines seen though paper.

IMPORTANT:
When using a window for tracing, do not let the sun shine directly in your eyes!

Tip

Erasing some of the guide lines on the original, even though you don't have to, will make tracing easier.

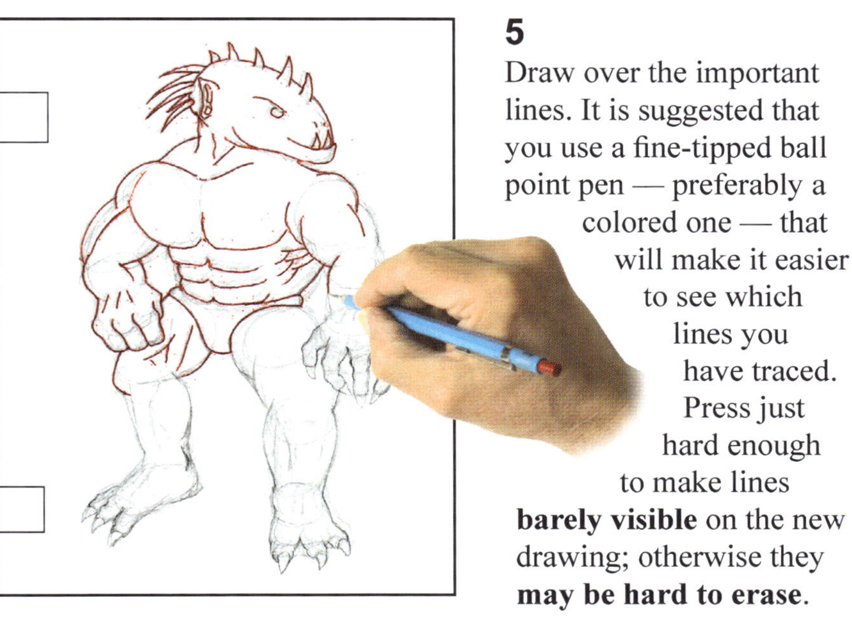

5

Draw over the important lines. It is suggested that you use a fine-tipped ball point pen — preferably a colored one — that will make it easier to see which lines you have traced. Press just hard enough to make lines **barely visible** on the new drawing; otherwise they **may be hard to erase**.

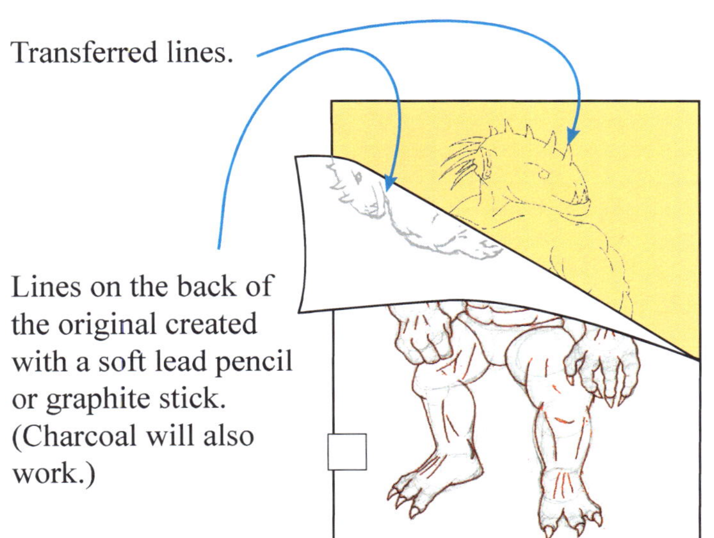

Lines traced on the back of the original with a white colored pencil or, better yet, a white pastel pencil.

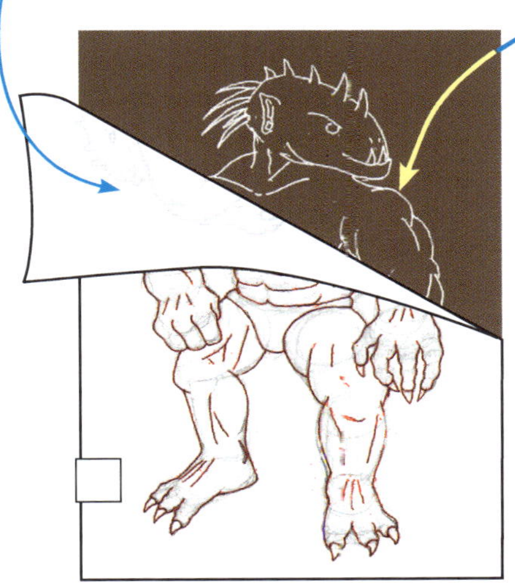

Transferred lines.

Method C: Transfer with Transfer Paper

Next Page:

The following method uses *transfer paper* for copying drawings to opaque paper. Available from art and hobby stores, transfer paper should be wax-free and specifically for artists. Graphite paper makes gray lines on light colored paper. Despite the manufacturer's claims, the lines are typically difficult to make and hard to erase, so **I prefer method B above**. Saral brand white paper, on the other hand, produces good easy-to-erase white lines on darker colored paper.

Transfer Paper Method (Contined)

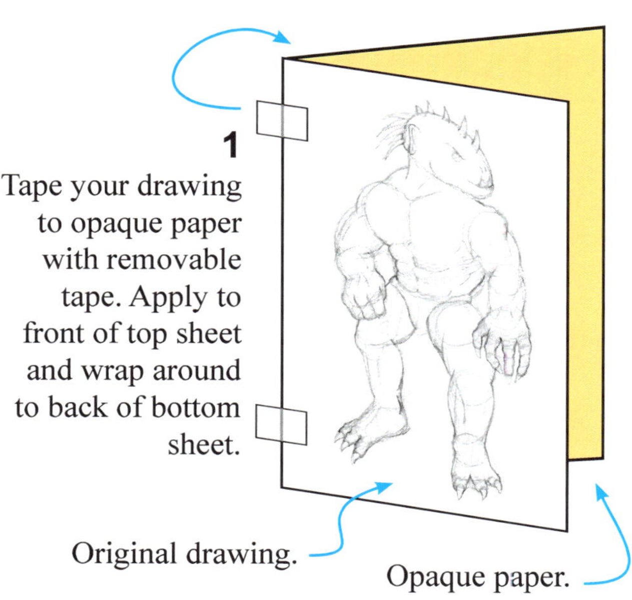

1

Tape your drawing to opaque paper with removable tape. Apply to front of top sheet and wrap around to back of bottom sheet.

Original drawing.

Opaque paper.

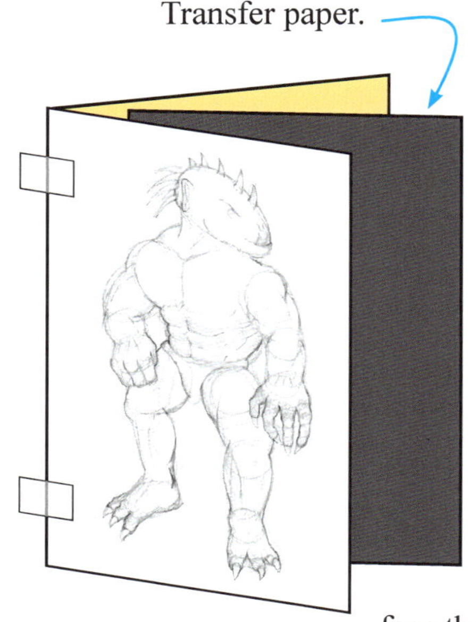

Transfer paper.

2

Insert a sheet of transfer paper between the top and bottom sheets. If your opaque paper is light, use black or gray transfer paper.

If it is dark, use white transfer paper.

Have the side of transfer paper that will leave a mark face the opaque paper.

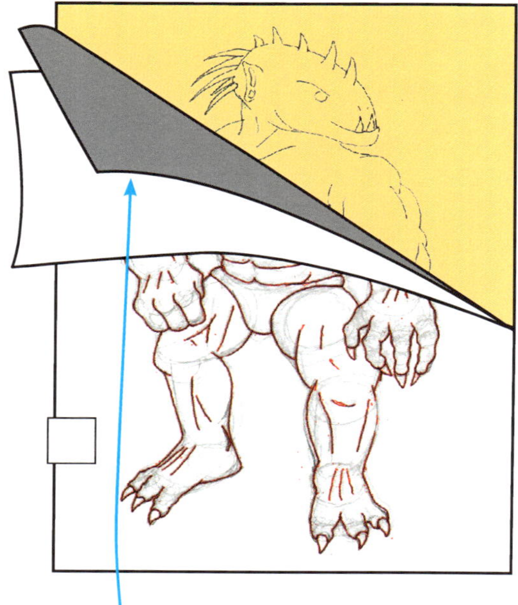

Black or gray transfer paper for light opaque paper, maybe, but method B works better.

3

When you first start, flip the paper and check that lines are copied onto the opaque paper — not back onto your original drawing. Continue checking as you trace the drawing to be sure lines are strong enough to see but not too strong.

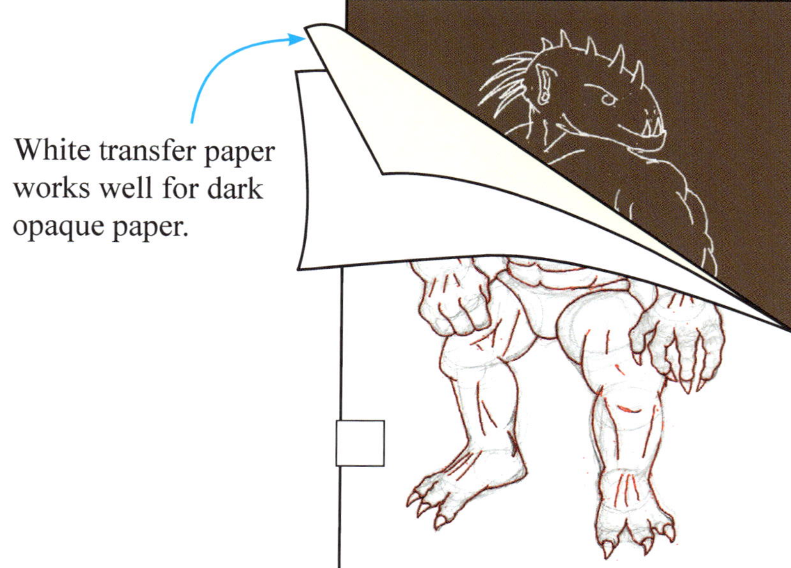

White transfer paper works well for dark opaque paper.

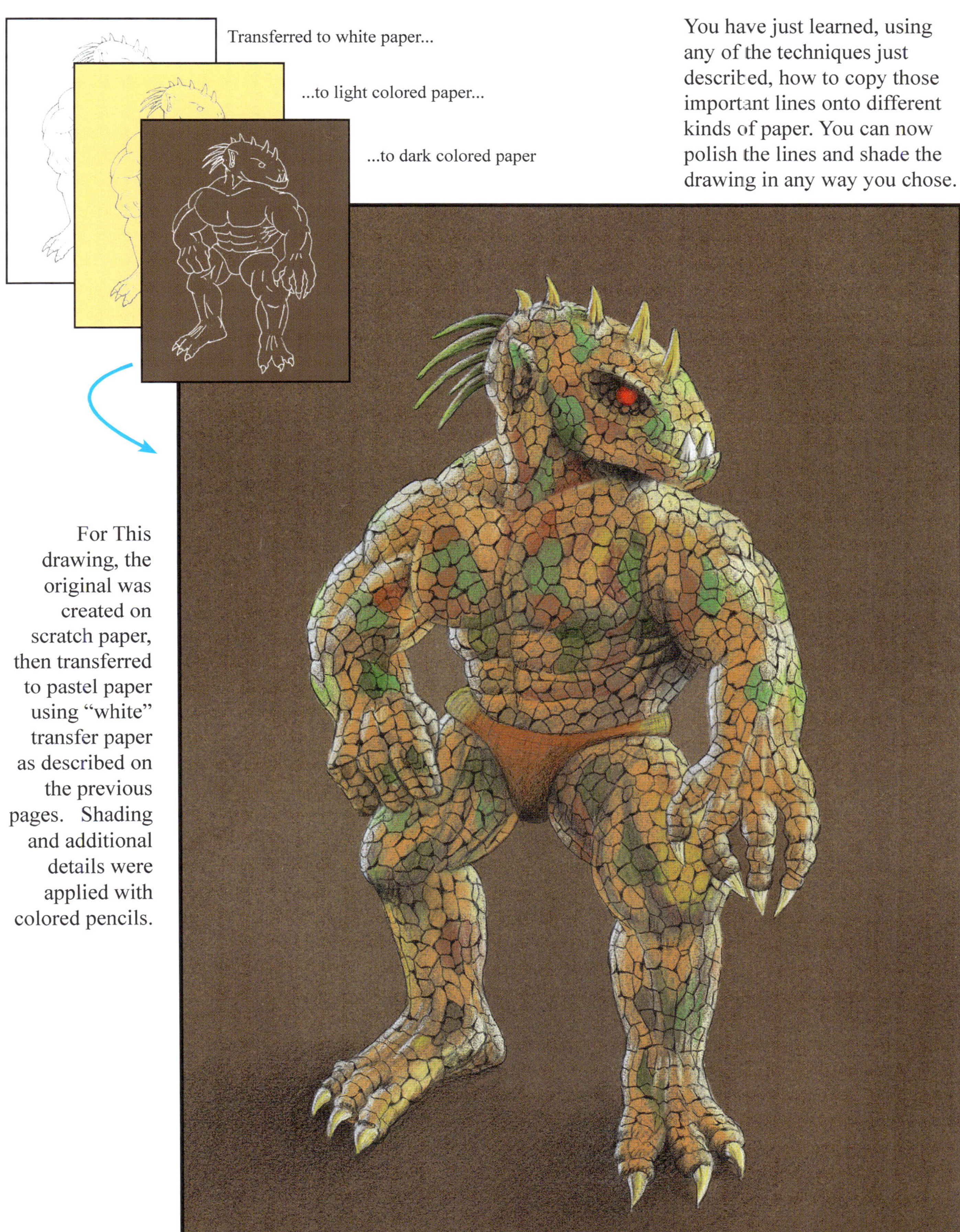

You have just learned, using any of the techniques just described, how to copy those important lines onto different kinds of paper. You can now polish the lines and shade the drawing in any way you chose.

For This drawing, the original was created on scratch paper, then transferred to pastel paper using “white” transfer paper as described on the previous pages. Shading and additional details were applied with colored pencils.

Here's Something About SYMMETRY

If features on the left side of your monster or alien are almost identical those on its right — if the features "mirror" each other — your creature has *symmetry* (sem-eh-tree): it is *symmetrical*.

This monster is

Not Symmetrical.*

The features on its left side may be *similar* to those on its right, but the *sizes*, *shapes*, and *locations* are much different.

This is not necessarily a bad thing: he is a *monster*, after all: such distortions may not matter. They may, in fact, make him more creepy than he would be if his features were symmetrical.

The features of many monsters are, however, pretty much alike on both their left and right sides; they are symmetrical. You'll learn how to draw monsters that have symmetry on the next few pages … *if* that is your wish!

(*A monster that is not symmetrical would be *asymmetrical*.)

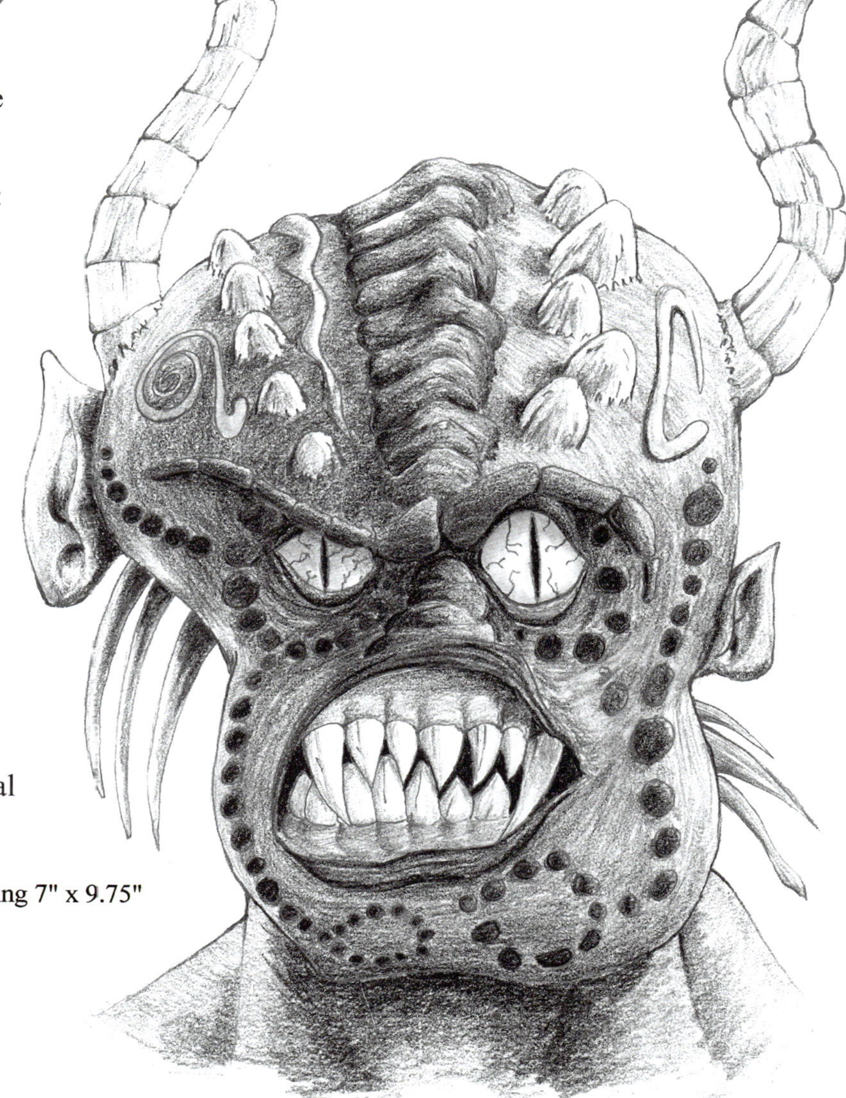

Original drawing 7" x 9.75"

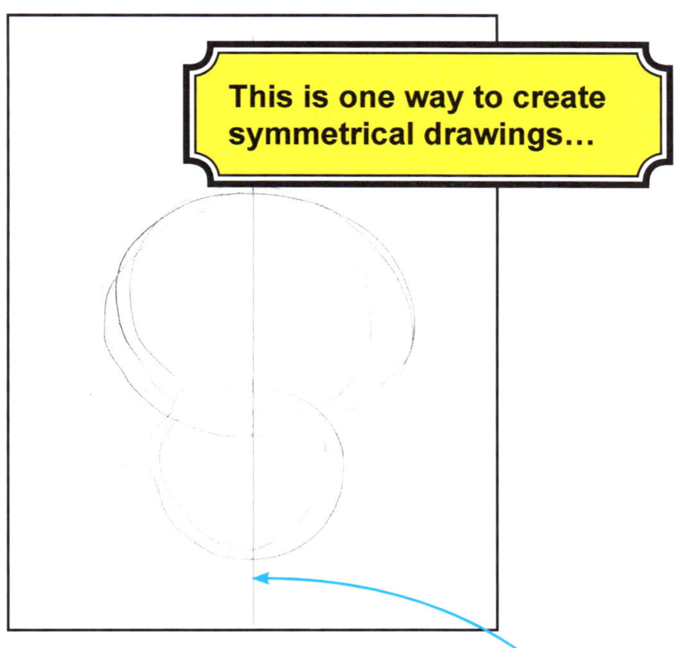

1

Start with simple shapes, such as light circles, on **tracing paper** (available at most hobby stores) or fairly **thin plain paper**.

Using a ruler, draw a straight vertical center line dividing the shapes in half.

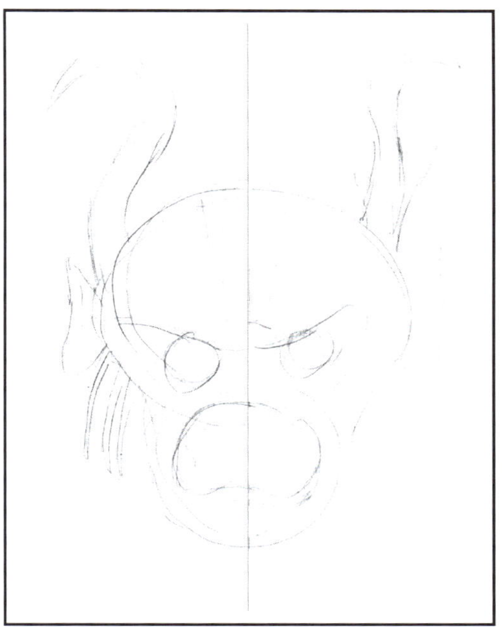

2

Continue with very light guide lines. At first, sketch on both the left and right sides of the vertical line to get an idea of the over-all shape of your creature.

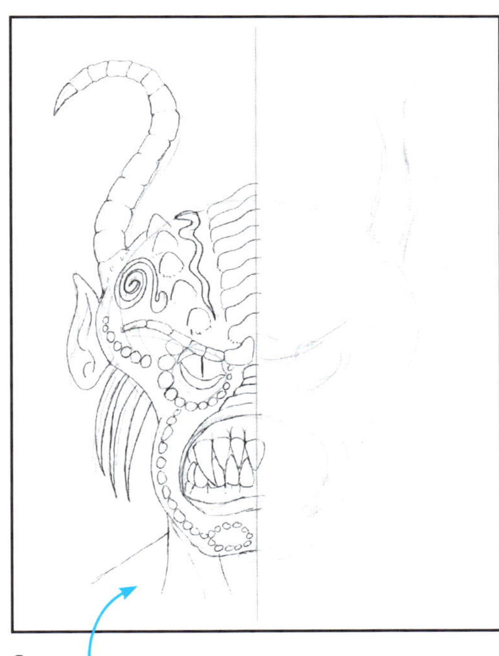

3

When ready, make heavier solid lines of the sort you'll want to keep in the final drawing. **Focus on one side only**: In this lesson, the left side is chosen.

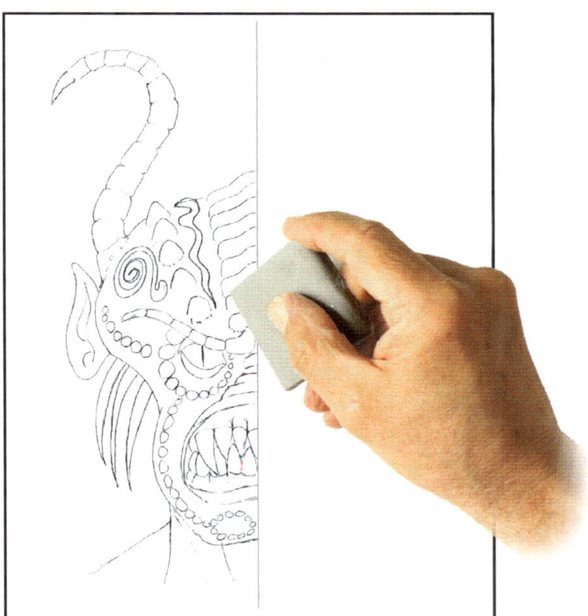

4

Go over the drawing with a kneaded eraser so the light lines on both sides disappear while the darker ones one the left — the ones you want to keep — remain. You may want to darken those lines again. Don't erase the center line! (Learn more about kneaded erasers on page 11.)

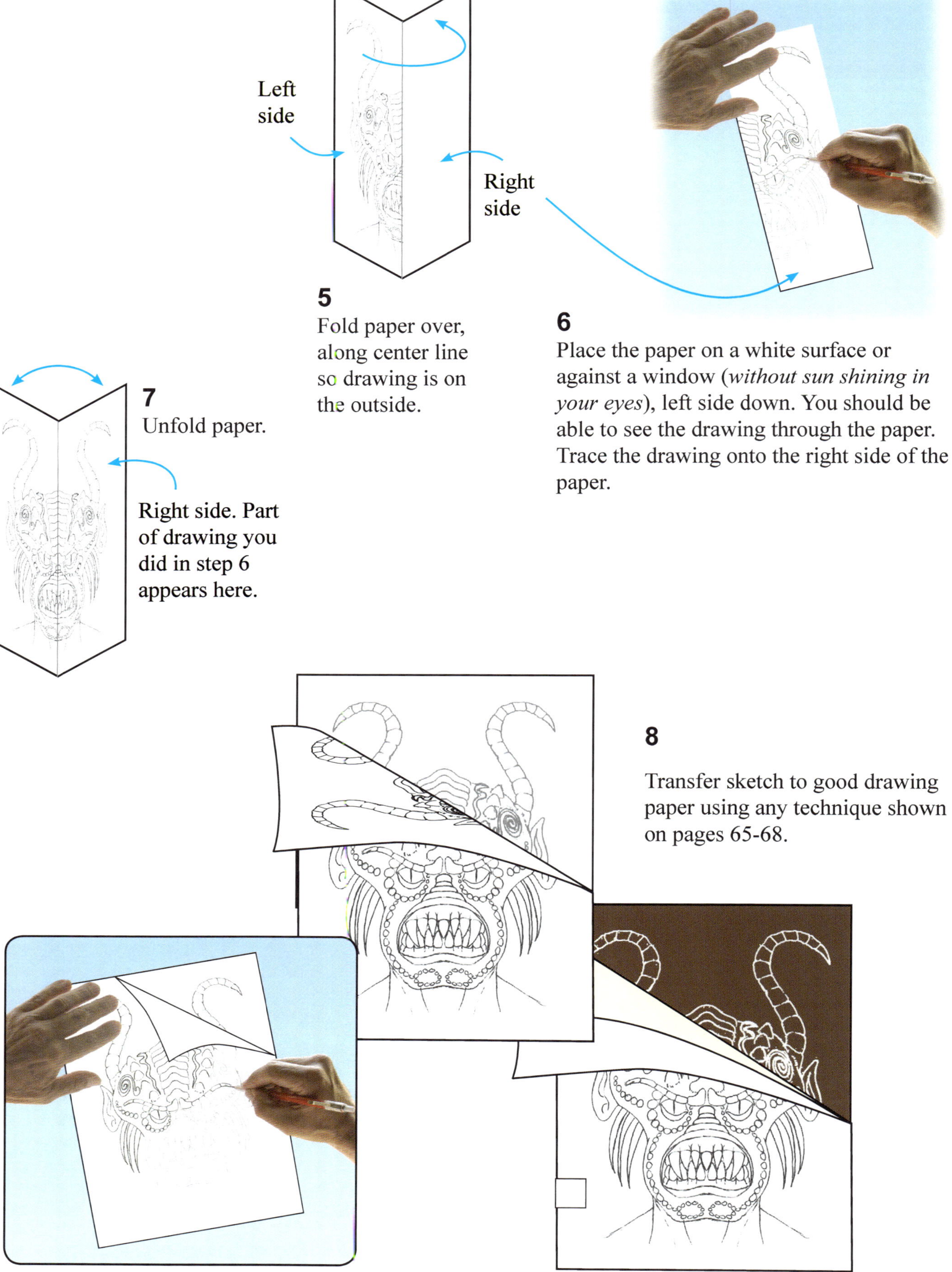

5

Fold paper over, along center line so drawing is on the outside.

6

Place the paper on a white surface or against a window (*without sun shining in your eyes*), left side down. You should be able to see the drawing through the paper. Trace the drawing onto the right side of the paper.

7

Unfold paper.

8

Transfer sketch to good drawing paper using any technique shown on pages 65-68.

The monster is now

SYMMETRICAL.

The features on his left are very similar to those on his right, even though they face opposite directions.

(The shading may differ, due to the light that falls on him, but that doesn't detract from his symmetry, as defined in this book.)

You may have the skills necessary to make symmetrical drawings freehand, without aids. If so, congratulations! You have more talent than I!

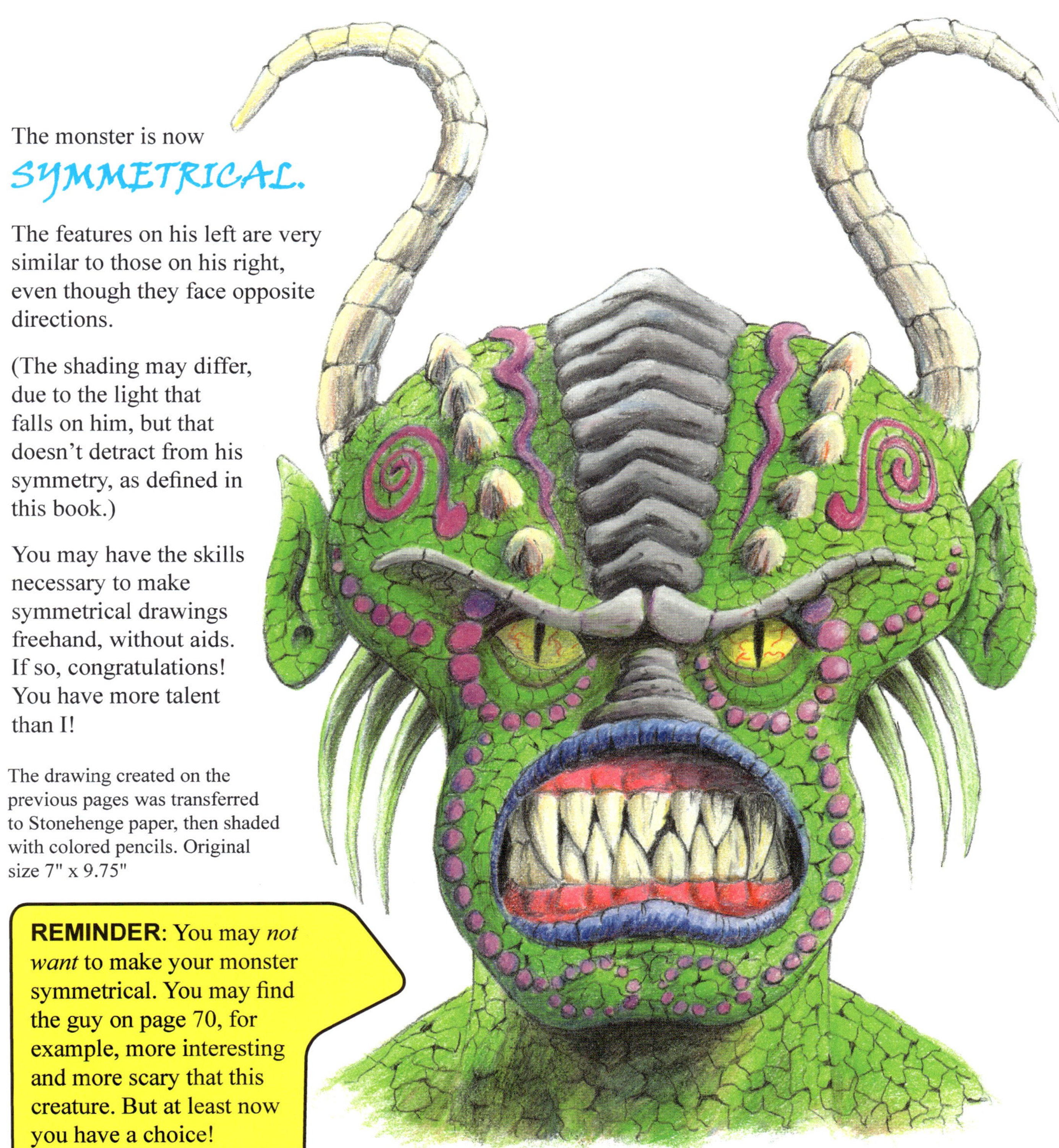

The drawing created on the previous pages was transferred to Stonehenge paper, then shaded with colored pencils. Original size 7" x 9.75"

REMINDER: You may *not want* to make your monster symmetrical. You may find the guy on page 70, for example, more interesting and more scary that this creature. But at least now you have a choice!

Nearly every monster or alien in this book which directly faces you, the viewer, was created using a method similar to the one just described.

Perhaps you can figure out other methods as well.

Draw a DRAGON!

While many drawings start with circles, this one starts with a simple curved line...

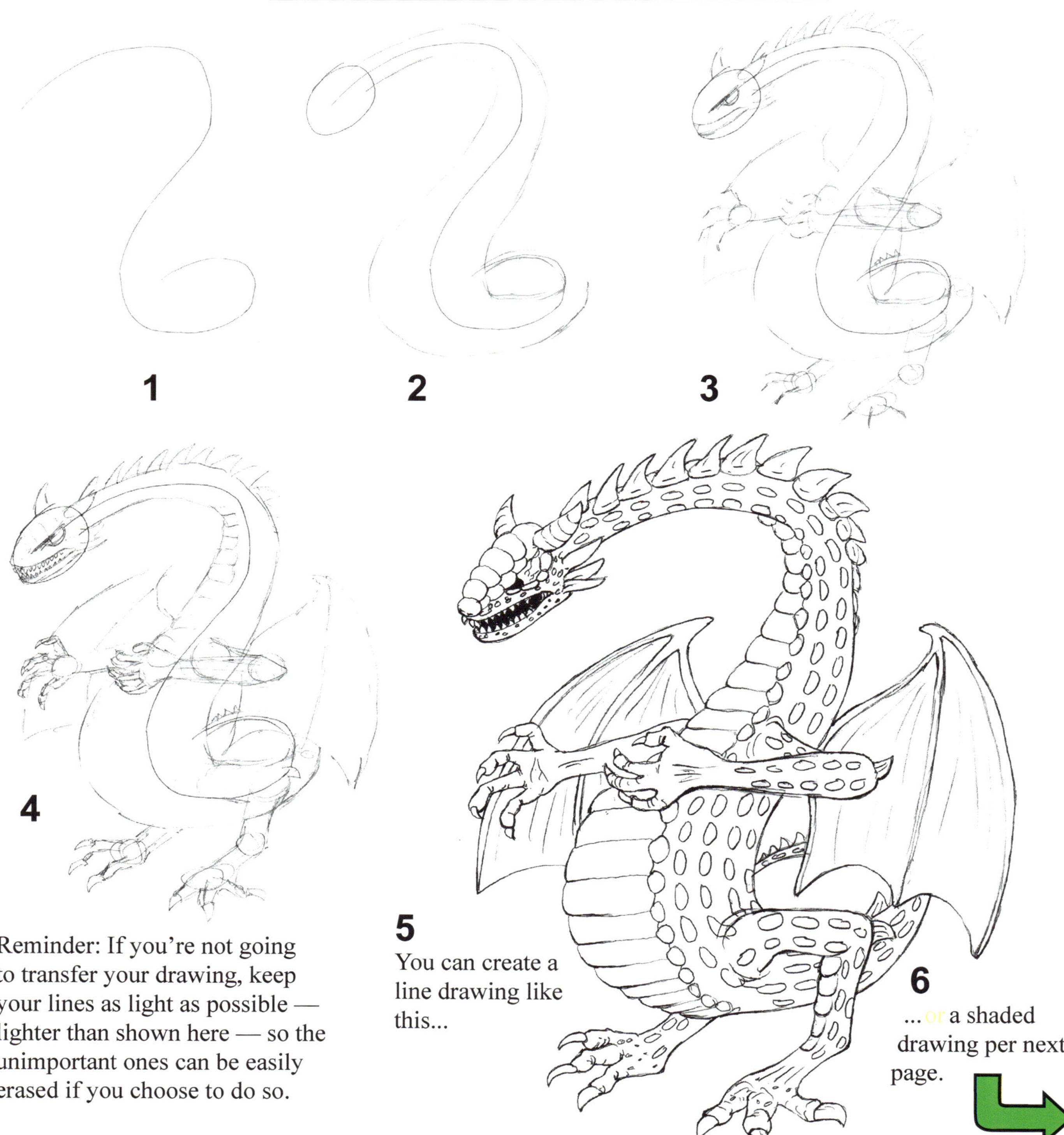

Reminder: If you're not going to transfer your drawing, keep your lines as light as possible — lighter than shown here — so the unimportant ones can be easily erased if you choose to do so.

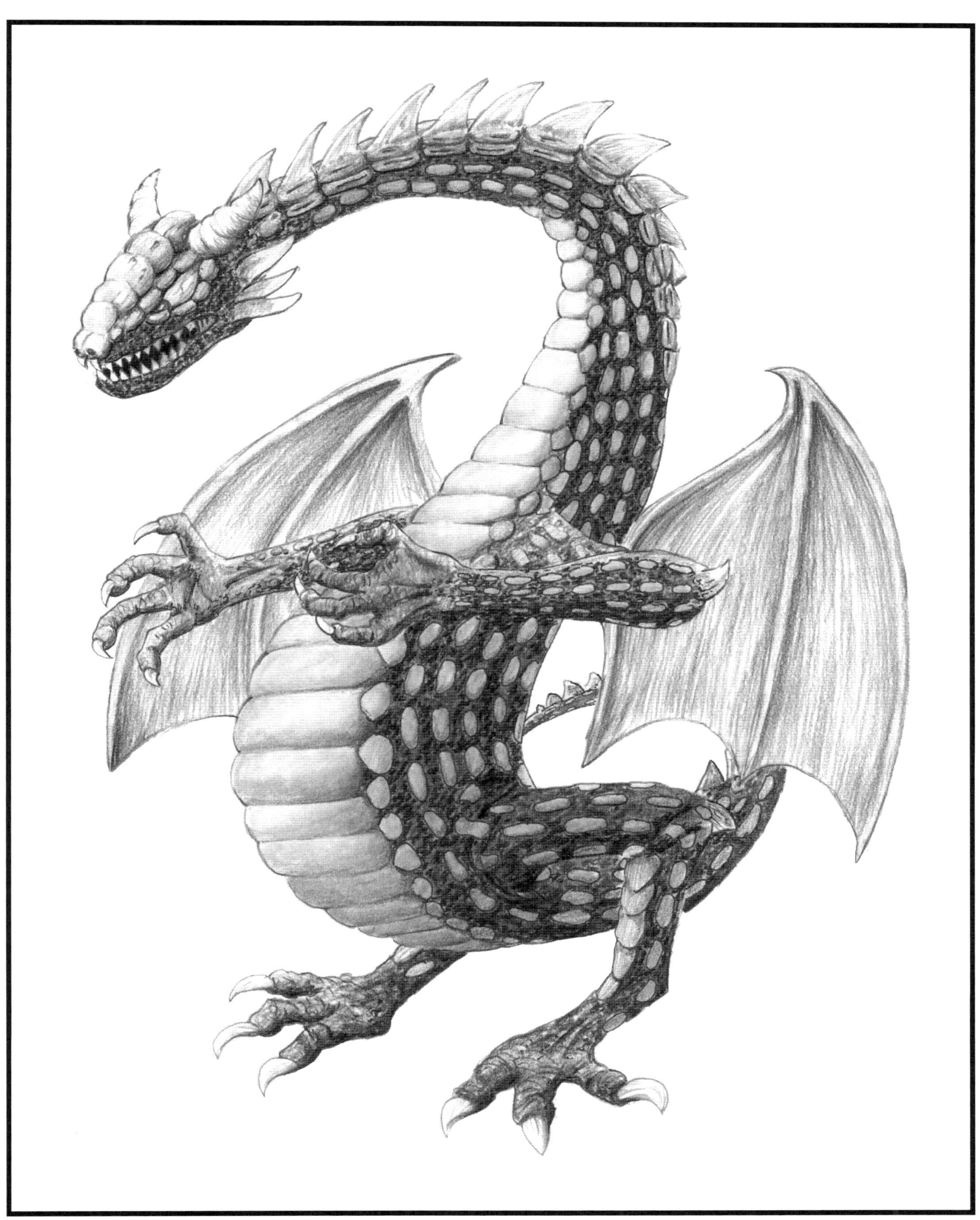

Original on Stonehenge paper, 9.5" x 12.5".

Keep it CLEAN!

Here's how to keep from smearing a pencil drawing with your hand...and clean the smear when it happens.

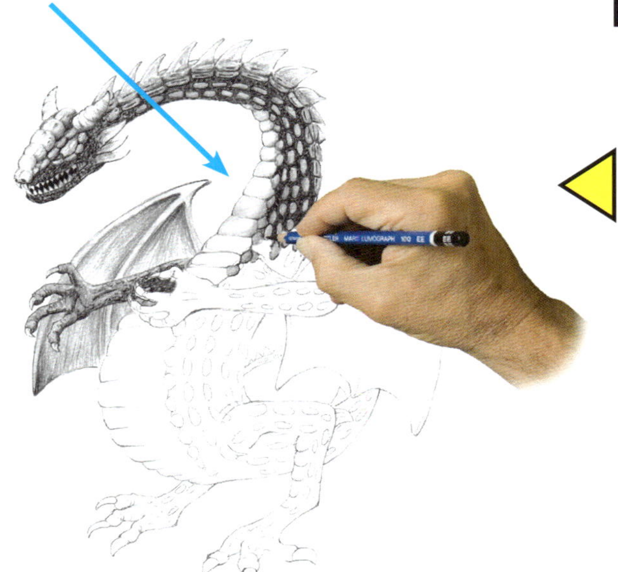

Shade from the top down — from the upper left if you're right handed, from the upper right if you're left handed. This keeps the palm of your hand off the shaded part.

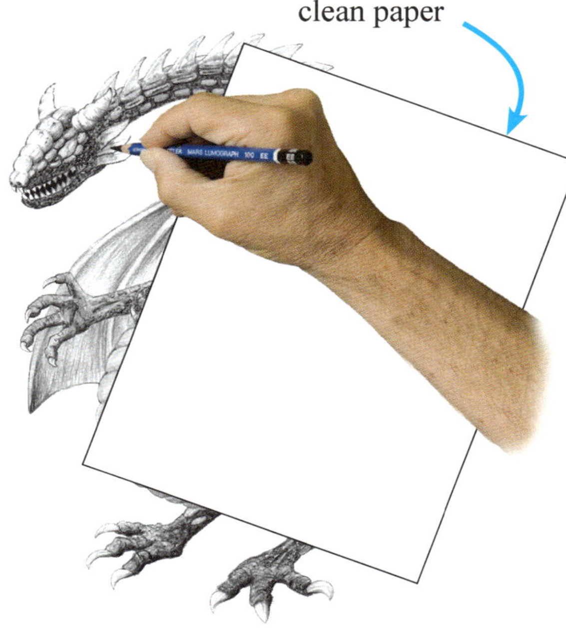

When you return to the upper part of the drawing to touch it up, place a clean, blank sheet of paper over the drawing and let the palm of your hand rest on the protective paper, not on the drawing.

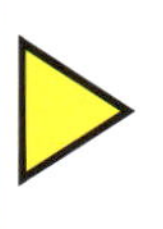

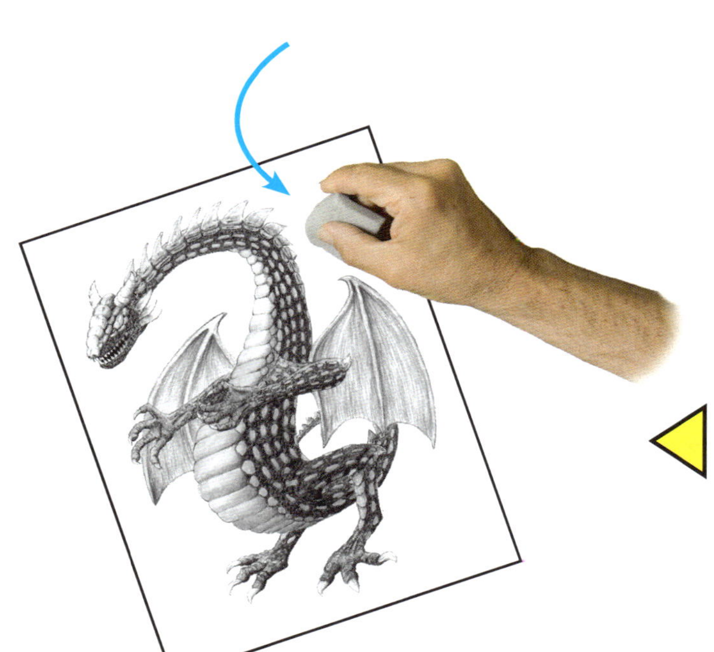

Despite your best efforts, you will (if you are like me) probably get some light smudge marks on the paper surrounding the drawing.

Clean the should-be-white area with a kneaded eraser, rounded at the end. It will soak up the misapplied graphite and not leave eraser crumbs! (More about kneaded erasers on page 11.)

PROTECT *your* DRAWING!

To keep graphite pencil drawings from smudging when handled, and colored pencil drawings from developing a waxy "bloom" on their surface, apply a *fixative*, as shown on this and the next page.

CAUTION!
Breathing fumes from fixatives can be
DANGEROUS TO YOUR HEALTH!
This is true even of so-called "odorless" fixatives.

AVOID breathing fixative fumes by following the directions on this and the next page. Read the label on the fixative can for a complete list of instructions and precautions. If you are young, have an adult fix your drawings for you.

It is suggested that you fix your drawing outside if it is a fairly nice day (60^{0}F or more) and there is little or no breeze.

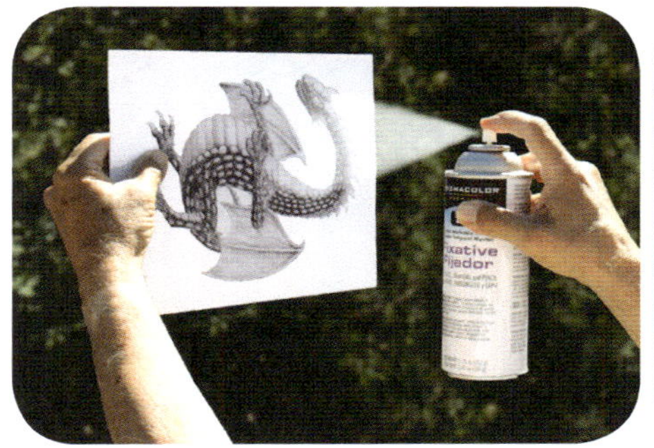

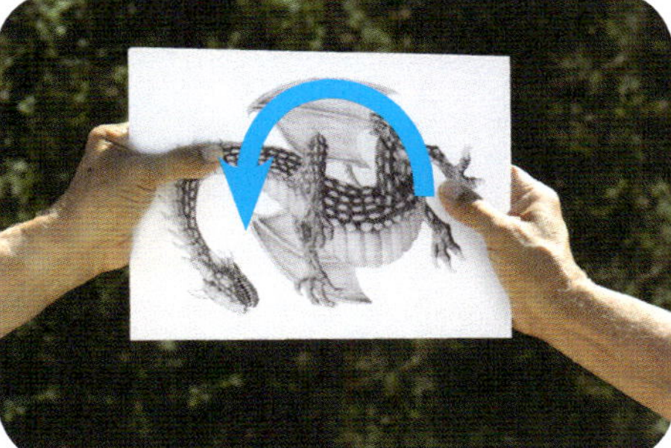

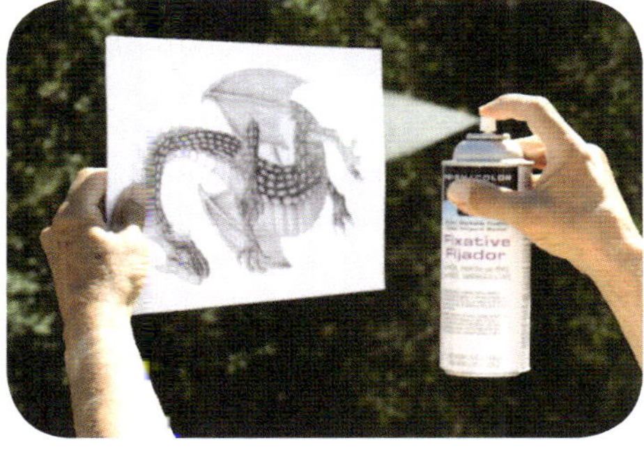

1
Hold the drawing by the edge at arm's length. Spray half of the drawing on the side opposite your hand, **holding your breath** as you do so. If there is a breeze, spray so that the breeze carries the fumes away from you. When finished, back away from the area where you were spraying for a few seconds and resume breathing. (Duh!)

2
Rotate the drawing half way around.

3
Hold your breath again and spray the other half of the drawing as you did in step 1. Back away from the area and *stop holding your breath!*

See note regarding second coat next page.

After applying fixative, hold can upside down and spray away from you, preferably outdoors, until liquid has cleared nozzle. This will help keep fixative from spattering on your drawing next time.

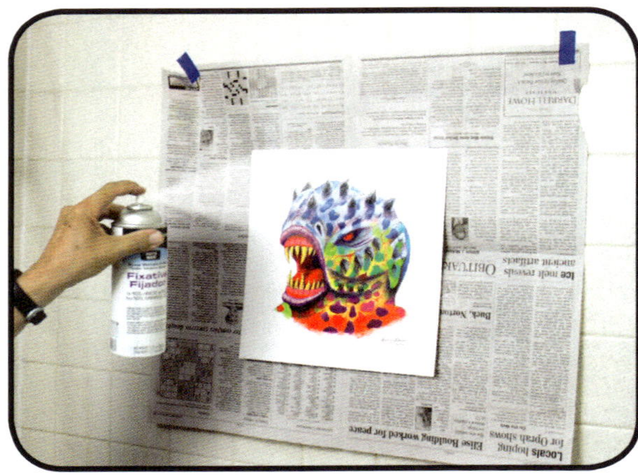

If you wish to apply a second coat of fixative, spray in the opposite direction of the first; e.g., if you sprayed left-to-right the first time, spray up-and-down the second time. (Do this when spraying outdoors as well.)

If the weather does not permit you to fix your drawing outdoors (too cold and/or too windy), you'll need to do it inside. One possibility:

1 Attach sheets of newspaper to the wall of a shower or bathtub with masking tape or removable tape. Be sure the sheets are large enough so that when you spray to the edge of the drawing, excess spray does not get on the wall.

2 Attach your drawing to the newspaper using *removable* tape. Be sure it's removable — otherwise you might tear your artwork! Scotch® removable tape works well.

3 Turn on the bathroom fan. Hold your breath. Spray the entire drawing. This should take just a few seconds. Leave the room and close the door. Resume breathing. (If your bathroom doesn't have a fan, open the window.)

4 When you're confident the fumes have left the room, return and, if you want, repeat step 3.

Remember that colored pencil drawings require an application of fixative on completion. If a few days or weeks have passed without fixing, first wipe surface of drawing with a soft cloth to remove wax "bloom", then apply fixative.

The ANIMAL CONNECTION

Our very own planet is, and was, populated by an enormous variety of very weird, strange, often scary animals and insects that can provide you with great ideas for monster and alien bodies, skin types, eyes, teeth, horns, claws, and other stuff.

Browse your local library and nearby book stores (including used book stores) for books about bugs, reptiles, dinosaurs, insects, sea life, and such. At the library, review back issues of *National Geographic* magazine. Search the internet for pictures, using keywords for the kinds of creatures that might interest you. Include the word "images" in your search. *BigstockPhoto.com* is a great source for many photos and illustrations.

Represented on this and the next two pages is a tiny fraction of real earth creatures that are (and were) out there.

(**NOTES**: The colors for the styracosaurus, mosquito, and cat flea are imagined by the artist.) Drawings were created with colored pencils — originals about twice as large as those shown. Shaded backgrounds of the caterpillar and mosquito were rendered digitally.)

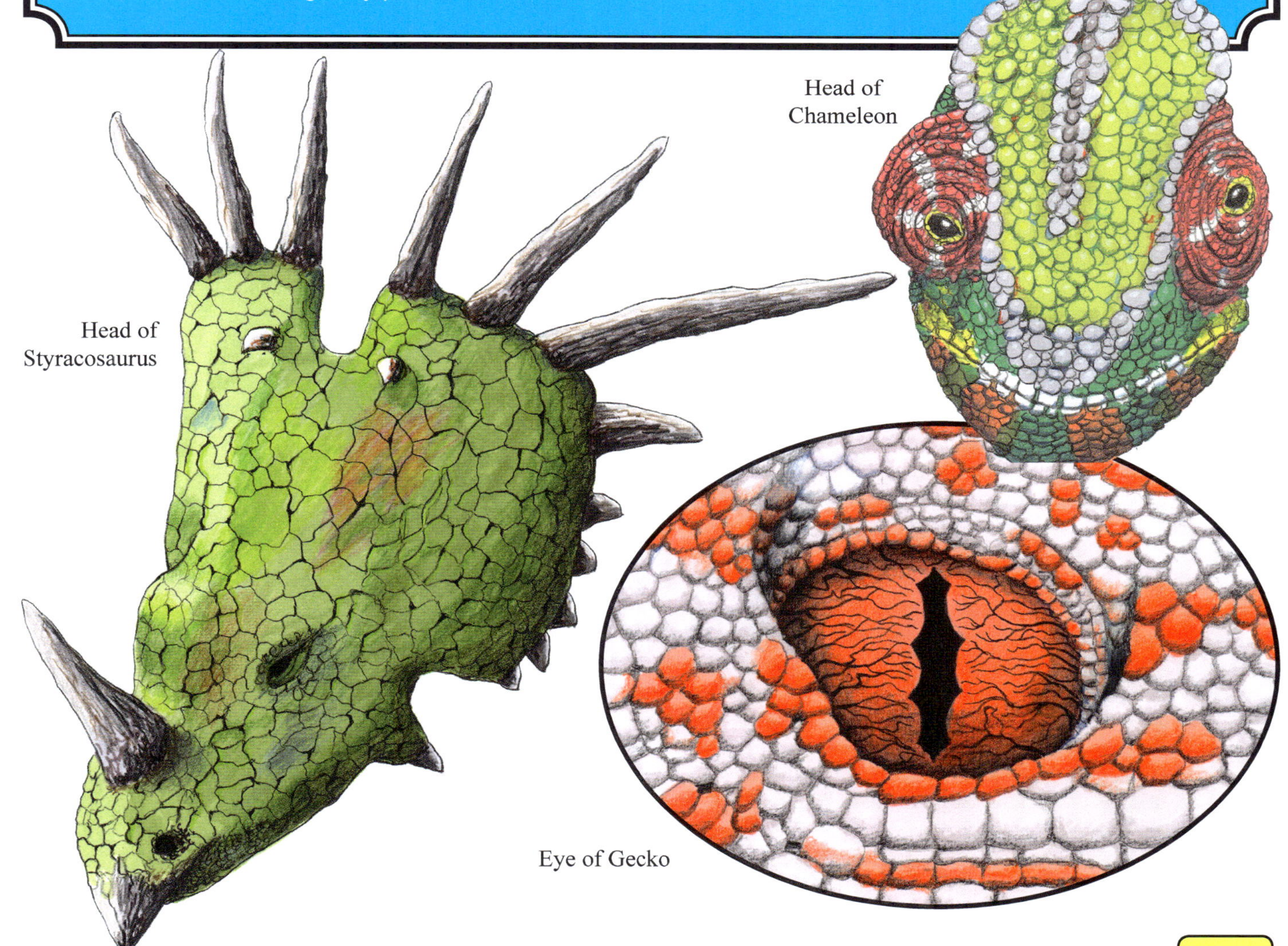

Head of Chameleon

Head of Styracosaurus

Eye of Gecko

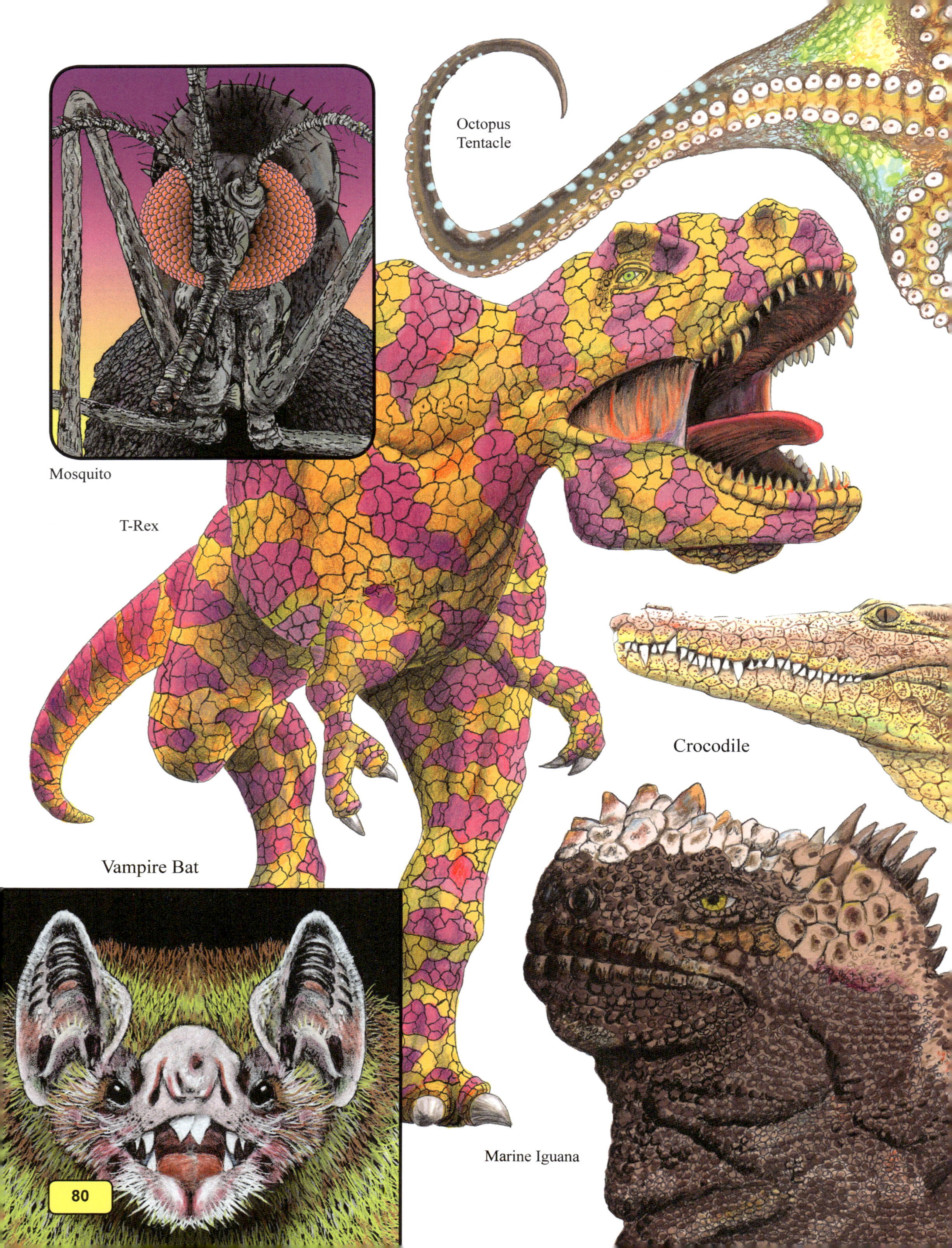
Octopus
Tentacle
Mosquito
T-Rex
Crocodile
Vampire Bat
Marine Iguana

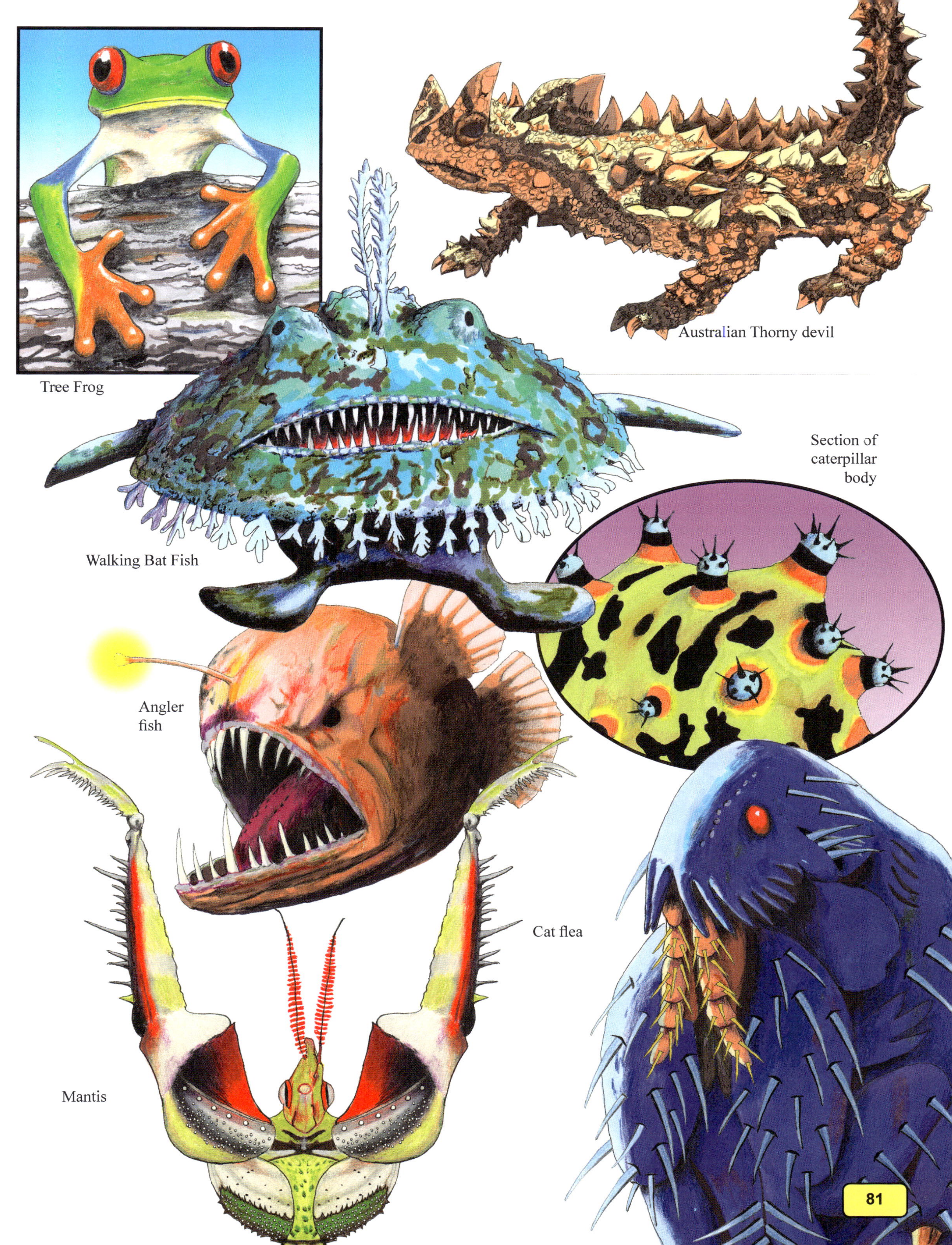
Tree Frog
Australian Thorny devil
Section of
caterpillar
body
Walking Bat Fish
Angler
fish
Cat flea
Mantis

Monster and Alien ANATOMY and the HUMAN CONNECTION

You can make more realistic monsters and aliens if you draw them with realistic anatomy. Do this by studying *human* anatomy and applying what you learn to non-human creatures. Notice the role muscles, bones, and tendons play in outward appearance.

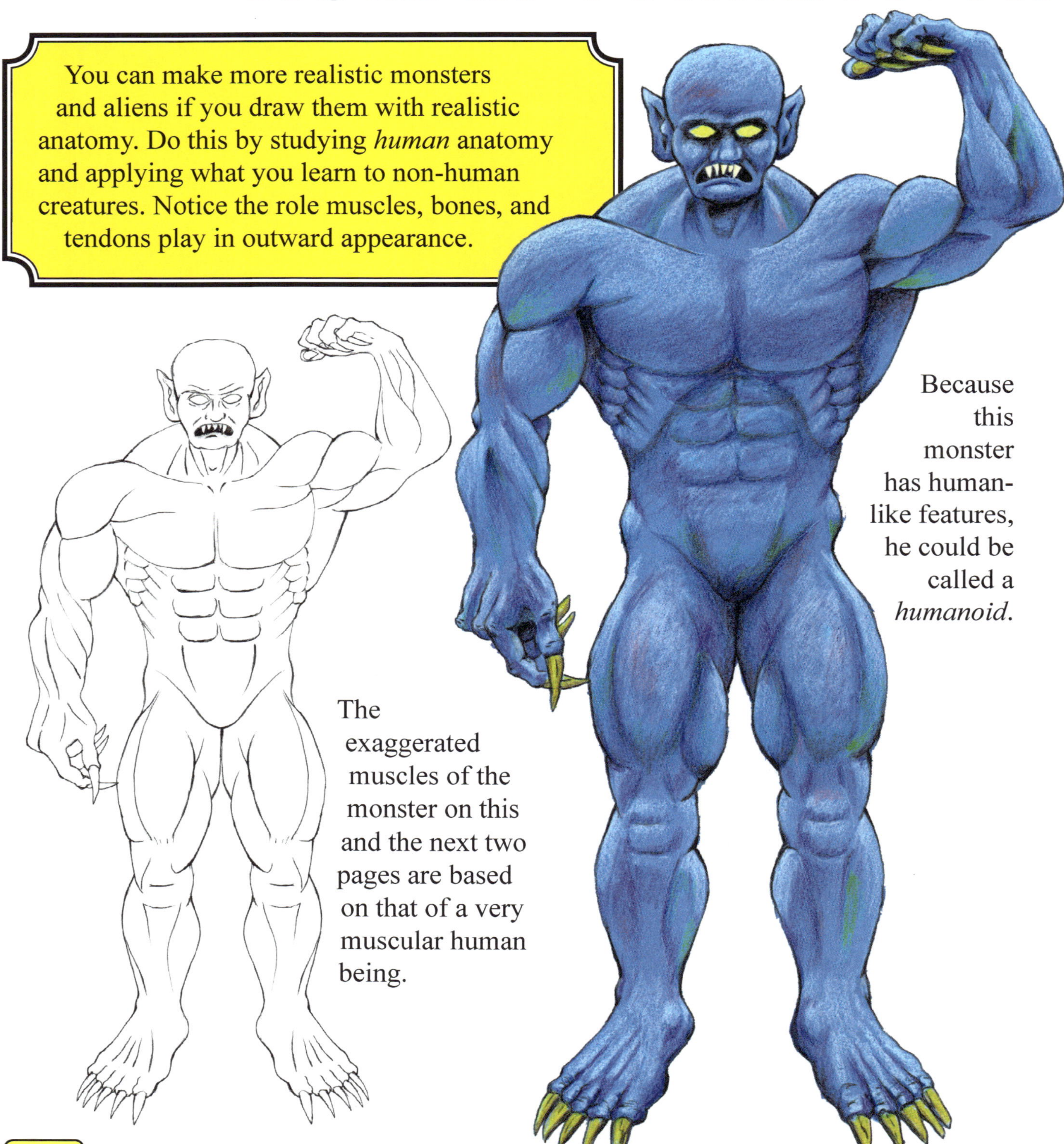

The exaggerated muscles of the monster on this and the next two pages are based on that of a very muscular human being.

Because this monster has human-like features, he could be called a *humanoid*.

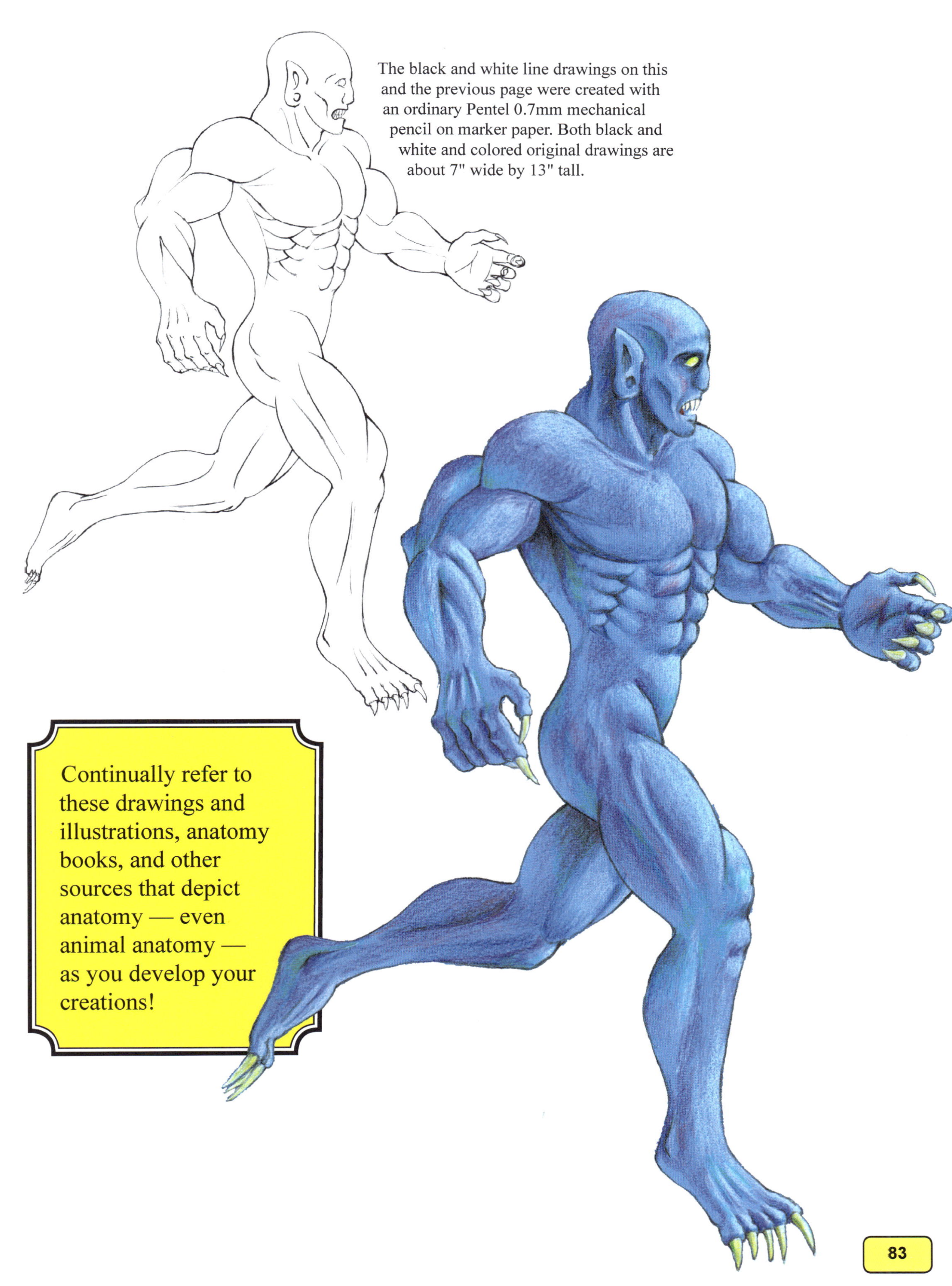

The black and white line drawings on this and the previous page were created with an ordinary Pentel 0.7mm mechanical pencil on marker paper. Both black and white and colored original drawings are about 7" wide by 13" tall.

Continually refer to these drawings and illustrations, anatomy books, and other sources that depict anatomy — even animal anatomy — as you develop your creations!

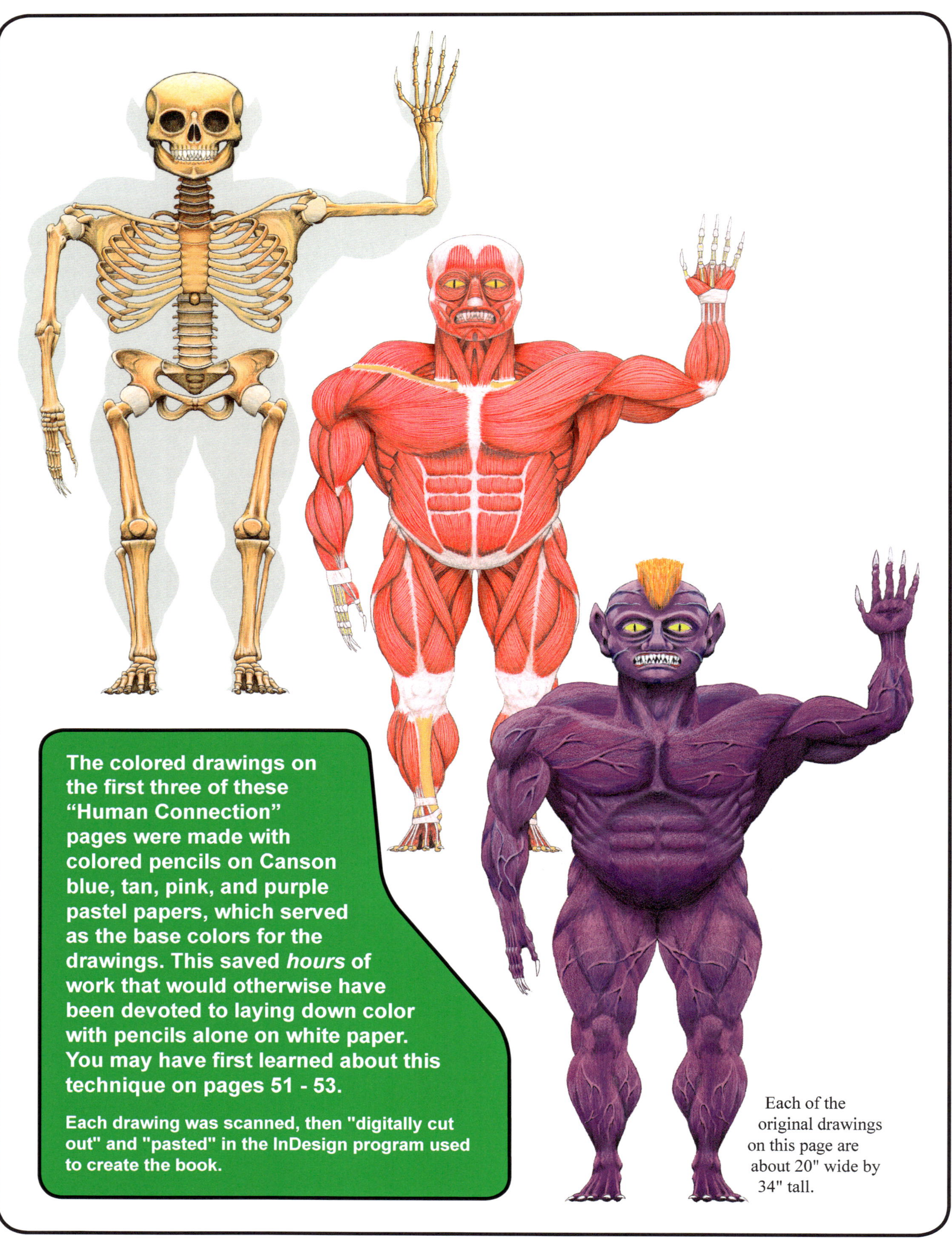

The colored drawings on the first three of these “Human Connection” pages were made with colored pencils on Canson blue, tan, pink, and purple pastel papers, which served as the base colors for the drawings. This saved *hours* of work that would otherwise have been devoted to laying down color with pencils alone on white paper. You may have first learned about this technique on pages 51 - 53.

Each drawing was scanned, then "digitally cut out" and "pasted" in the InDesign program used to create the book.

Each of the original drawings on this page are about 20" wide by 34" tall.

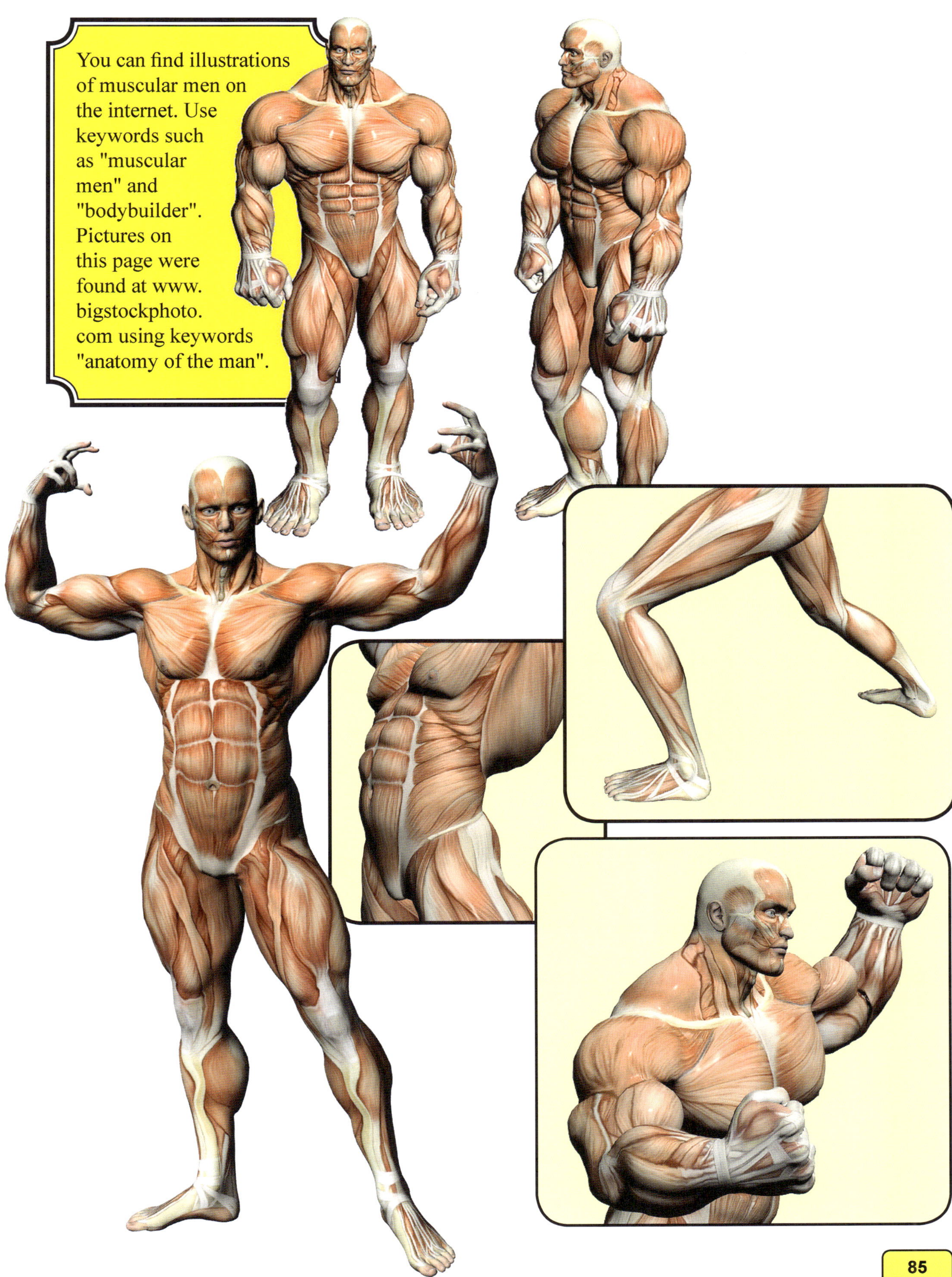

You can find illustrations of muscular men on the internet. Use keywords such as "muscular men" and "bodybuilder". Pictures on this page were found at www.bigstockphoto.com using keywords "anatomy of the man".

Monster and Alien

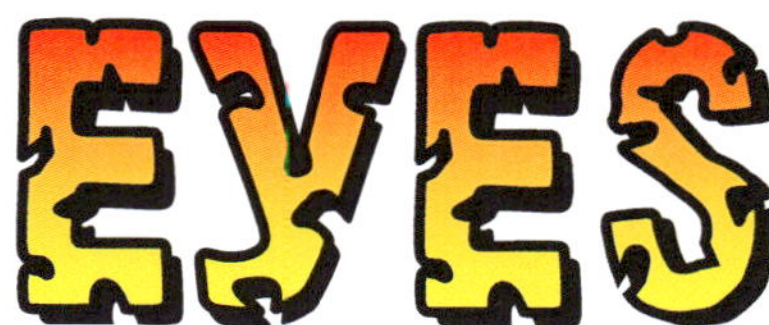

The eyes of monsters and aliens that are *similar* to ours are humanoid, or human-like. Study the illustration below and learn how to make appealing and realistic humanoid eyes.

Different colors should be included to make the eyes more realistic. Look carefully and you'll see additional lines of red, blue, yellow, dark green, and brown added to the iris's light green color.

The eyelid casts a shadow that is especially visible on the iris.

Sparkle: A reflection of the light source.

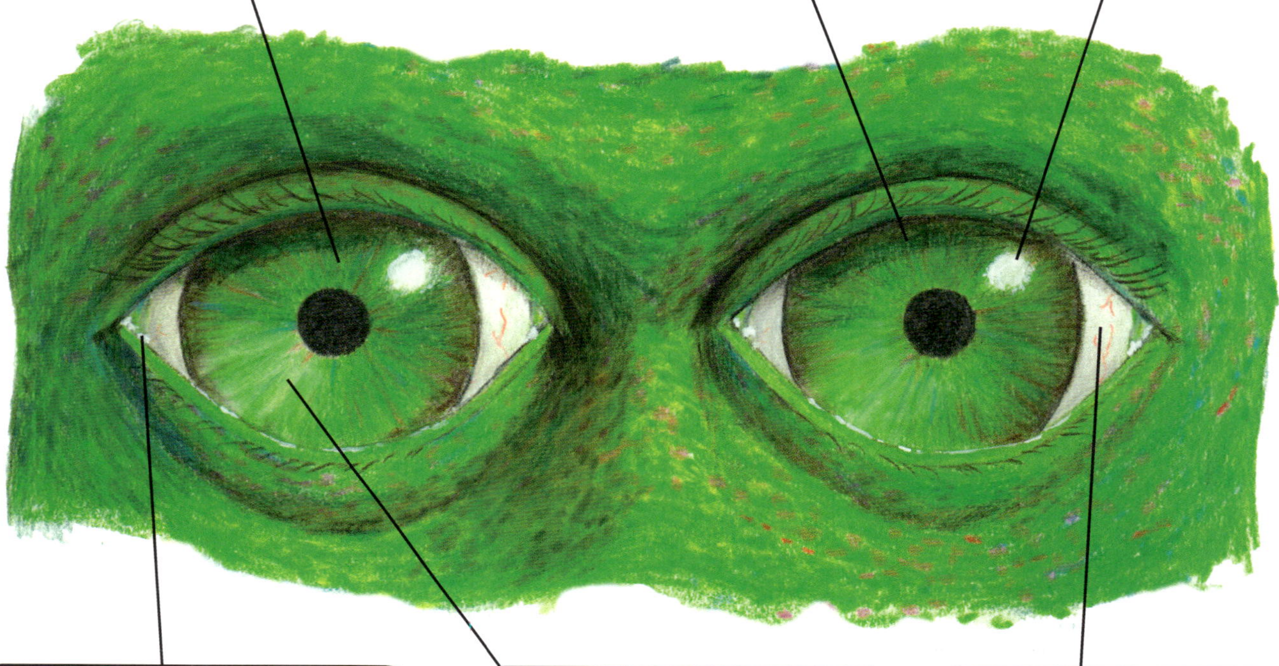

You *may* wish to add bits of white at the edges of the eyes. This indicates moisture — present in the eyes of us humans and many monsters and aliens.

The eyes' lenses focus light on the side *opposite* the sparkle, causing that part of the iris to be brighter. Here the sparkle is on the *upper right*, so the *lower left* of the iris is brighter than the rest.

Be sure to include some shading in the eyeballs, even if they are white. Notice that the parts of the eyeballs facing the light have less shading than those facing away from the light. Only the brightest parts of the eyeballs were not shaded.

This drawing was made on BFK Rives paper with Prismacolor® Premier colored pencils. The white sparkle in the eyes and the white moisture at the edges were made with titanium white fluid acrylic paint after the rest of the drawing was done. The original is about 10-1/2 inches wide.

"Oh, Those Alien Eyes, Those Great Big Alien Eyes..."*

It is rumored that a UFO crashed in 1947 near Roswell, New Mexico, and that an alien body was recovered from the crash site. The creature's likeness — or what people *think* was its likeness — inspired countless images similar to this fellow in cartoons, movies and other places.

You can make his hypnotic, super-sized eyes pure black with watercolor, fluid marker, or a black colored pencil.

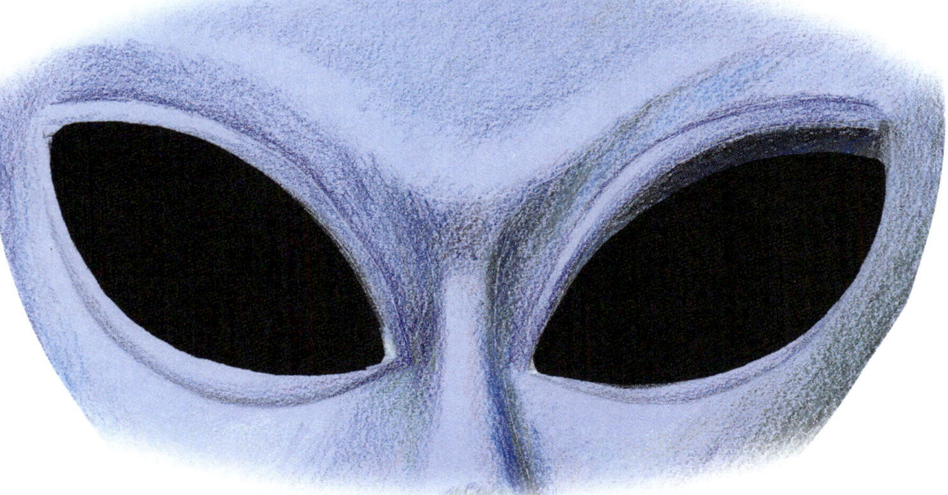

Here ink from a broad-tipped black marker was first applied on drawing paper. To give his eyes a diffuse, steely look, colored pencils were then used to apply white, gray, blue, and green, a little at a time. Finally, the colors were blended together with a colorless colored pencil blender (described on page 15).

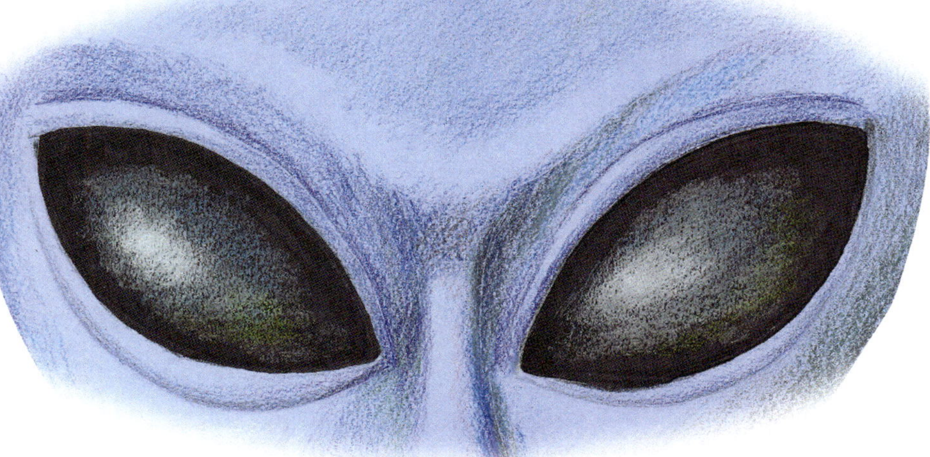

*For you youngsters in the audience, this page's title is inspired by lyrics from an old tune: "Oh, those beautiful eyes, those great big beautiful eyes..."

How I created black, shiny, glossy eyes

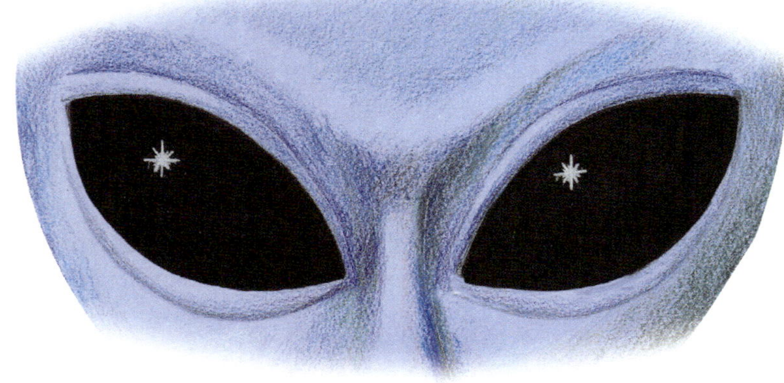

1

I first applied a black liquid marker to the eyes, then used a white colored pencil to create a reflection of the sun.

2

Then I lightly applied light blue, brown, and green with colored pencils. I wanted to show a reflection of the nearby landscape in his eyes.

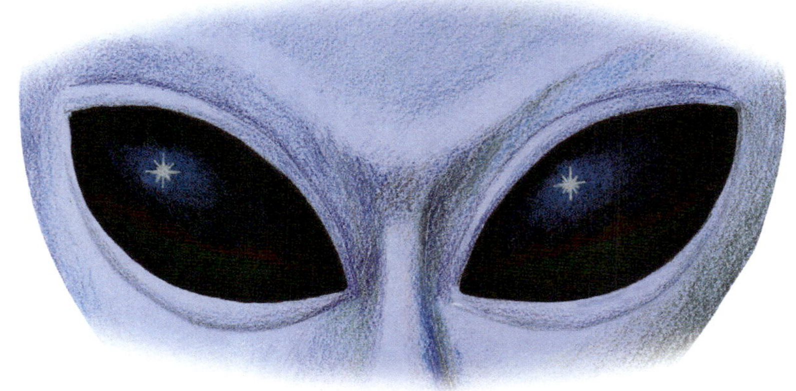

3

Another, heavier layer of light blue, brown, green, plus a darker blue was applied.

The reflection of the sun was made whiter with titanium white fluid acrylic paint.

If I had made the other landscape colors brighter, they would have "drowned out" the dark, sinister look of the eyes, so I left them as shown.

Reminder: Whatever colors you choose, if you're using colored pencils, apply them in layers — a little at a time, as shown on pages 49 & 50 and elsewhere.

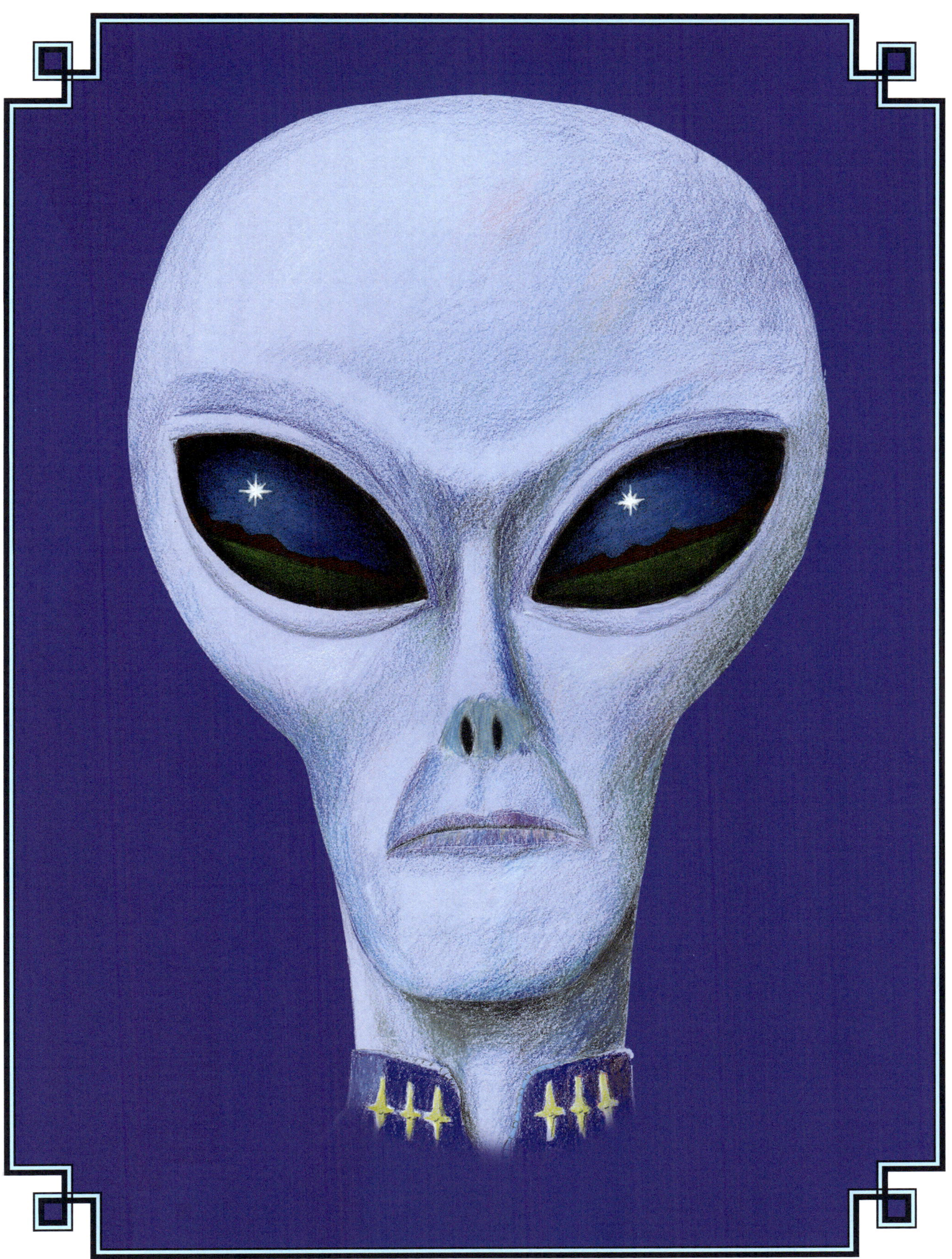

Head drawn on blue pastel paper with assorted Prismacolor® colored pencils (and a touch of white acrylic paint). Background digitally darkened. The original drawing is about 11" x 14".

Make Those Eyes Glow!

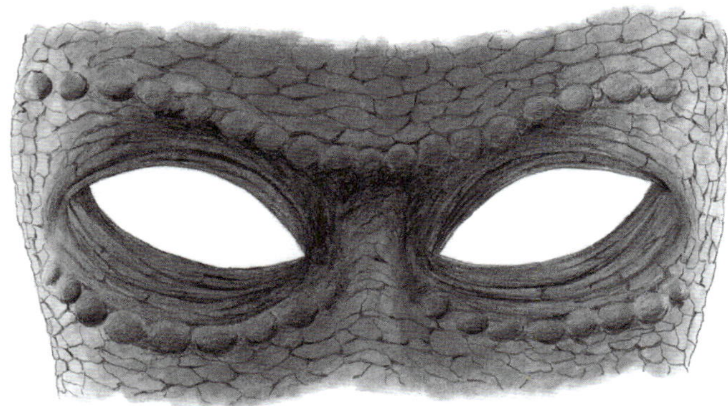

Some monsters have eyes that glow...even in the dark.

Their eyes will appear to glow brighter if they are blurred around the edges...

...and will appear to glow still brighter if they have streaks of light, "star points", radiating from their centers.

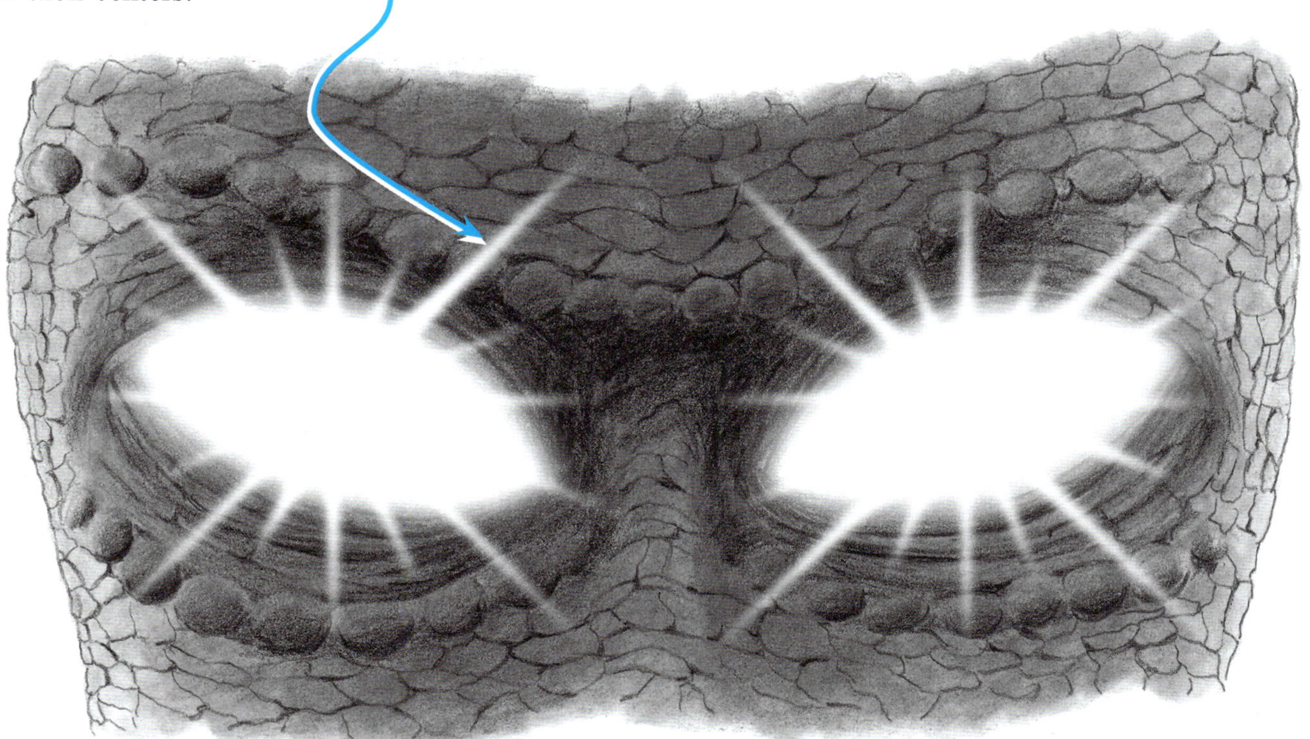

Use any of these styles to make the creatures' eyes glow — with sharp edges, fuzzy edges, star points, or any other method you might think of. See how to make blurred edges and star points on the next page.

TIPS for making glowing eyes in a pencil drawing

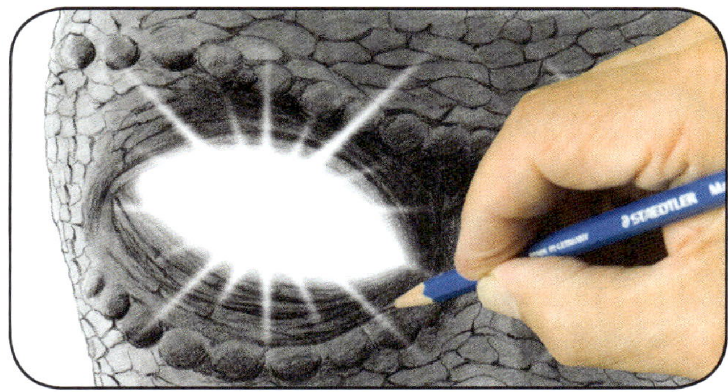

Press *very lightly* with your pencil around the edges of the eyes and the star points. Use an HB or lighter lead.

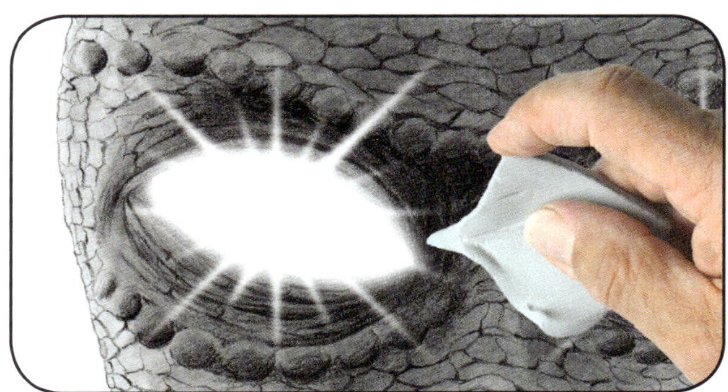

You can perfect the fuzziness of your edges with a kneaded eraser and/or a pencil eraser.

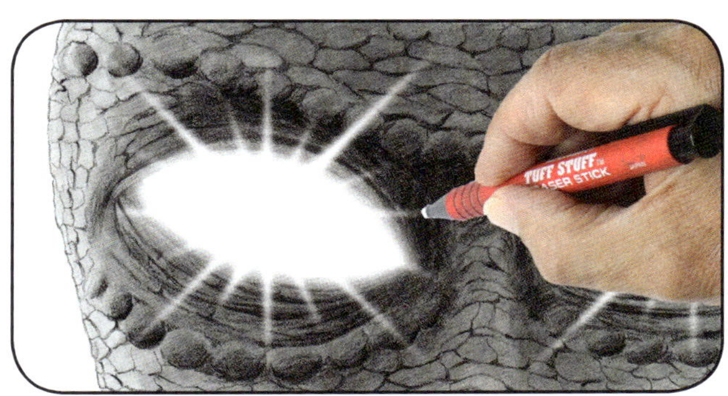

To guide you in making star points it is suggested...

1
...that you first make four long lines, radiating exactly from the center of the eye, spaced equally apart.

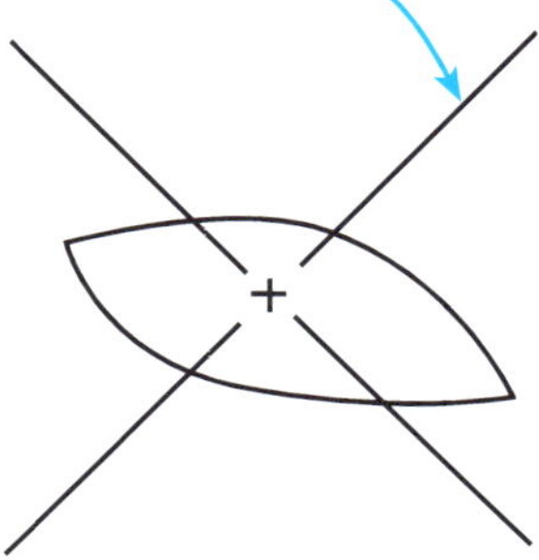

2
Then make four medium-length lines and place them between the long lines.

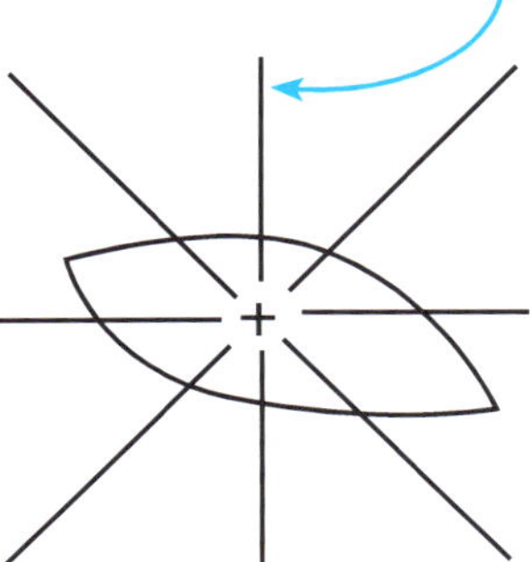

3
And finally make eight short lines and place them between the medium and long lines.

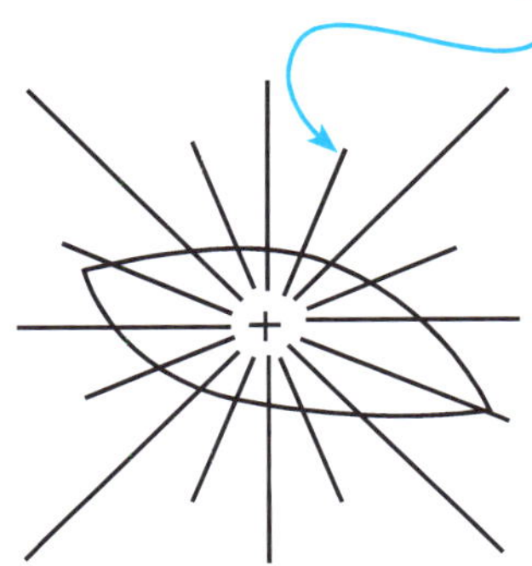

Make Those Eyes SINISTER!

The eyes on this fellow are perhaps scary enough. But notice that they don't have much depth, and the face looks kind of flat. Also, does his dark mouth draw more of your attention than his eyes?

I darkened the area around the eyes. Do you think this makes them a little bit more scary? Are *your* eyes more drawn to his?

Other parts of the face were darkened a little also, because with the eye area darker, some other parts appeared *too* light.

Head drawn on Arches "Satin" paper with graphite lead pencils and smoothed with a stump (see pages 41-46). Gray background created with Adobe Photoshop.

Original about 8" x 10".

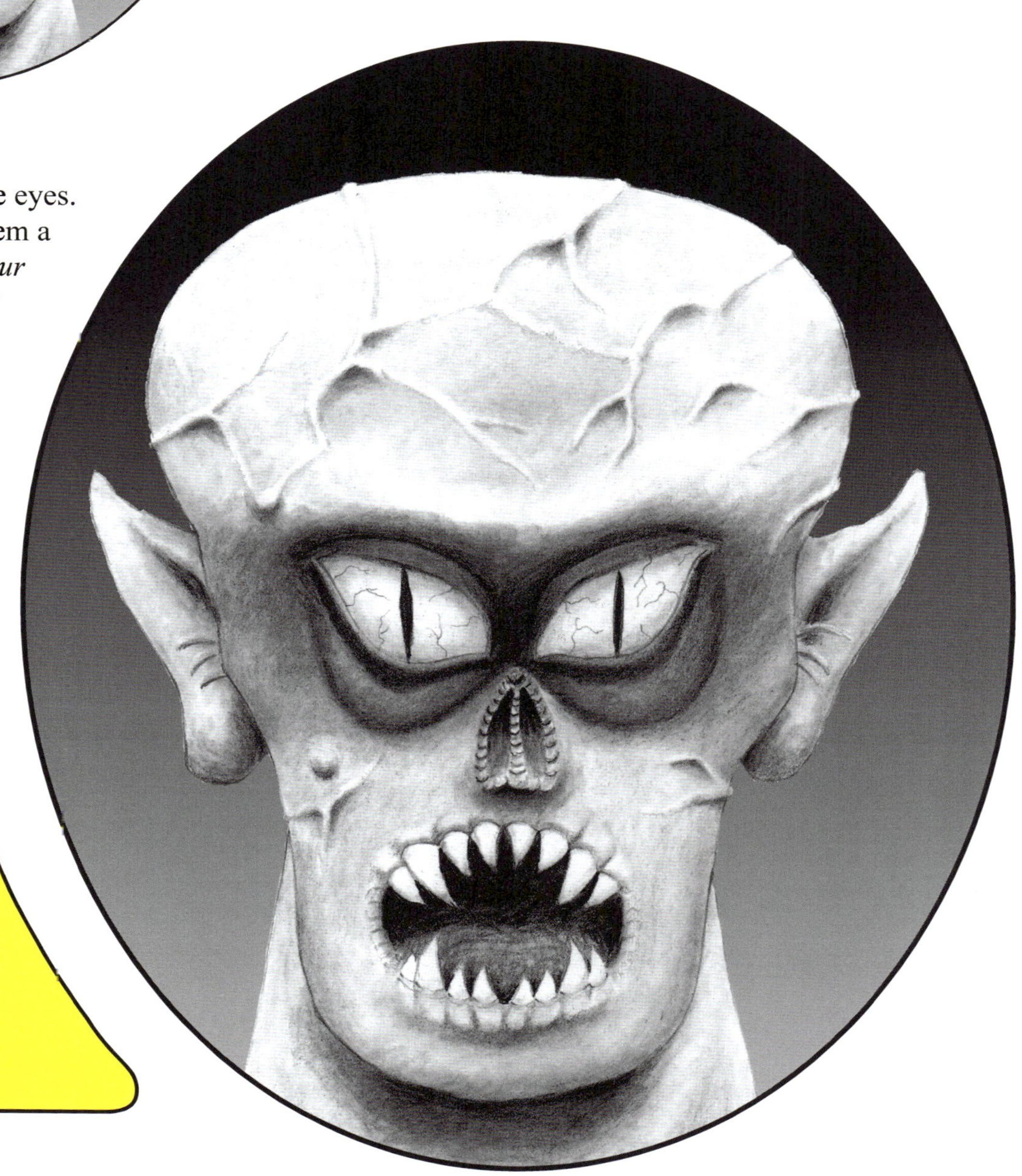

Surrounding the eyes with a darker color makes them more sinister and more readily attracts the attention of the viewer.

Make Those Eyes THREATENING!

Partially hiding eyes beneath a furrowed brow makes them quite threatening!

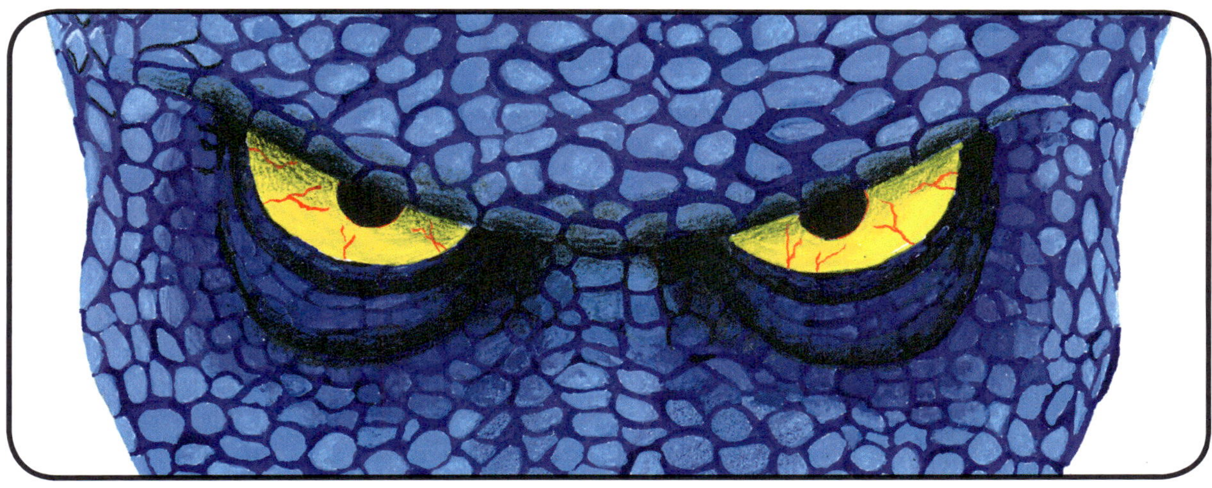

When LESS is sometimes MORE

Not having irises in the eyes can make them *more* creepy.

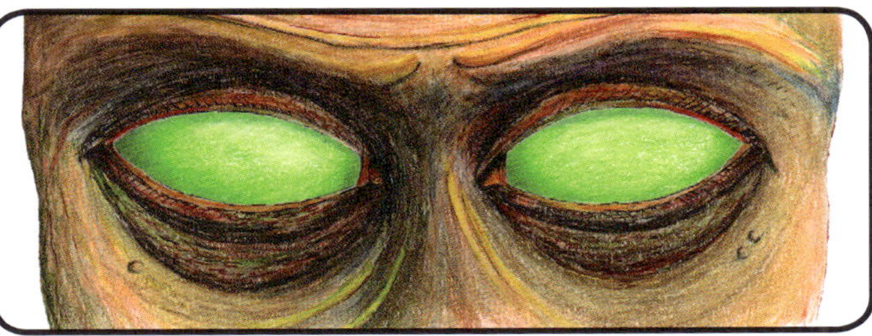

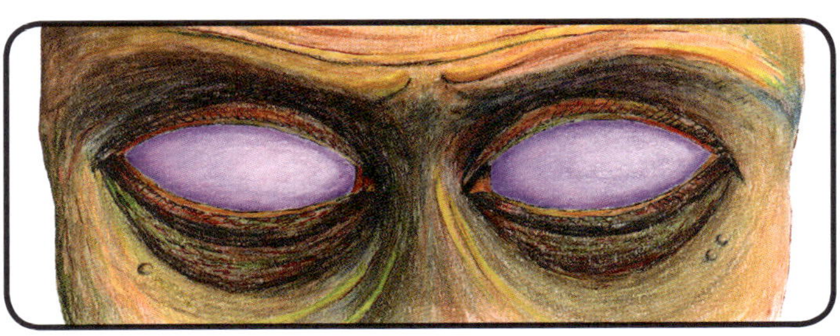

Monster and alien eyes can be any color you choose.

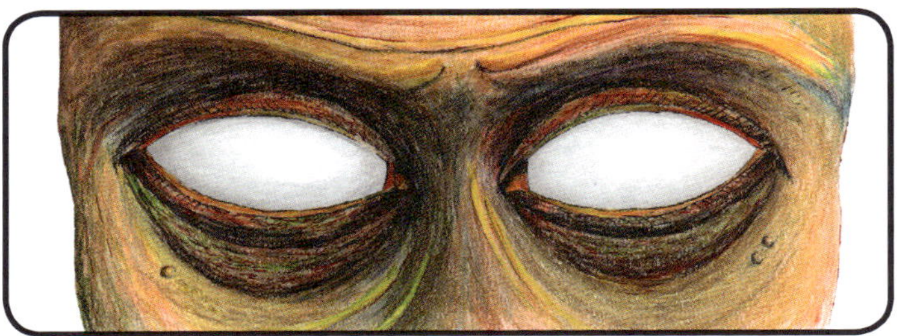

Using Circle Templates to Create Circular Eyes

Templates, such as those shown on this page, will help you draw nearly perfect circles — useful for eyeballs of some monsters and aliens. They are available at hobby and art supply stores. You can also get templates for ellipses and curves in a variety of shapes.

Most creatures who don't live in water have eyelids, which help spread moisture across the eyes. Some monsters, however, apparently do not have eyelids at all, making their eyes look especially weird.

1
You can use a template to draw eyeballs...

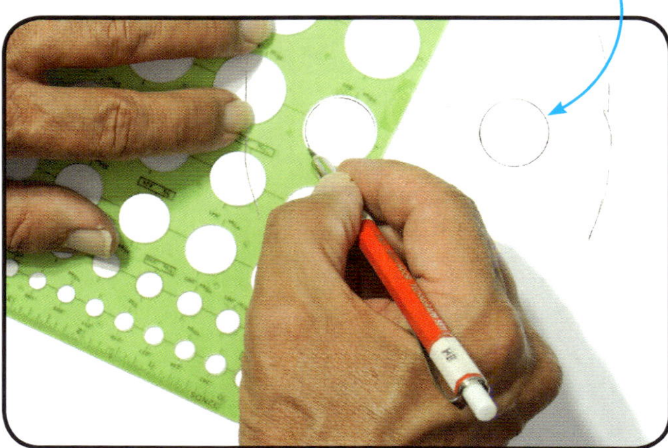

2
...and irises and / or pupils. It doesn't matter in which order.

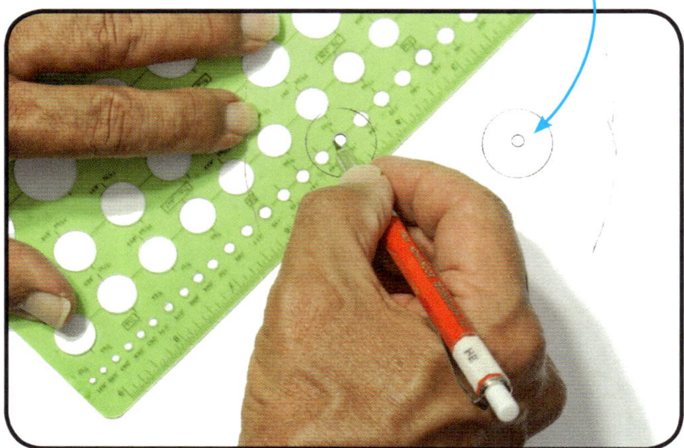

3
Finish with additional features and shading of your choosing.

This illustration, whose original size is about 9", wide, was created on Stonehenge paper with HB, 6B, and 8B pencils. A stub was used for smoother shading (see pages 41-46).

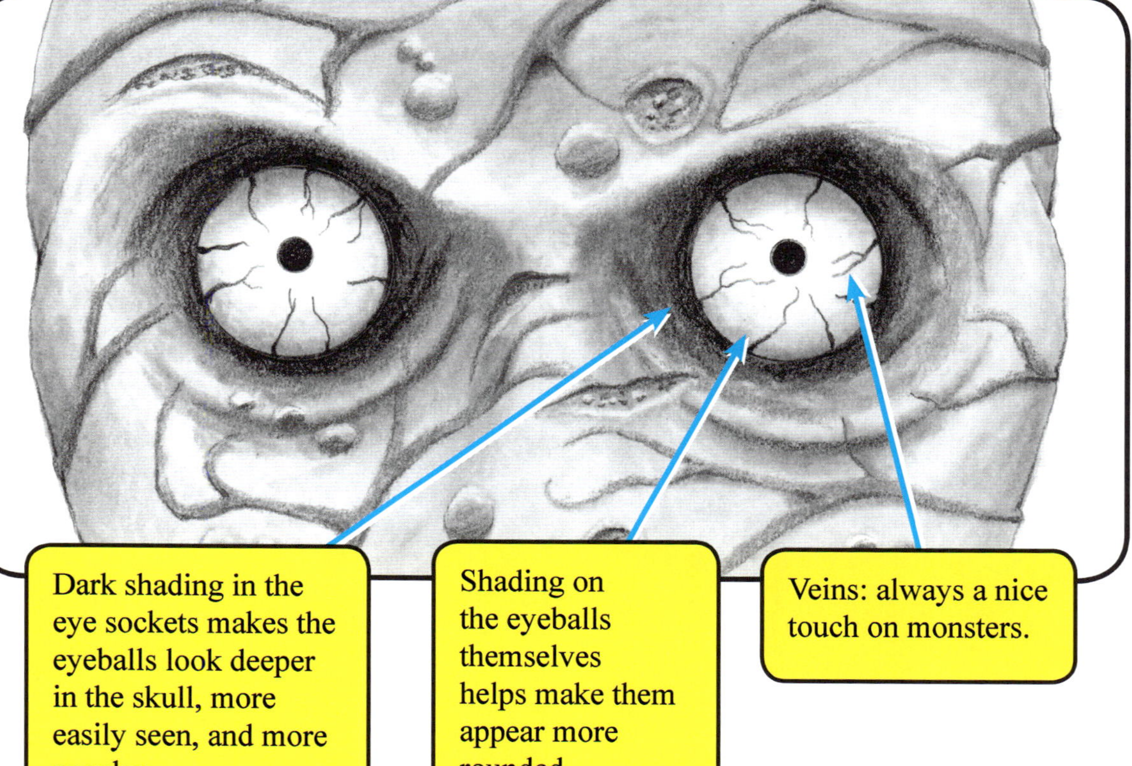

Dark shading in the eye sockets makes the eyeballs look deeper in the skull, more easily seen, and more spooky.

Shading on the eyeballs themselves helps make them appear more rounded.

Veins: always a nice touch on monsters.

Bug Eyes

Some monsters and aliens have eyes that look like those of insects — bug eyes. As you'll see on the next pages, earth insect eyes can provide good ideas for very interesting monster and alien bug-like eyes.

Drawing of mosquito. Color imagined by the artist.

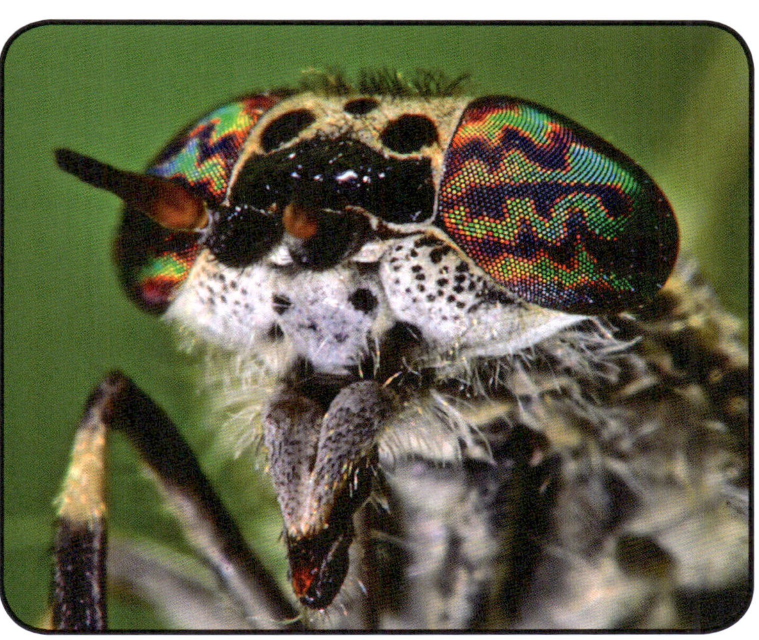

Photos above and lower left courtesy Bigstockphoto.com

Science

Rather than having two eyes with one lens on each eye that captures a complete image as ours do, many earth insects have compound eyes — clusters of tiny individual lenses, each of which sees just a piece of an image, like pixels in a digital photograph. The insect's brain assembles the pieces into an image that somewhat makes sense (to the insect, that is).

Create Compound Bug Eyes — an Easy Method

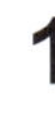

1
Draw or paint your basic creature.
(If you wish, you could leave these eyes as they are: they look pretty cool already.)

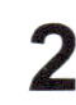

2
Make some grid lines. Note that they are curved to follow the curve of the eyeball.

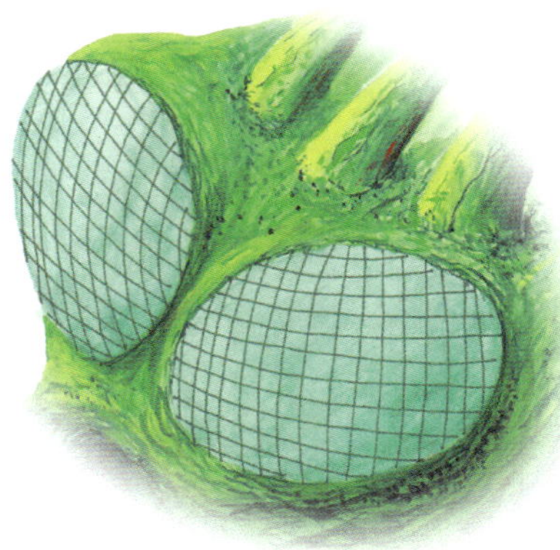

3
Draw circles inside the squares formed by the grid lines.

4
Fill in the gaps between the circles. For this illustration, the basic creature was painted with transparent watercolor on watercolor paper. Dark green and black Sharpie® "ultra fine point" markers were used for the grid lines and circles.

This illustration is about half the original size (7" x 8.5").

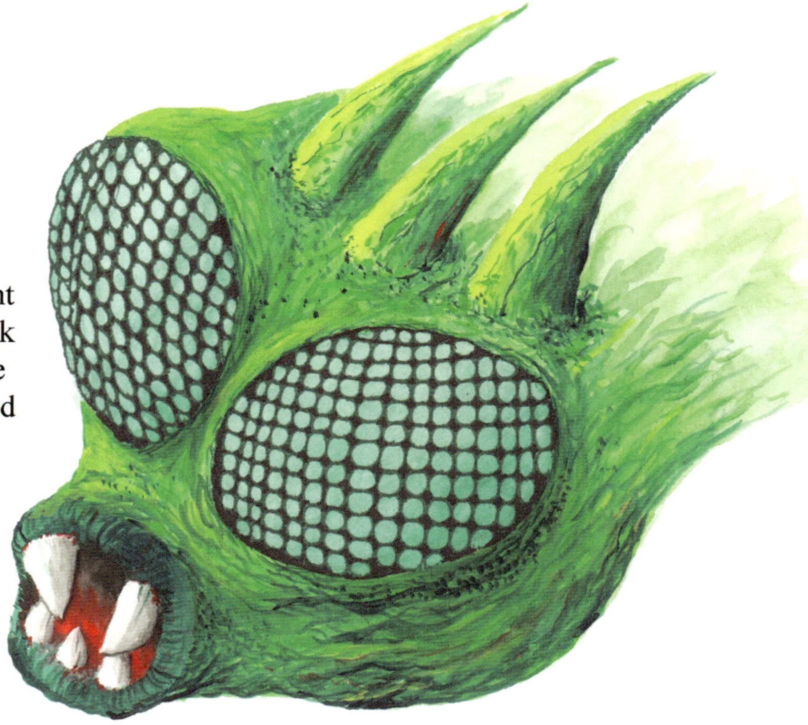

Compound Bug Eyes — Another Easy Method

As you can see in the photographs on page 95, an insect eye can consist of hundreds of little lenses. Drawing all those itty-bitty lenses can be quite difficult and take a long time. Using the technique shown on this page will enable you to draw, easily and quickly, what *looks like* a lot of little lenses.

Basic drawing.

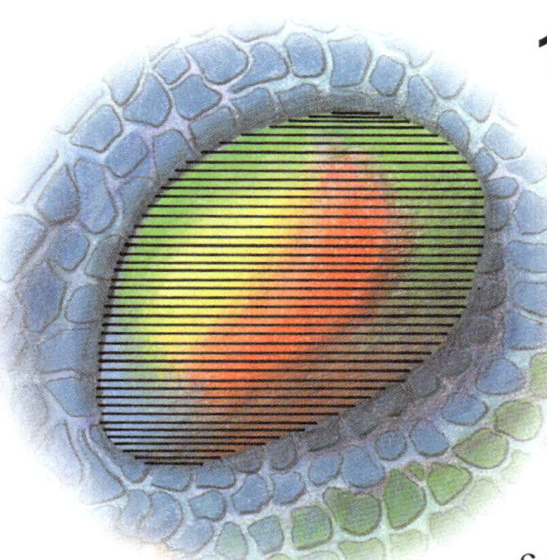

1

Draw parallel lines, evenly spaced. You can use a ruler if you wish. Either a Sharpie "ultra fine point" marker or a sharp black pencil would be a good choice.

If you use a marker, "fixing" the drawing first may give you sharper lines (more about fixatives pages 17 and 77 & 78).

Parallel lines

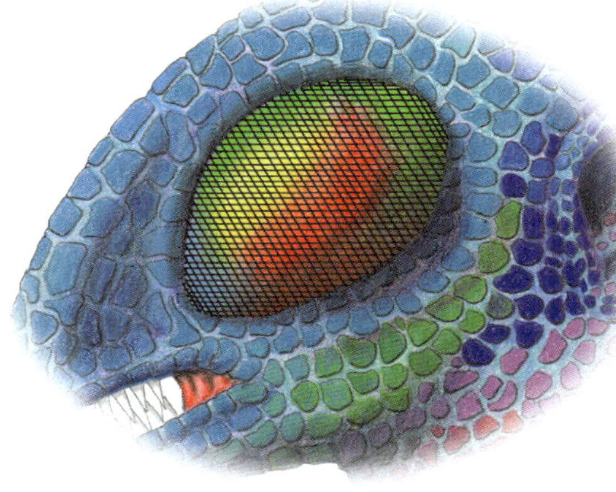

2

Draw more lines, at an angle shown, which is *about* 60^0 to the first lines.

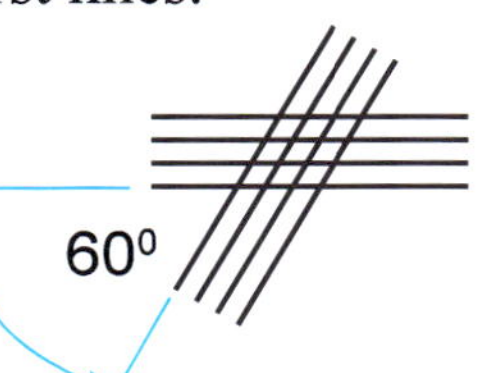

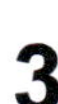

3

Finally, a third set of lines.

They can cross each other precisely, like this...

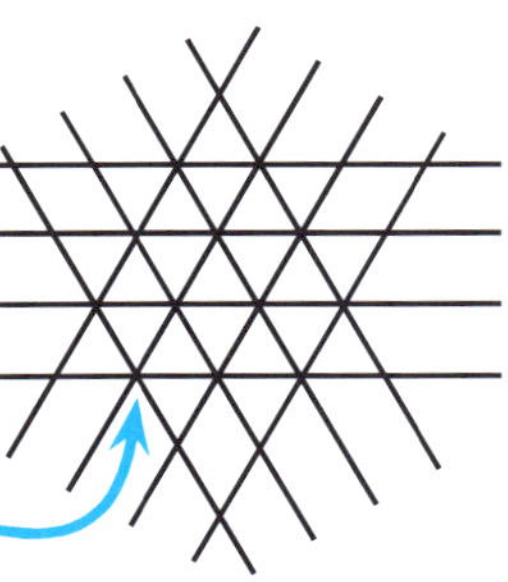

...or not so precisely, like this, which *may* produce a better illusion of circles.

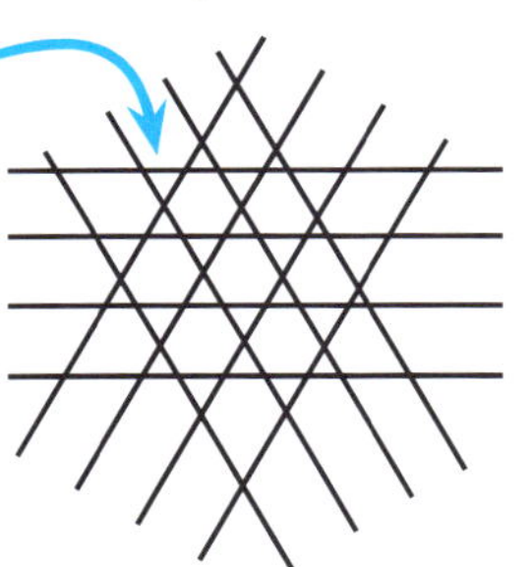

You experiment, and see which works best!

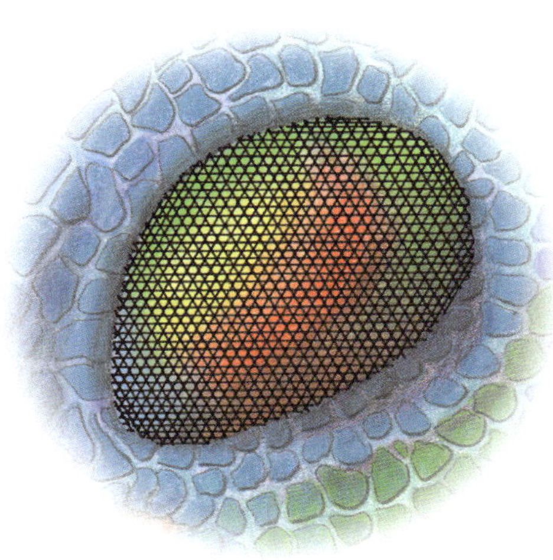

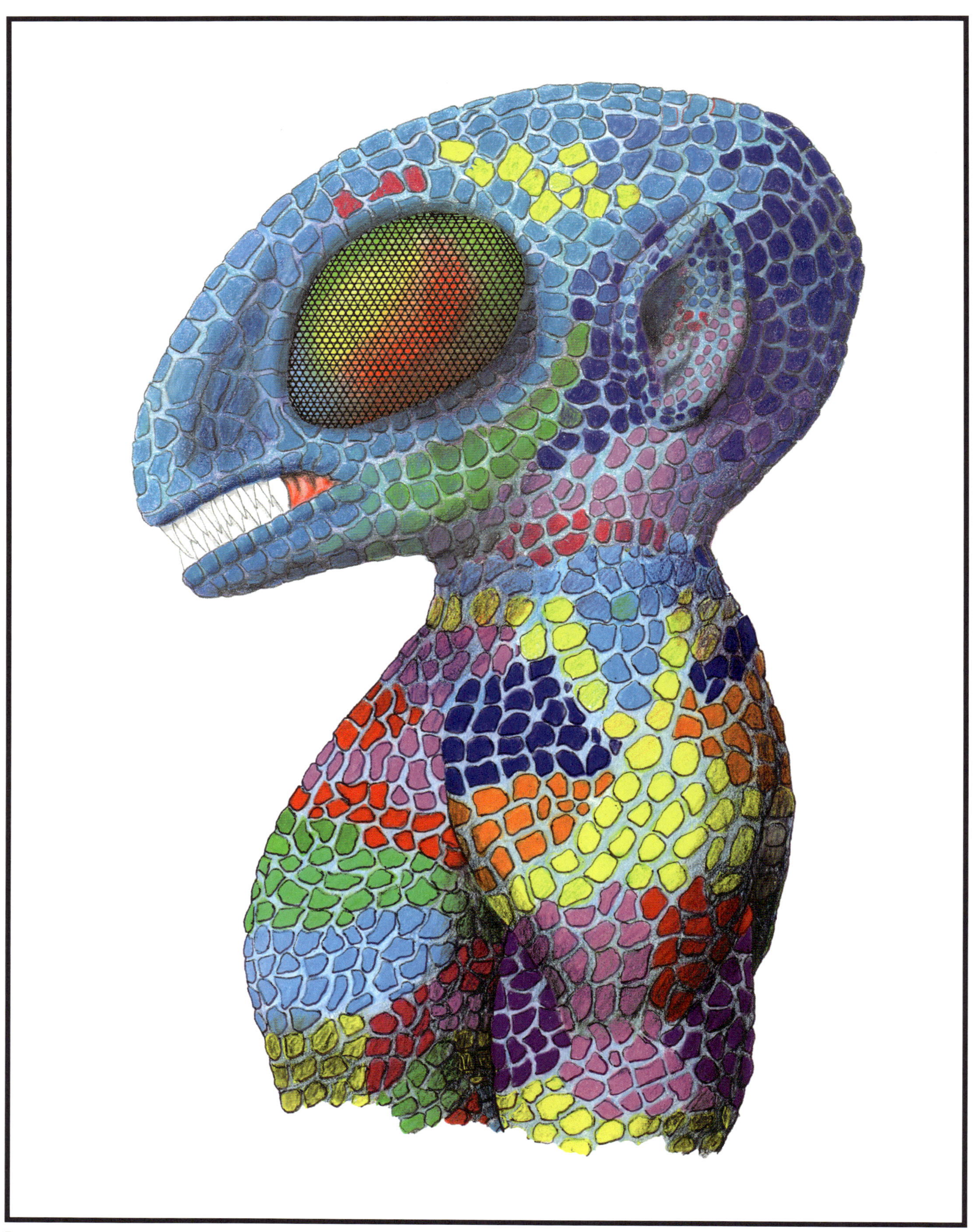

Drawn on Canson paper with colored pencils. Black outlines made with Sharpie marker pen, black colored pencil, and 8B lead pencil.

Original size about 10" x 15".

Compound Bug Eyes: An Interesting Pattern

Inspired by insect eyes similar to this one.
(Photo from www.bigstockphoto.com.)

1
Make an over-all sketch of your creature.

2
Make two *very light* lines that cross each other in the center of the eye. I suggest using an HB lead — it will be easier to erase than a lighter H lead.

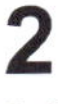

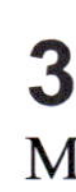

3
Make "tick marks" on each line to help guide you in making a grid. The marks should be **closer together as they approach the outer edge of the eye**.

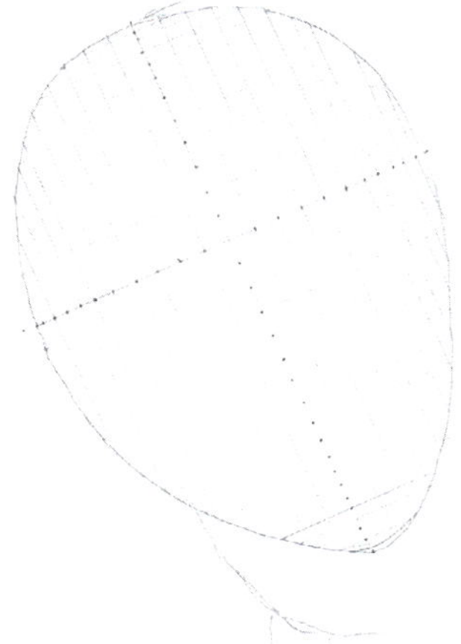

4
Make very light grid lines perpendicular to each other, using the tick marks as a guide. A ruler was used here. You can make *slightly* curved lines if you wish. The lines should form squares in the eye's center. Keep your pencil sharp!

5
Starting at the center, begin making circles.

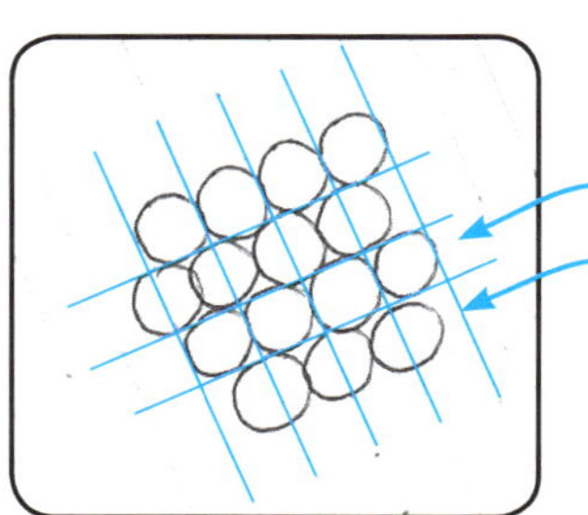

Note that the circles are *offset* from each other, which means that...

...in one row they occupy squares...

... and in the next row they're over grid lines.

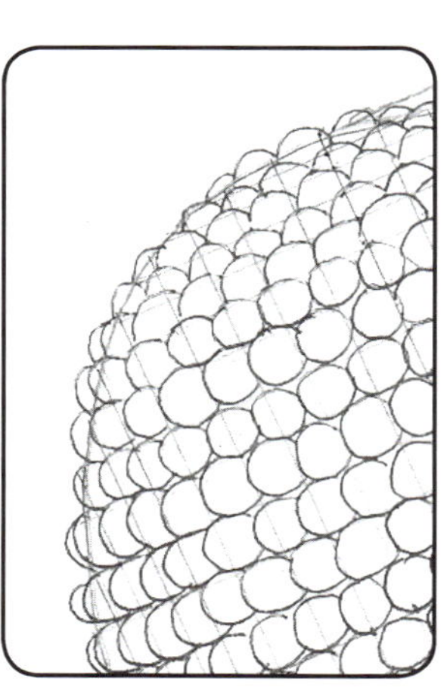

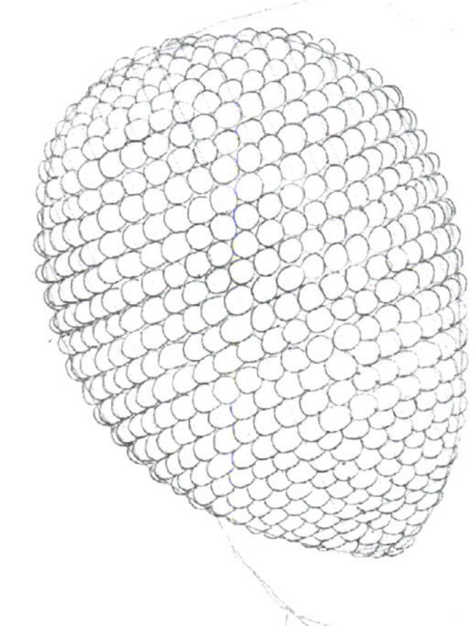

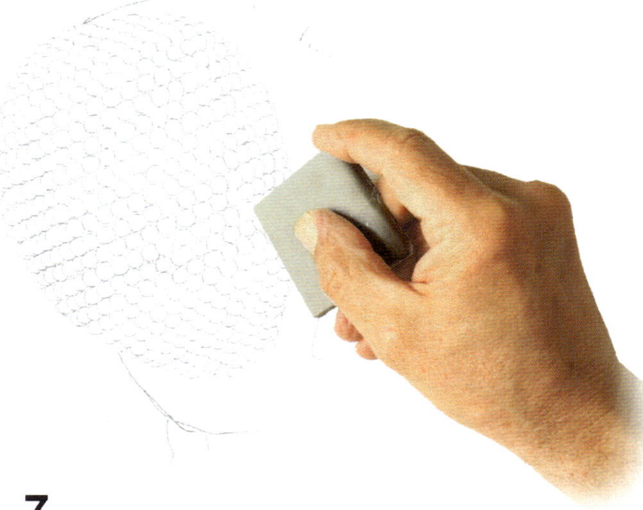

6

Finish making circles. The closer they are to the edge of the eye, the more they should overlap each other. Their lines should be a bit darker than the grid lines, but still quite light.

7

Run a kneaded eraser over the drawing. This should all but eliminate the grid lines and lighten the circles. Make sure the circles are just barely visible, so that the graphite (pencil lead) does not "corrupt" the colors that come next...

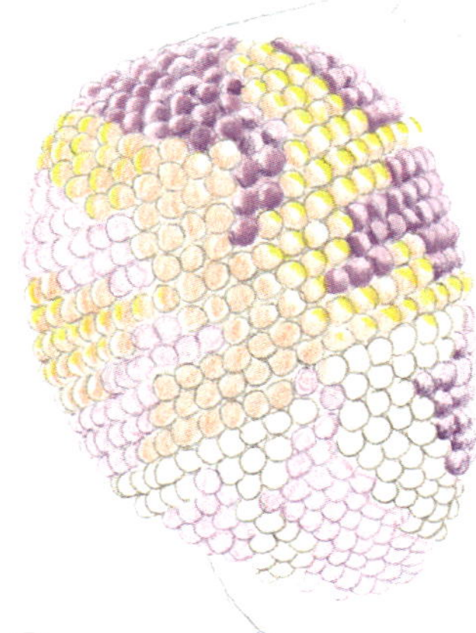

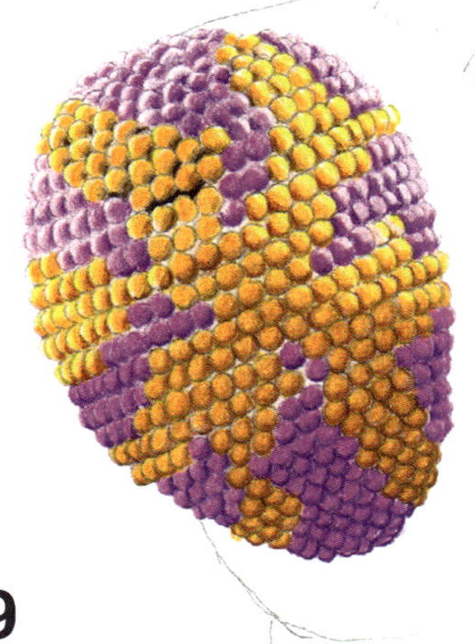

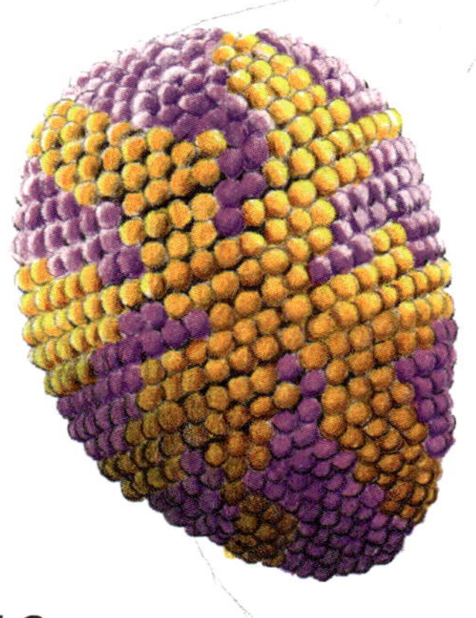

8

Assuming you're using colored pencils, lightly draw a pattern. Use whichever colors you wish.

9

Lay down another layer of color. Shade each circle so it has a lighter side facing the light and a darker side facing away. This will make them more round, like little balls..

10

More color, with shading. Fill in spaces between the circles with black.

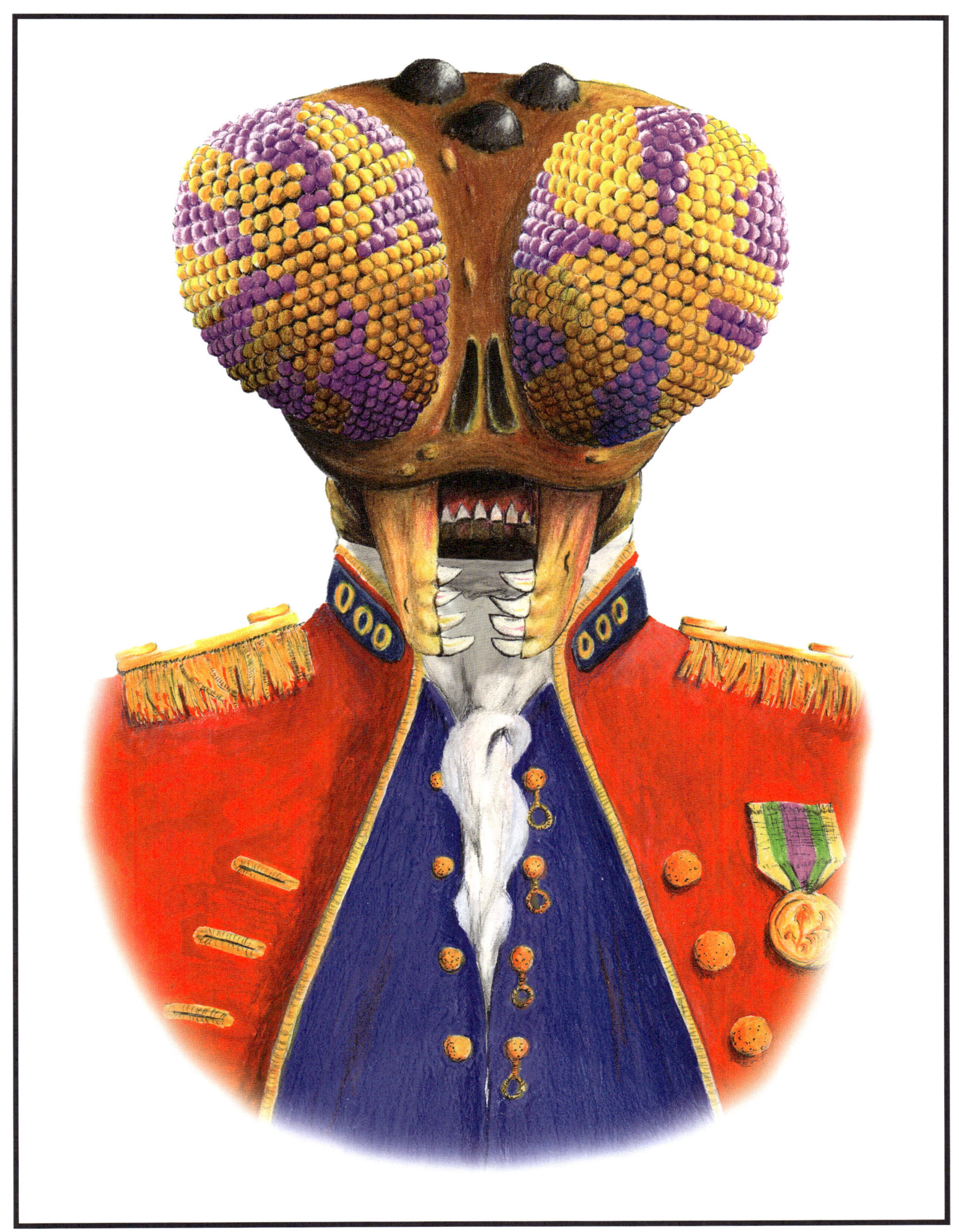

Orignal size 9" x 16"

11 Draw the other eye and complete your drawing! (Perhaps, to make the eyes somewhat alike, you could employ the "symmetry" technique demonstrated on pages 70-73.)

Bug Eye Variations

The whites of this creature's eyes were shaded with 6B and 8B graphite pencils, using the "smooth" technique illustrated on pages 41-46. The small black iris and veins were made with colored pencils.

Note how the instructions for "humanoid" eyes on page 86 were applied here.

Notice that the veins are slightly thicker as they near the outside of the eyeballs.

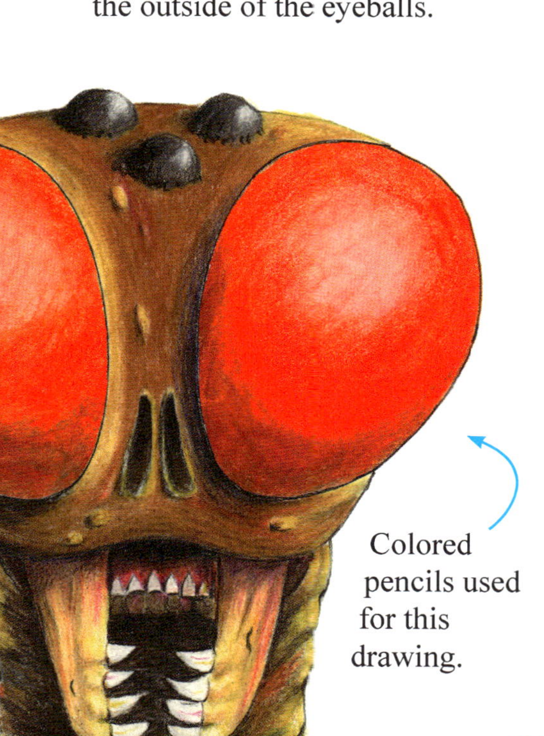

Colored pencils used for this drawing.

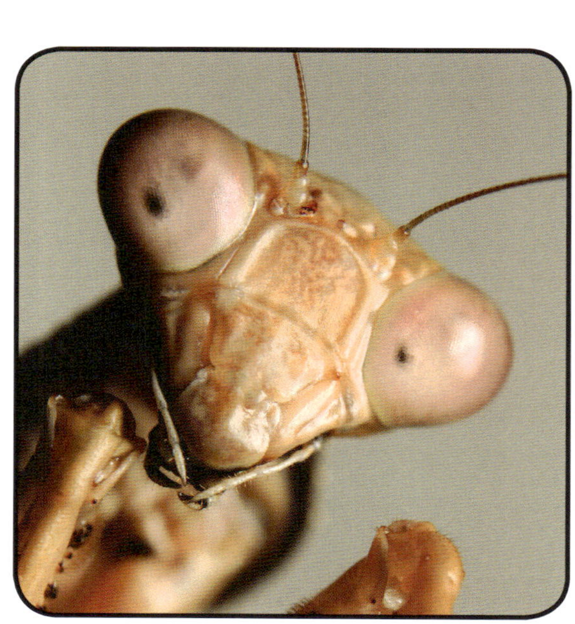

Look familiar? See how you can get ideas from nature? (Mantas photo from www.bigstockphoto.com)

OK! Maybe the eyes on this creature don't look like eyes. So? But does he look creepy? Isn't that the point?

Drawn with colored pencils on Canson® drawing paper. The original is about 9" wide.

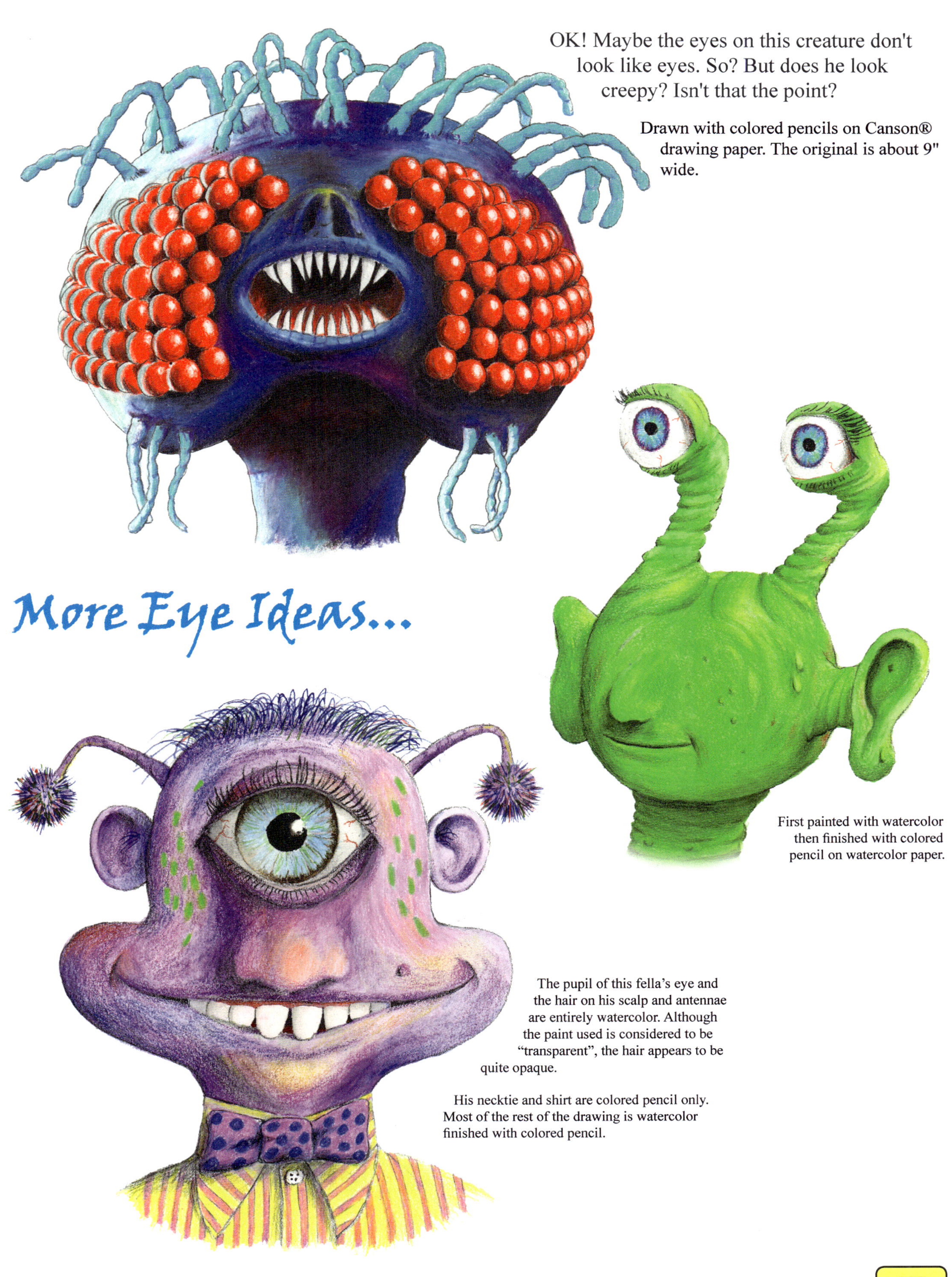

More Eye Ideas...

First painted with watercolor then finished with colored pencil on watercolor paper.

The pupil of this fella's eye and the hair on his scalp and antennae are entirely watercolor. Although the paint used is considered to be "transparent", the hair appears to be quite opaque.

His necktie and shirt are colored pencil only. Most of the rest of the drawing is watercolor finished with colored pencil.

Some pointers on TEETH

On the next few pages you'll discover different kinds of teeth. Use any of the samples, or a combination, as an inspiration for your drawings.

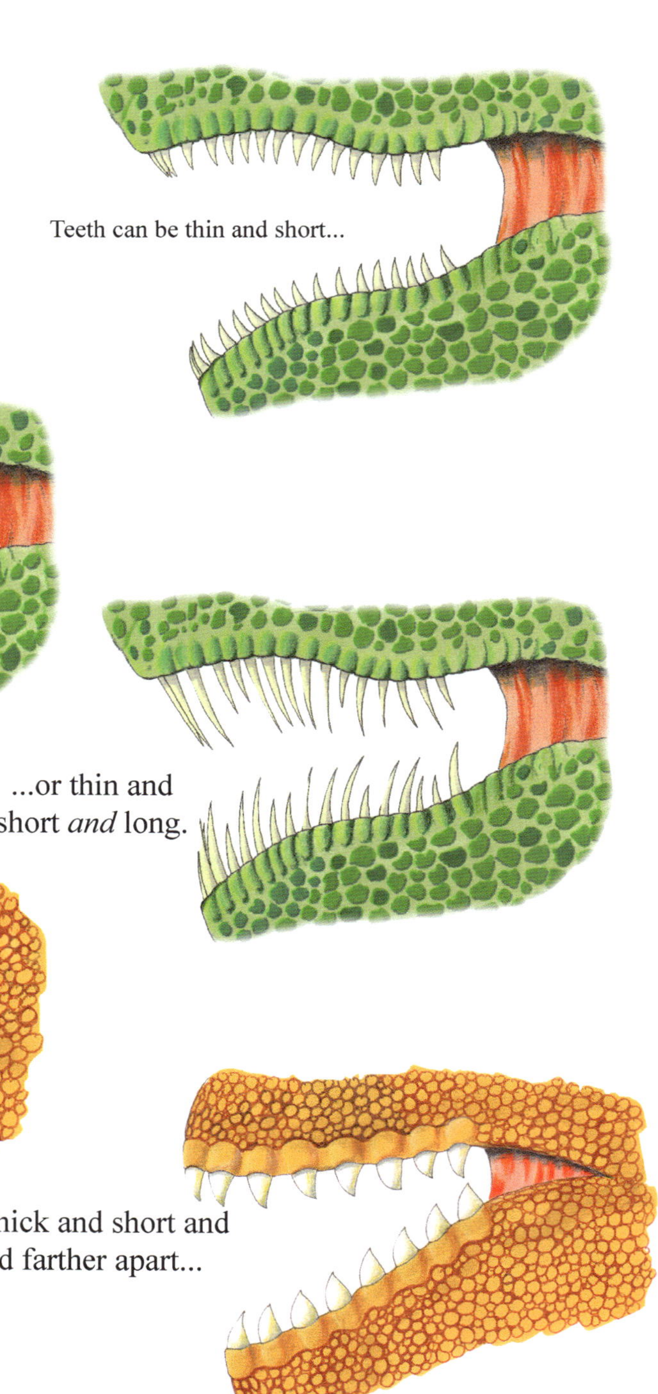

Teeth can be thin and short...

...or thin and long...

...or thin and short *and* long.

...or thick and short and spaced close together...

...or thick and short and spaced farther apart...

...or thick and long and spaced close together...

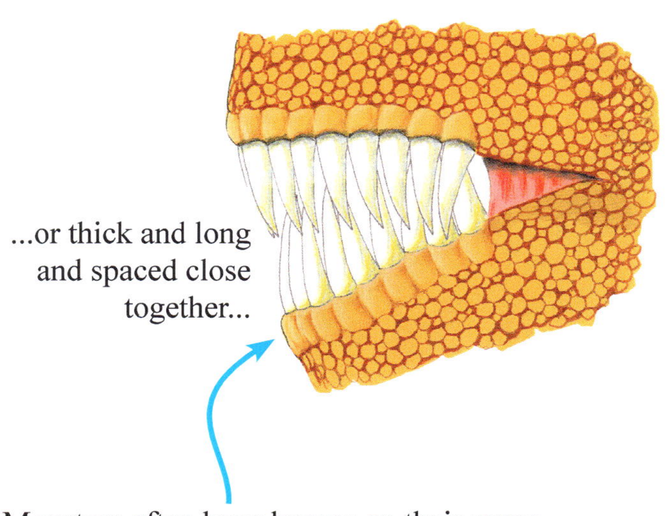

...or thick and short and long and *not* spaced close together.

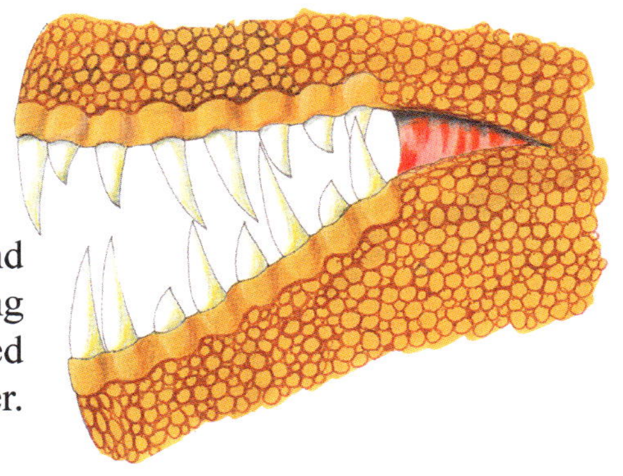

Monsters often have bumps on their gums at the bottom of each tooth.

Many creatures do not have lips — they just have thick "gums" like those shown here.

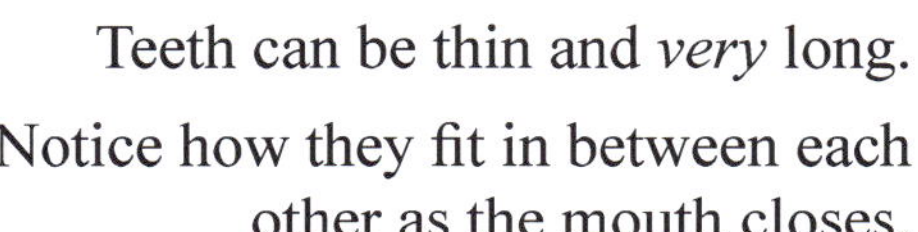

Teeth can be thin and *very* long.

Notice how they fit in between each other as the mouth closes.

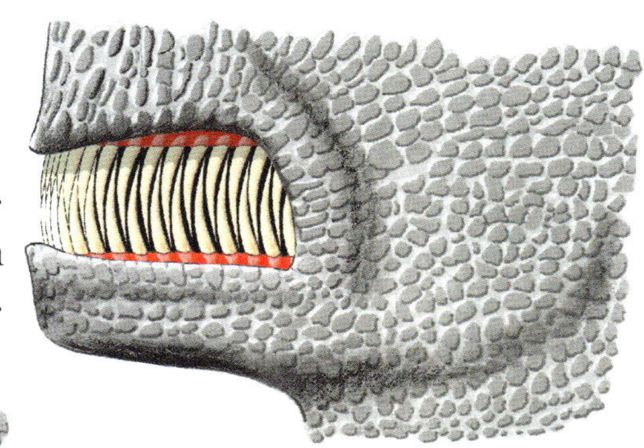

As shown above, some creatures don't have lips. But some do, like this one, more or less. (These are lips?)

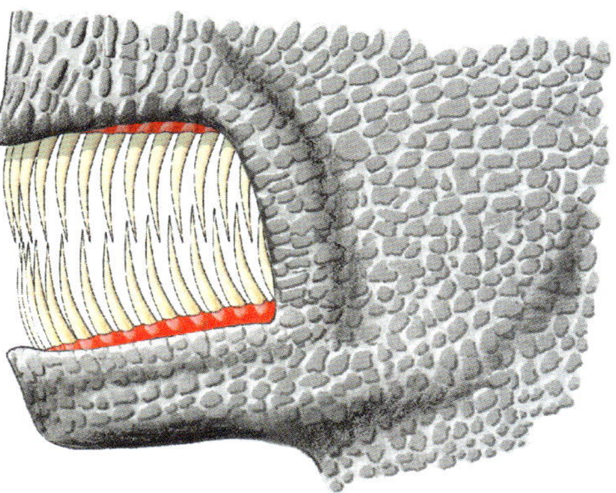

Inside gums — when there *are* inside gums — will also have bumps at the bottom of each tooth.

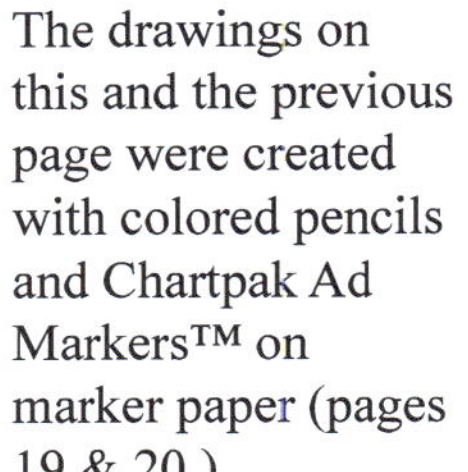

The drawings on this and the previous page were created with colored pencils and Chartpak Ad Markers™ on marker paper (pages 19 & 20.)

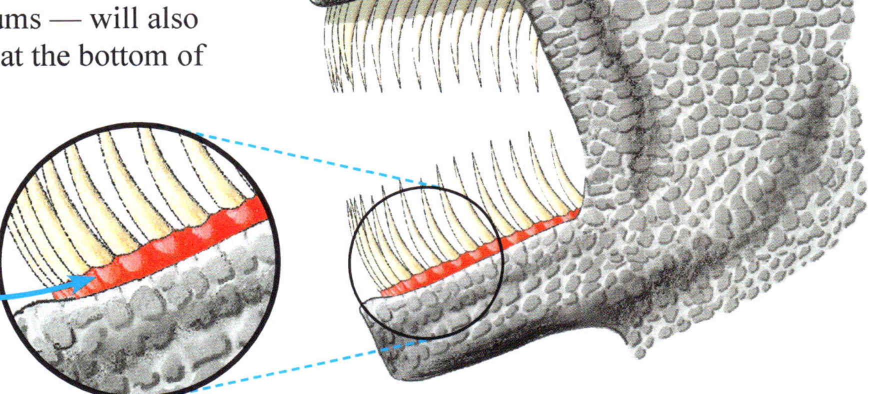

Fabulous Fantastic FANGS

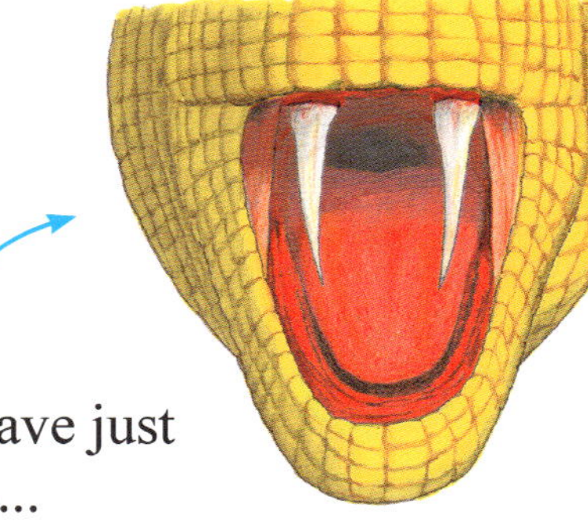

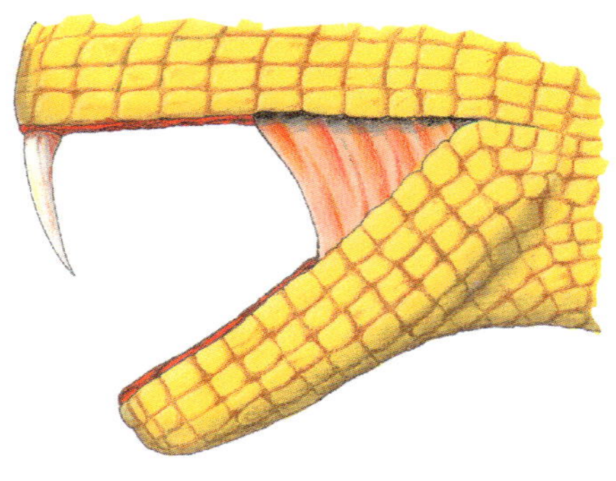

Monsters can have just two large fangs...

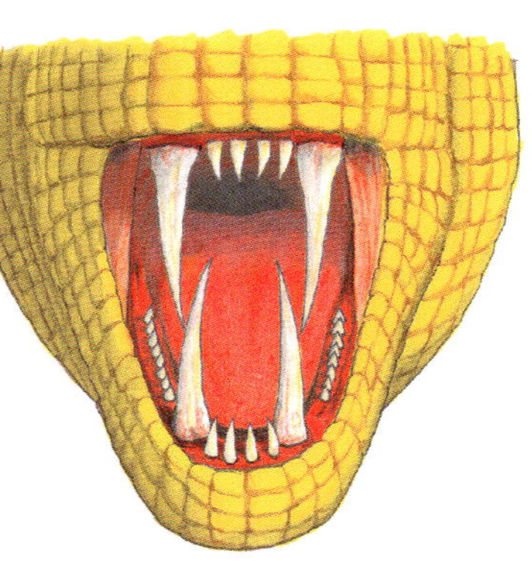

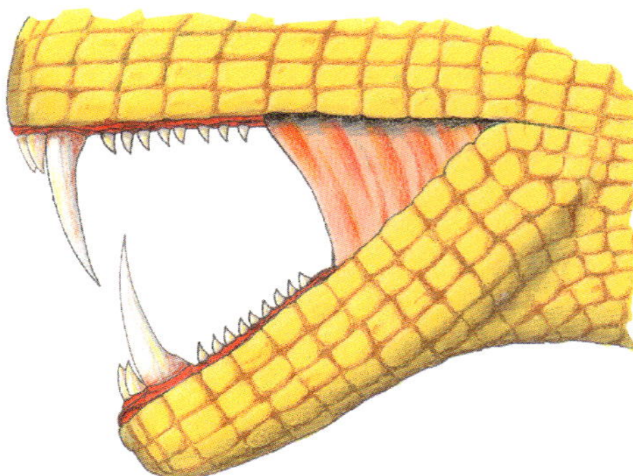

...or a combination of fangs and smaller teeth. Make up your own combination!

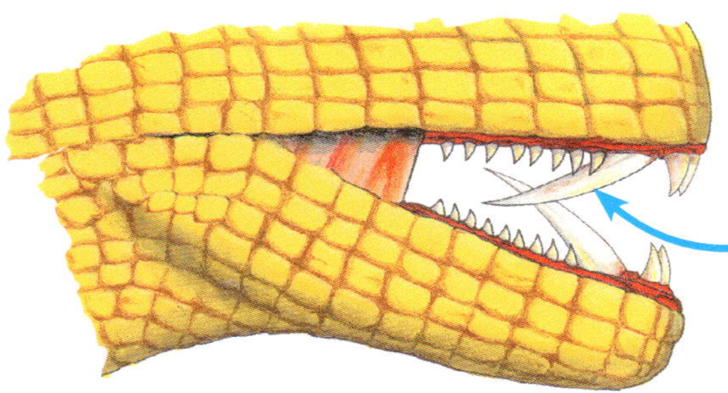

SCIENCE

Snakes' teeth are hinged. They swivel out of the way as the mouth closes to avoid puncturing themselves. (Earth snakes lack fangs on the bottoms of their mouths).

Slimy Slobber

White spots help make the slime look wet. If you've already colored the area, you can use an electric eraser or use thick white paint or a pen with white pigment.

A Sharpie black ultra fine point marker was used to outline shapes *after* fixative was applied over the colored pencil drawing (see pages 77 & 78).

Original about 6 -1/4" x 8-3/4".

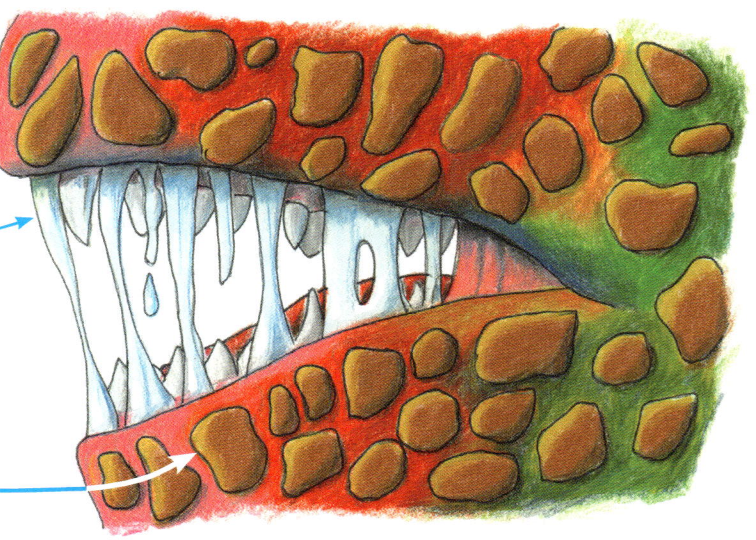

An Incisive Observation:

Many carnivorous (meat-eating) earth animals, such as dogs and cats, have two very long sharp teeth near the front of their mouths, top and bottom, called *incisors*. These are used for catching, killing, and eating their prey. Many monsters throughout the universe have incisors as well, so keep this in mind when you draw your monsters.

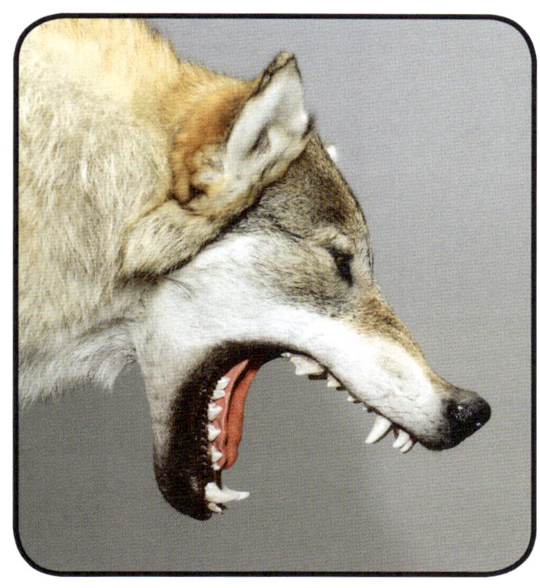

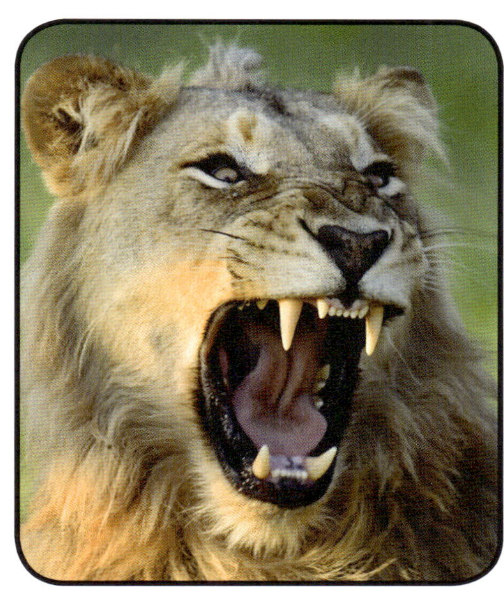

We humans also have incisors, but they are not nearly as long since we no longer use them to catch and kill our food.
Photos courtesy Bigstockphoto.com

The Tooth Lines: Curve Them!

Your creatures will look more realistic if their jaws and teeth follow curved lines.

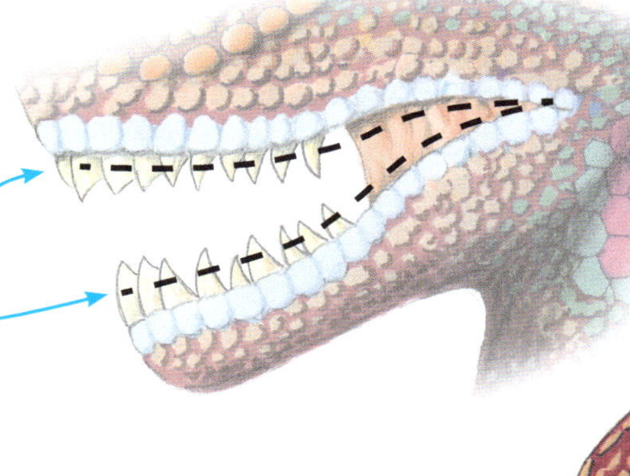

Creature with straight tooth lines: Not very realistic.

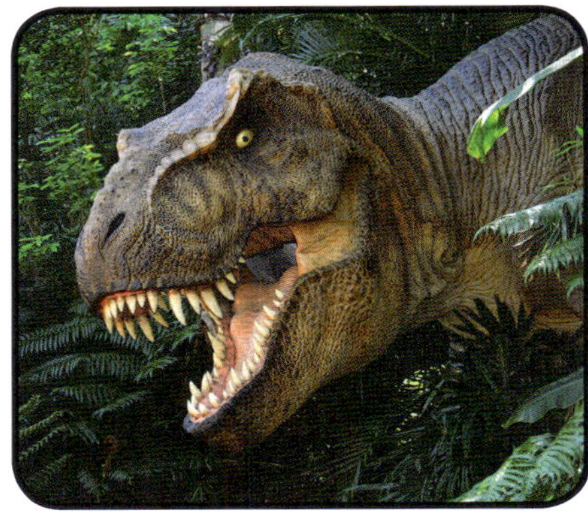

Curved tooth lines are common on dinosaurs and other earth animals.

T-Rex photo courtesy Bigstockphoto.com.

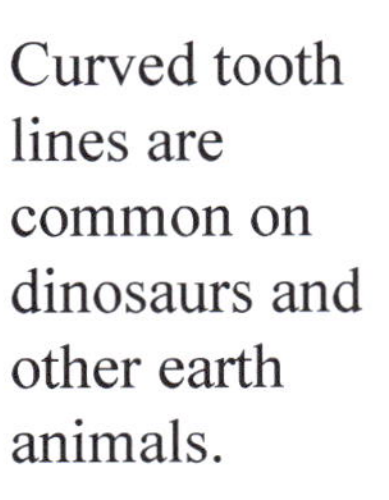

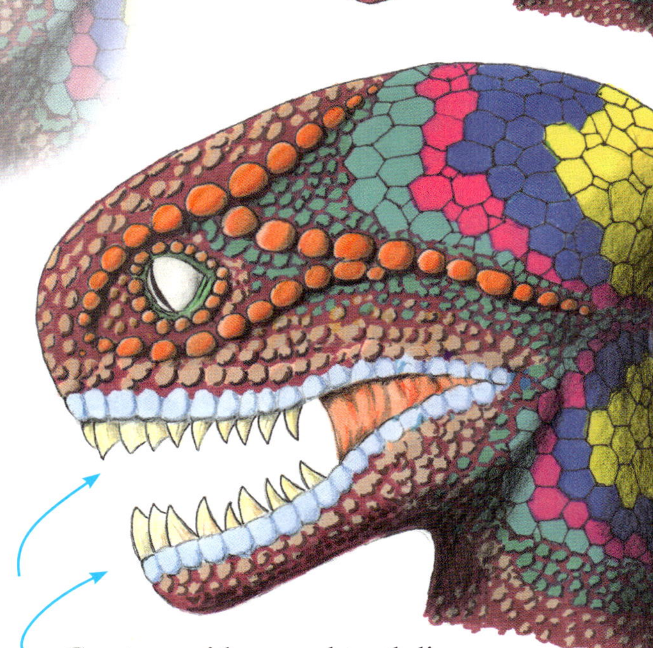

Creature with curved tooth lines.

A case for

Poor Dental Hygiene

A monster will likely be more menacing if its teeth are yellowish, scarred, and stained.

Note that the teeth bow outward, away from the mouth. This may add a bit to the monster's scariness.

White spots on teeth, gums, and lips are reflections of light, indicating moisture on these parts.

Red stains on teeth: could be blood!

Mostly dark purple and red were used to show ugly stains on the teeth and along the gum lines (as if the creature could care).

Grooves, or cracks, help trap dirt and other yucky stuff.

Drawn with colored pencils on Stonehenge paper. Original size 5.5" x 7".

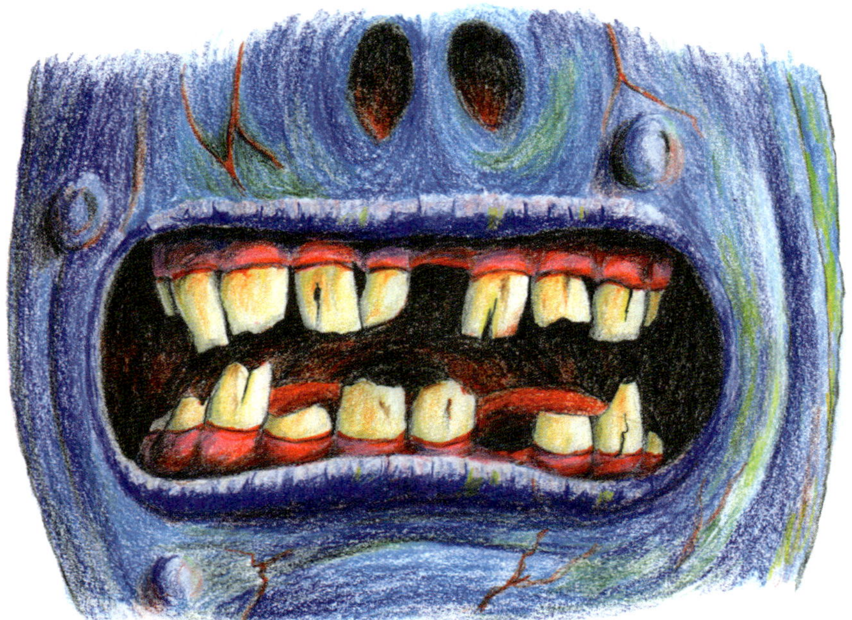

Drawn with about twenty colored pencils on Canson 702-6190 paper. Original size 6.5" x 8.5".

Monster teeth don't have to be sharp. In fact, many monsters have flat teeth, just like you and me.

This creature had sharp, perfect teeth at one time, but they have become broken and worn due to a bad habit of eating rocks, getting into fights, and refusing to brush after meals.

Notice some teeth are missing and others lean toward or away from each other.

Teeth-in-the-Round

Though quite rare, some monsters have teeth arranged in a circular pattern. One method to arrange teeth evenly is shown here.

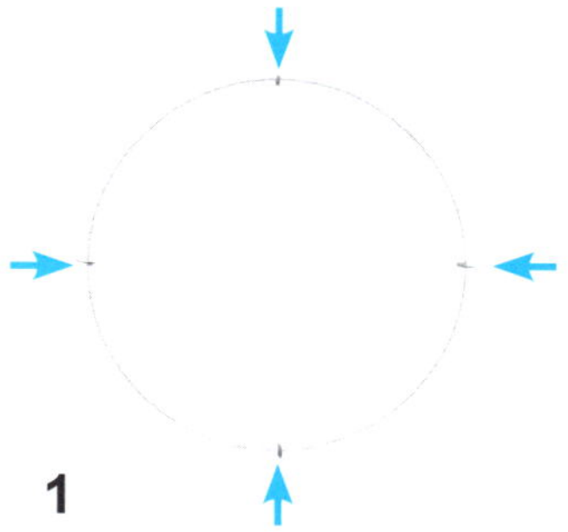

1
Make tic marks top, bottom, and sides of circle.

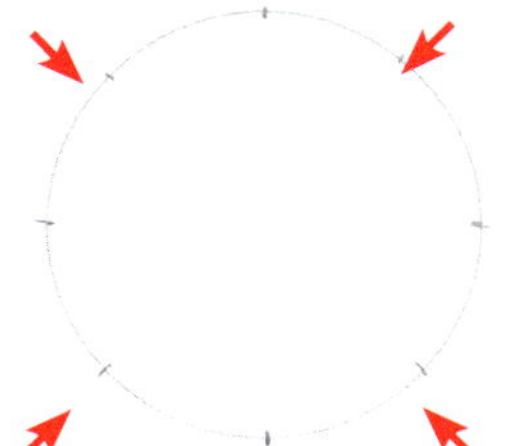

2
Make marks between first ones...

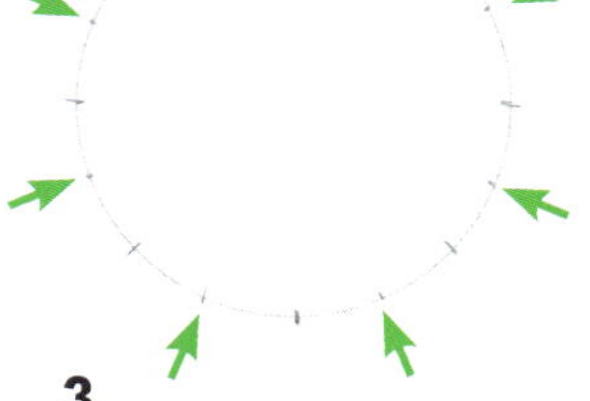

3
...and still more between ones you've just made.

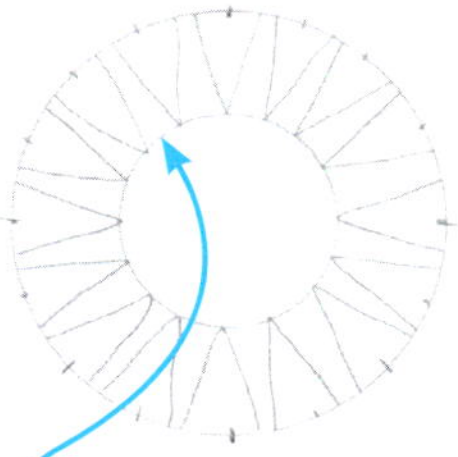

4
Draw teeth, using tic marks as guides.

An inner circle will help keep tooth lengths equal, if that's what you want.

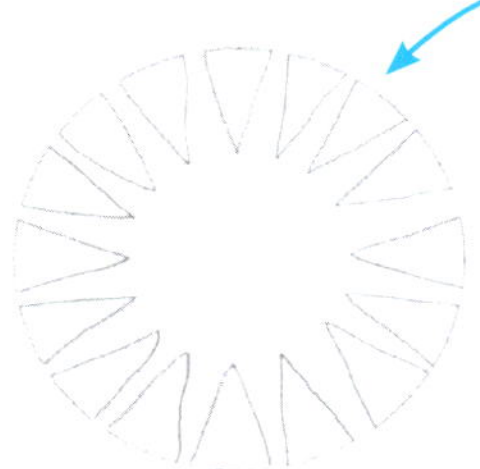

5
Erase unnecessary lines or transfer necessary ones to a new sheet of paper (pages 65-68). You can draw around the new set of teeth or center them on a drawing in progress.

Drawn mostly with colored pencils. Black lines were created with Micron pens after the drawing was fixed (Micron pens page 19; fixing drawings pages 77 & 78).

Original size about 9" wide x 6" tall.

NOTE: The fact that I used Strathmore 400 series "Drawing Medium" paper for this drawing doesn't mean I recommended it for colored pencil drawings. The paper's yellowish tint, apparent in the creature's shadow, got in the way of producing the more brilliant colors I wanted. I recommend using whiter stock for colored pencil drawings except when colored paper is used for effect (pages 51-53).

Slightly tinted paper can, however, be very nice for grayscale pencil drawings.

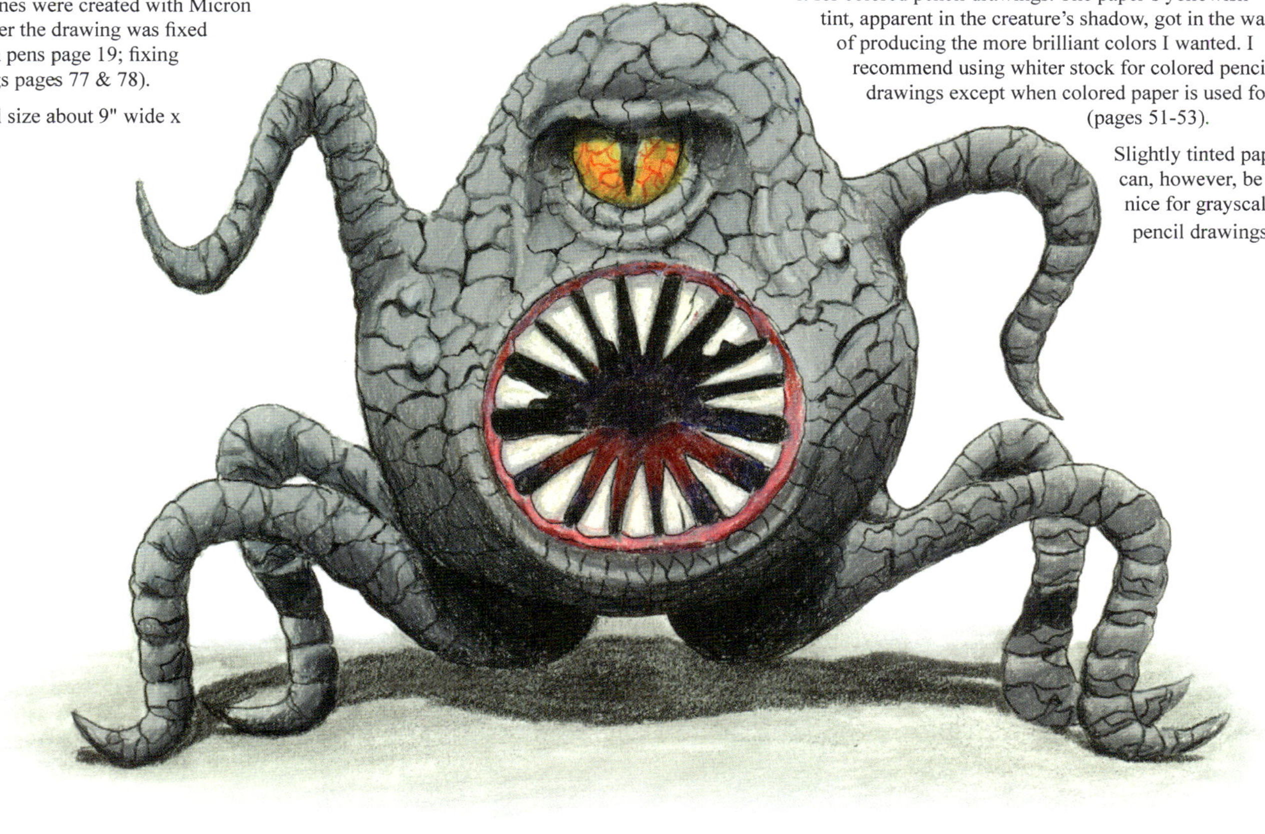

HORNS and BARBS

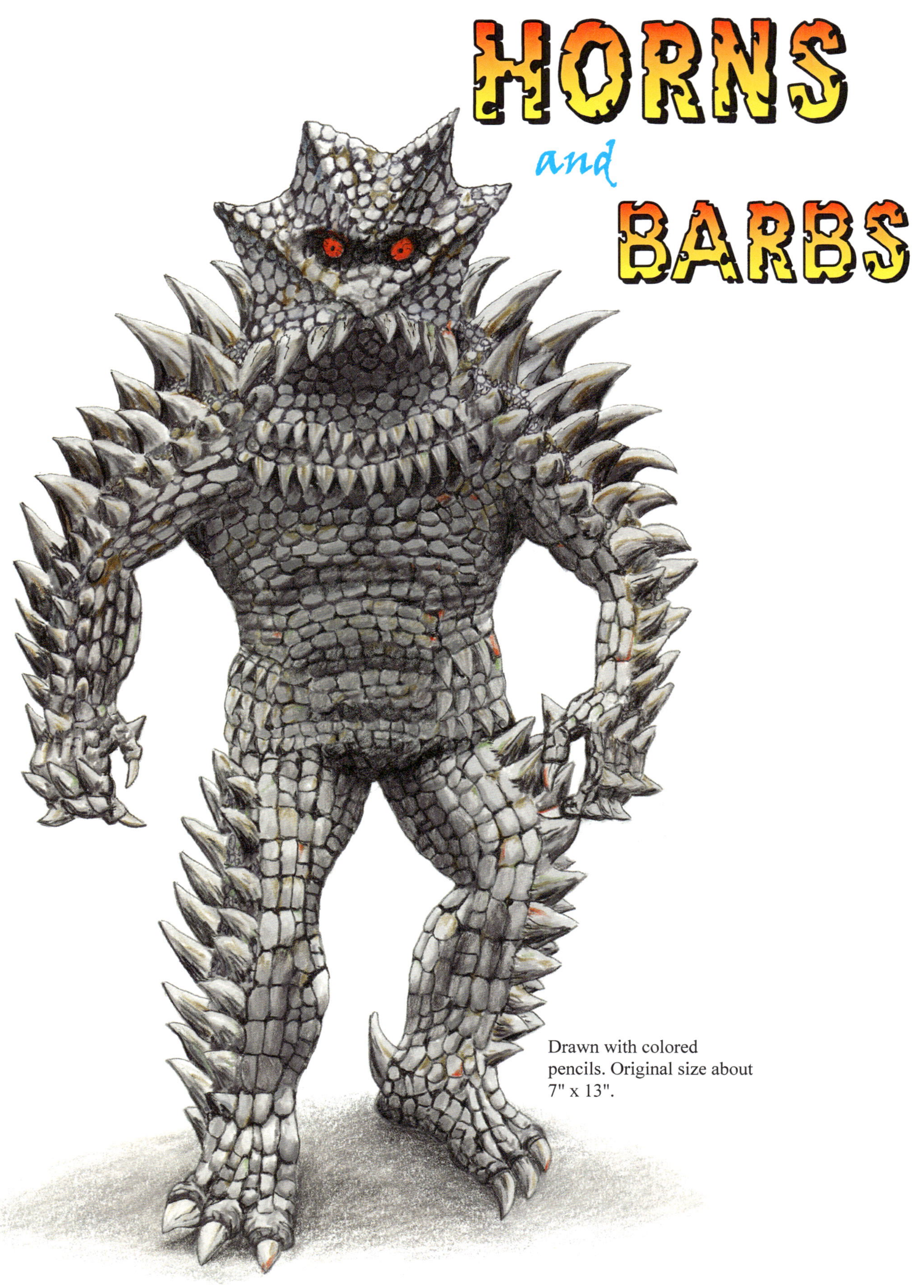

Drawn with colored pencils. Original size about 7" x 13".

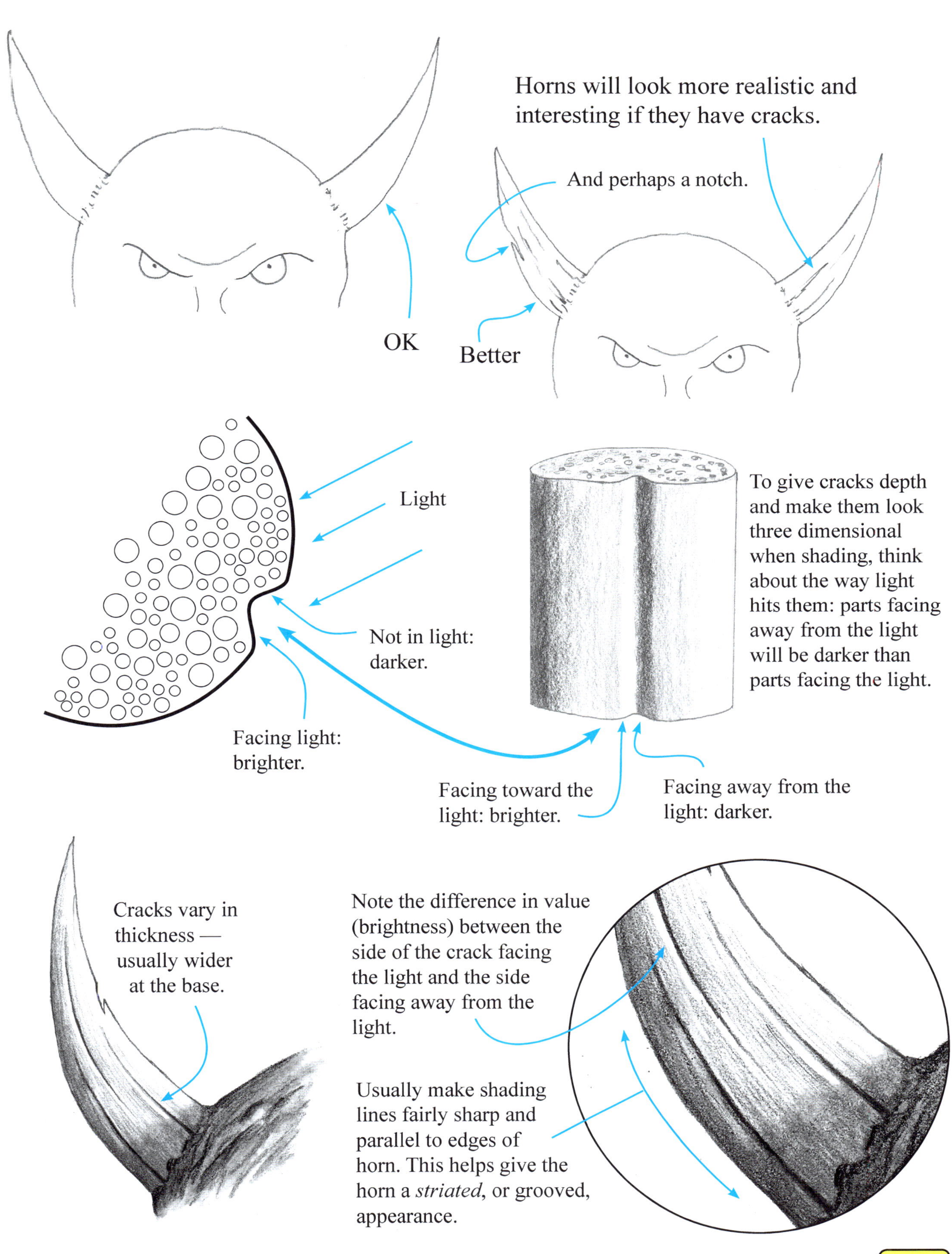
Horns will look more realistic and interesting if they have cracks.
And perhaps a notch.
OK
Better
Light
Not in light: darker.
Facing light: brighter.
To give cracks depth and make them look three dimensional when shading, think about the way light hits them: parts facing away from the light will be darker than parts facing the light.
Facing toward the light: brighter.
Facing away from the light: darker.
Cracks vary in thickness — usually wider at the base.
Note the difference in value (brightness) between the side of the crack facing the light and the side facing away from the light.
Usually make shading lines fairly sharp and parallel to edges of horn. This helps give the horn a *striated*, or grooved, appearance.

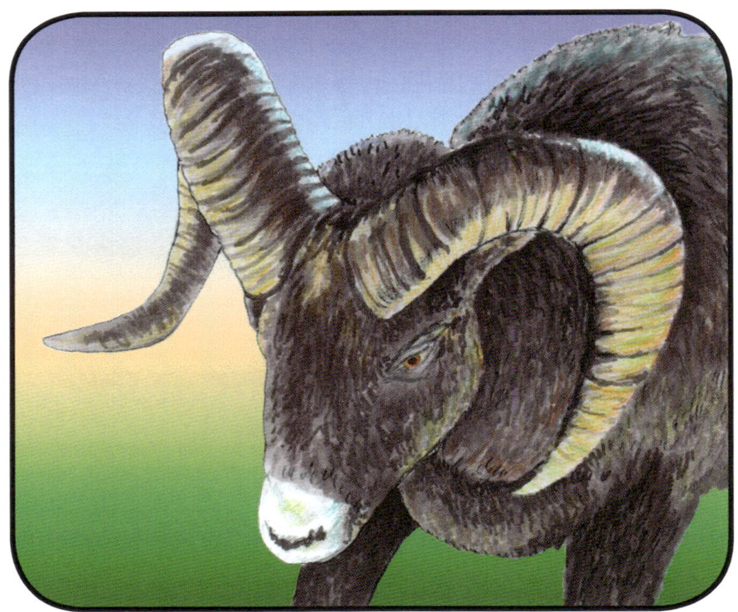

You can get ideas for horns from photographs and illustrations of real earth animals. The horns on the drawing below were inspired by those of a Rocky Mountain Big Horn Sheep (left).

Be sure to include dinosaurs in your search.

The background of the bighorn sheep, left, was created with Photoshop. The sheep itself was drawn with colored pencils...honest!

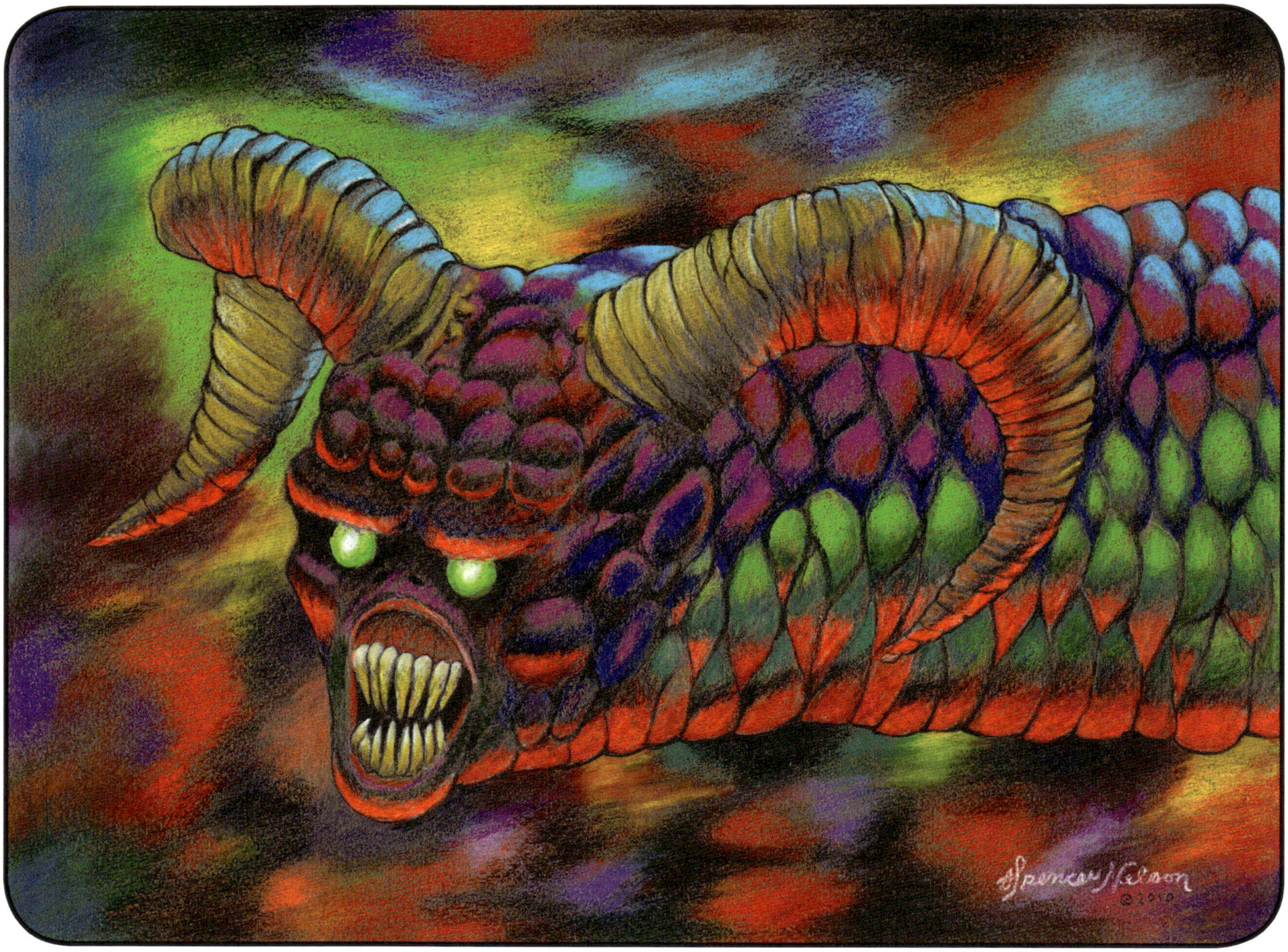

Drawn with colored pencils on brown Mi-Tientes pastel paper, 8.5" x 11". (Adobe Photoshop software used to increase color saturation.)

Horns can protrude from the side of a monster's head…and point down.

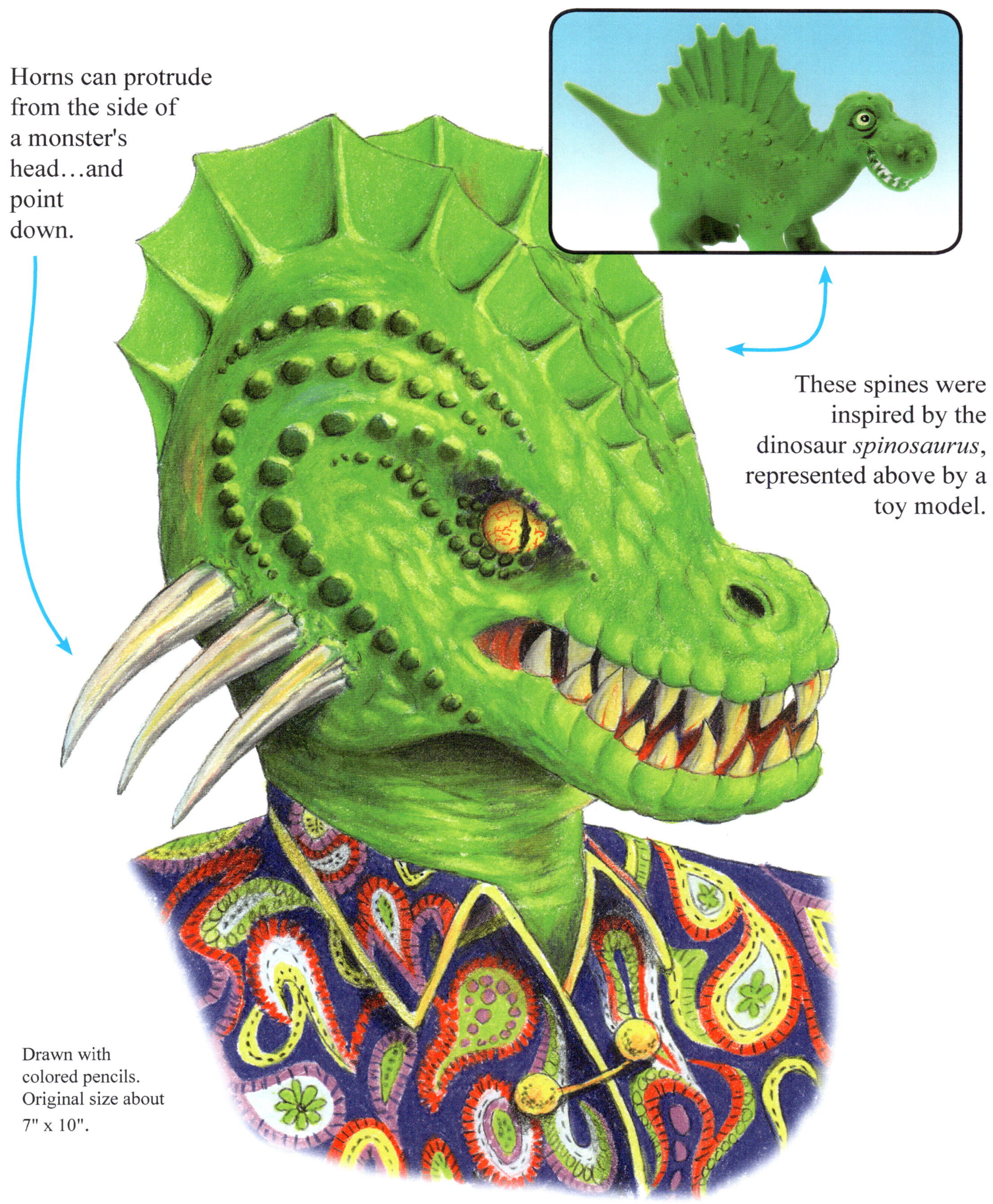

These spines were inspired by the dinosaur *spinosaurus*, represented above by a toy model.

Drawn with colored pencils. Original size about 7" x 10".

Here's EARS and NOSES

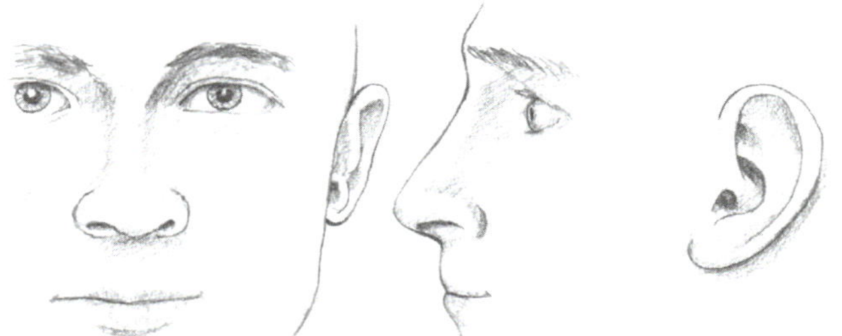

Monster and alien ears and noses are often similar to those of humans, but shaped differently. Study human ears and noses to get an idea of how to make creature ears and noses. Notice the similarities — and differences — in the drawings below.

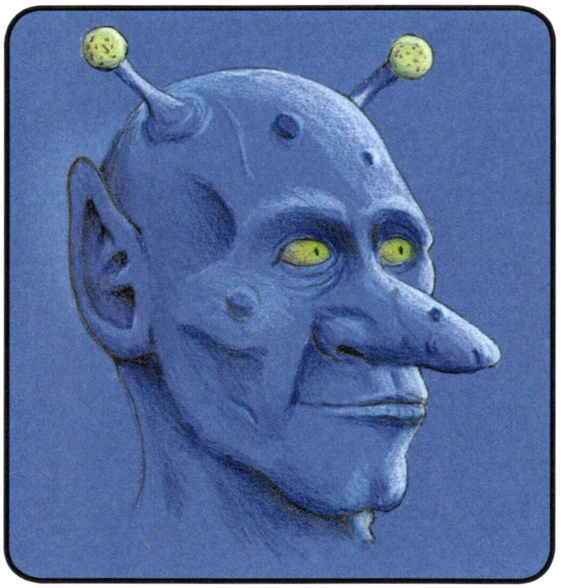

Original drawing 4.5" x 5.5"

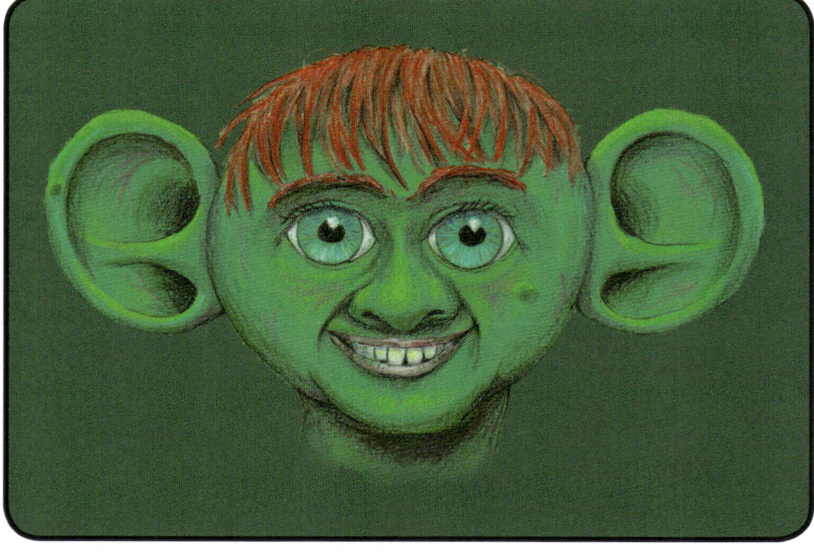

Original drawing 7.5" x 5". The three drawings with colored backgrounds were created with colored pencils on pastel papers. The green-eyed creature was drawn on Canson drawing paper with colored pencils and regular graphite pencils smoothed with a stump (pages 41 - 46).

Original drawing 4.5" x 7"

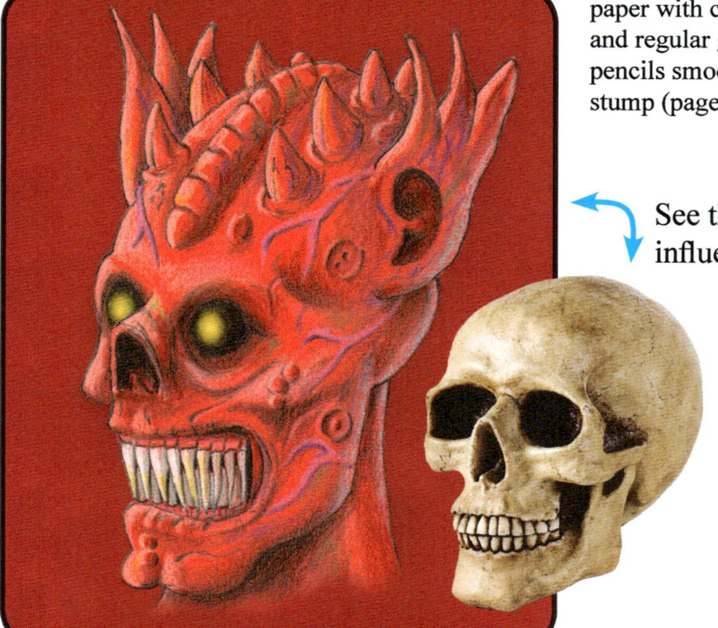

See the human influence?

Not all monster & alien ears & noses are human-like. Some are similar to earth animals, and in fact many monsters and aliens don't even have ears and noses.

Get a Handle on HANDS and CLAWS

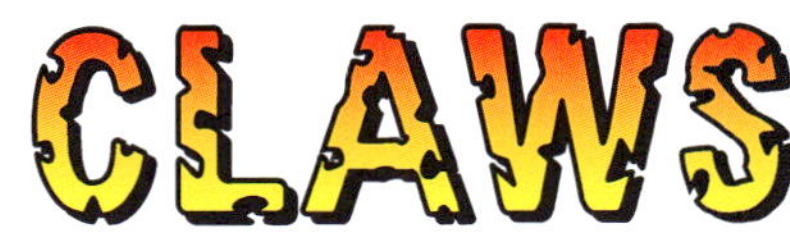

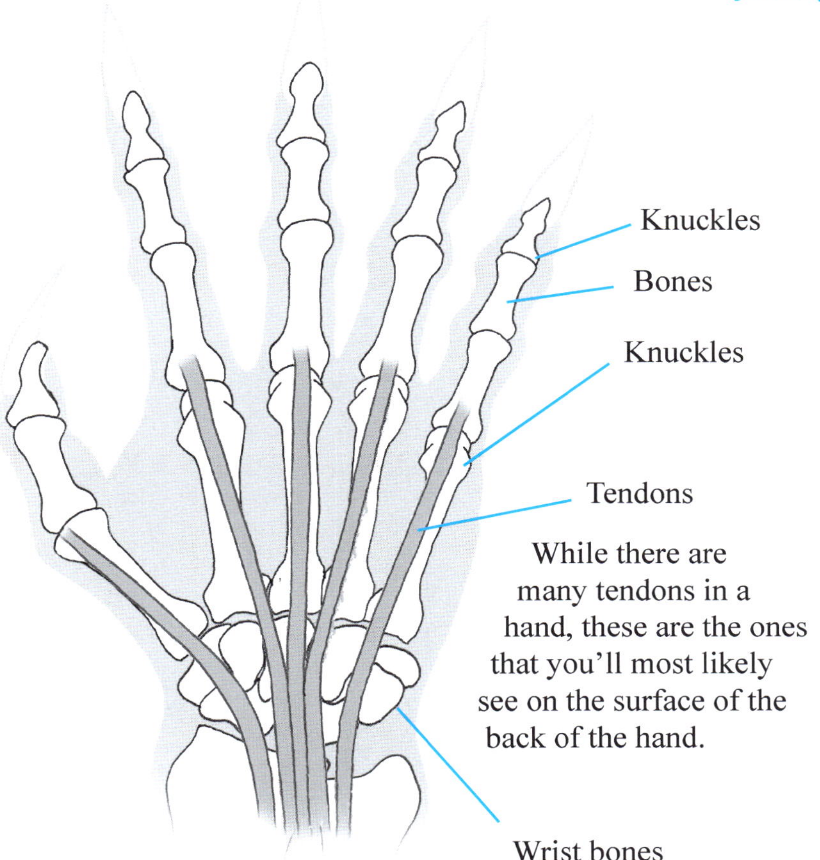

Bones and tendons play an important role in shaping the appearance of most hands.

Thinking about those bones and tendons as you draw will help you create more realistic hands — and claws.

Draw a Monster Hand

As with other parts of a monster or alien, there are many ways to draw hands. This is just one approach...

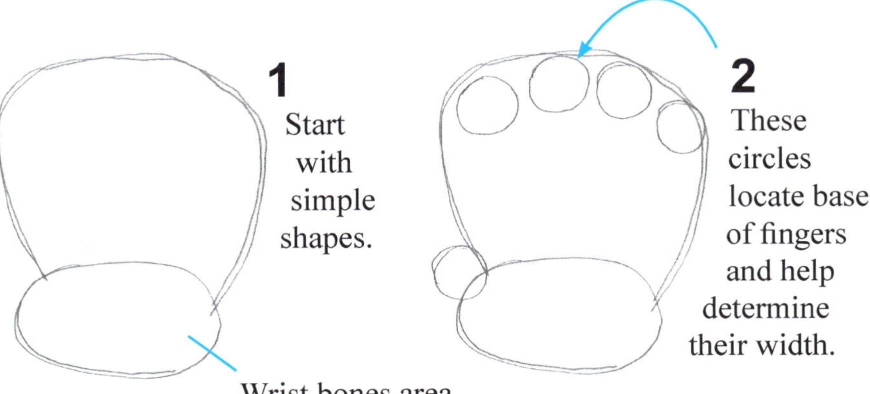

3

Straight lines will help you position fingers.

Small "tick marks" help determine locations of joints and length of fingers.

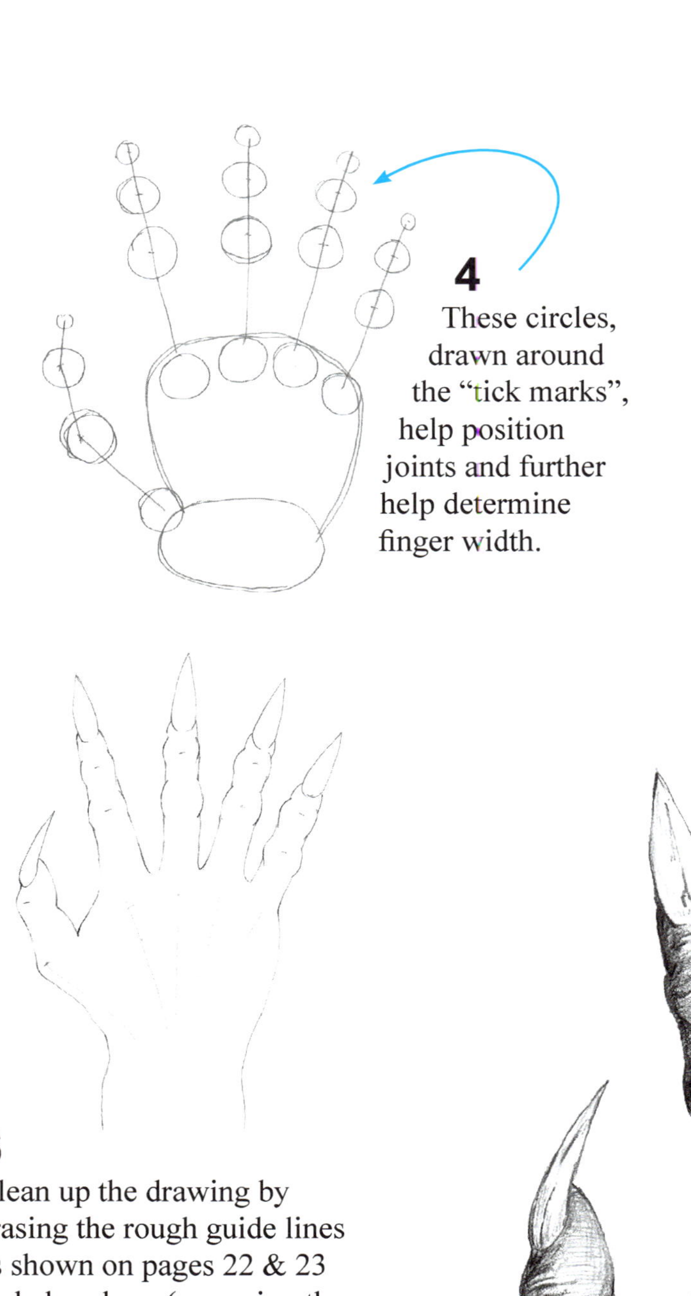

4

These circles, drawn around the "tick marks", help position joints and further help determine finger width.

5

Continuing with rough guide lines, you can start rendering the actual hand.

Remember to keep the lines very light.

6

Clean up the drawing by erasing the rough guide lines as shown on pages 22 & 23 and elsewhere (assuming the guide lines are light enough) or transfer the drawing to a new sheet of paper as illustrated on pages 65-68.

7

Shade the drawing, if you wish, in any style of your choosing. Of course, the hand you draw (or paint) will likely be part of a complete creature, so the style will be the same as the whole creature.

Knuckles

These ridges reveal tendons (not bones) just below the surface of the skin.

Note that they come together at the base.

Draw a Monster Hand — a different method

This is another way to draw a monster hand, using circles instead of "sticks" to indicate the fingers.

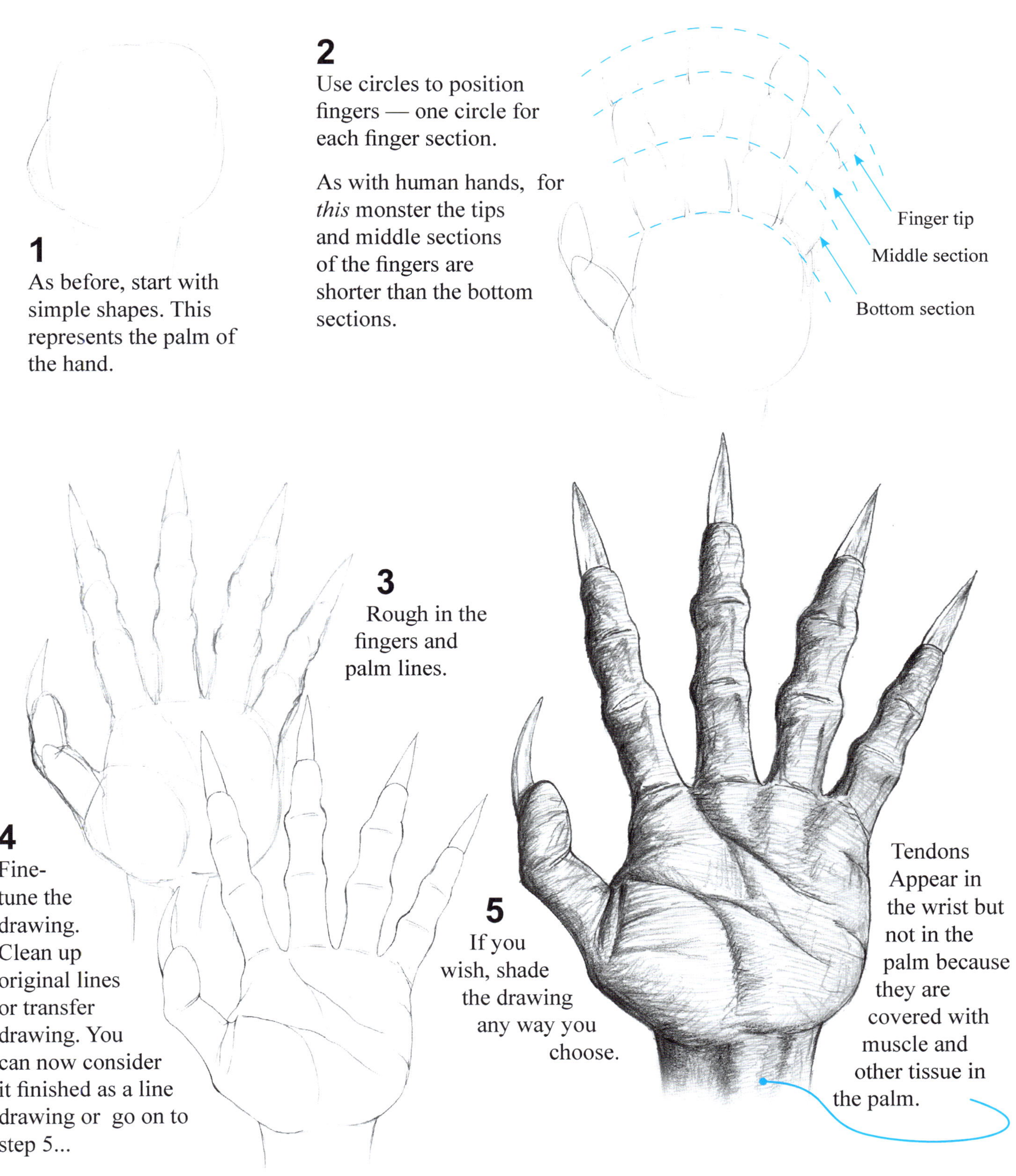

1

As before, start with simple shapes. This represents the palm of the hand.

2

Use circles to position fingers — one circle for each finger section.

As with human hands, for *this* monster the tips and middle sections of the fingers are shorter than the bottom sections.

3

Rough in the fingers and palm lines.

4

Fine-tune the drawing. Clean up original lines or transfer drawing. You can now consider it finished as a line drawing or go on to step 5...

5

If you wish, shade the drawing any way you choose.

Tendons Appear in the wrist but not in the palm because they are covered with muscle and other tissue in the palm.

Draw a Monster Hand — from the side

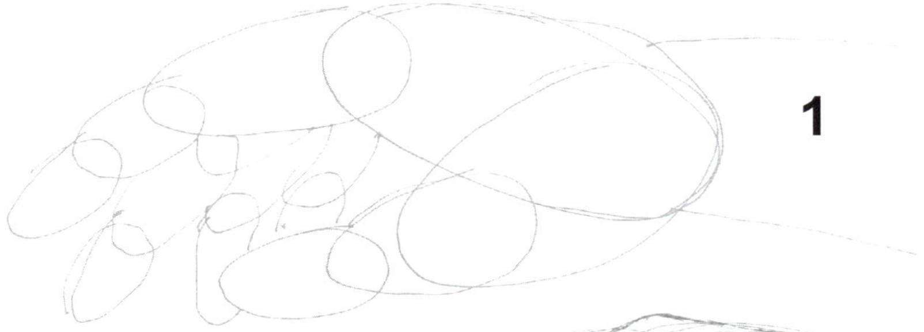

1

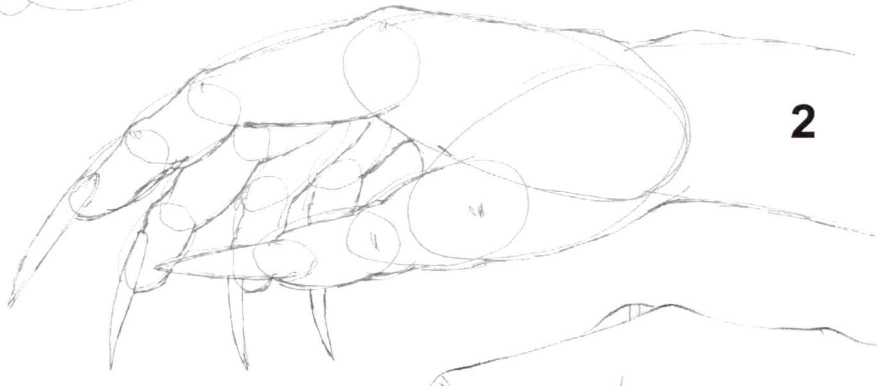

2

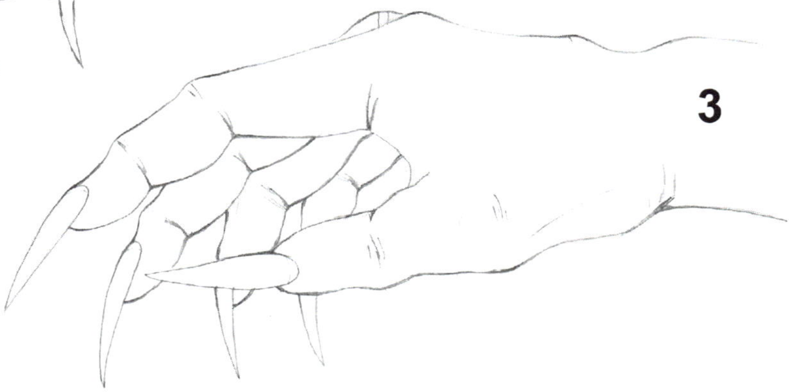

3

Final drawings on this and previous three pages made with 3H, HB, 3B, and 7B pencils on Canson 90lb. drawing paper.

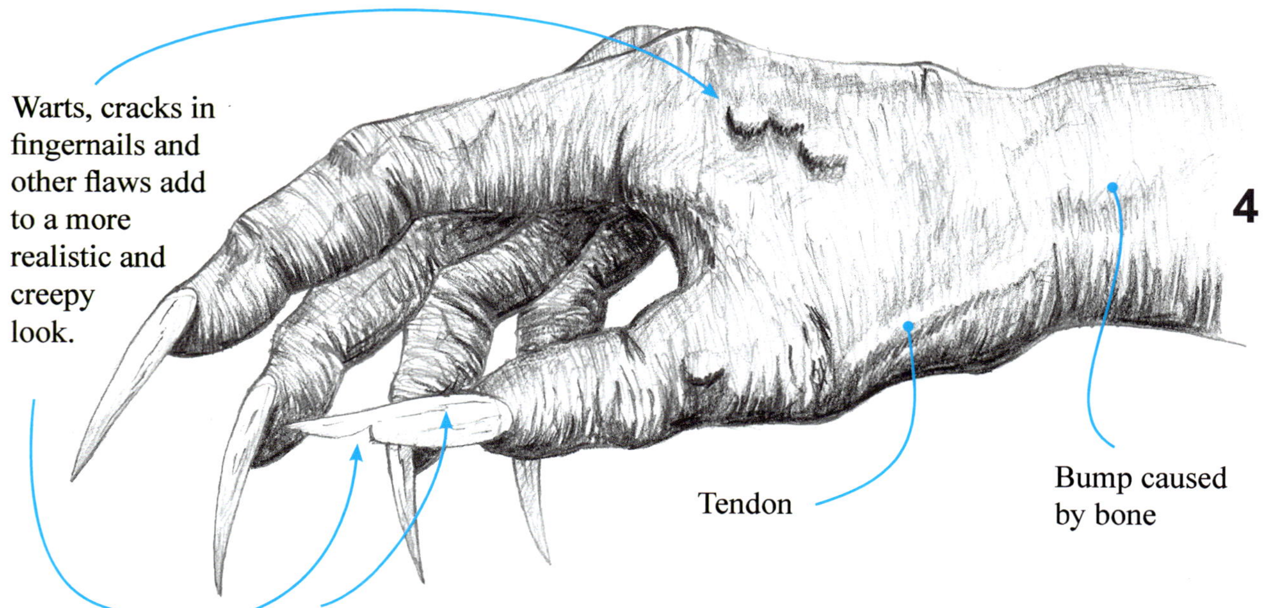

Draw a Monster Hand — from a different angle

The previous pages showed you views of hands as seen from simple angles that were fairly easy to draw (top, bottom, and side). Here, with the hand pointing toward you and with fingers curled downward, the angle is more challenging. **Before you start, read and understand steps 1 through 4; then, when you go back to step 1, it will make more sense.**

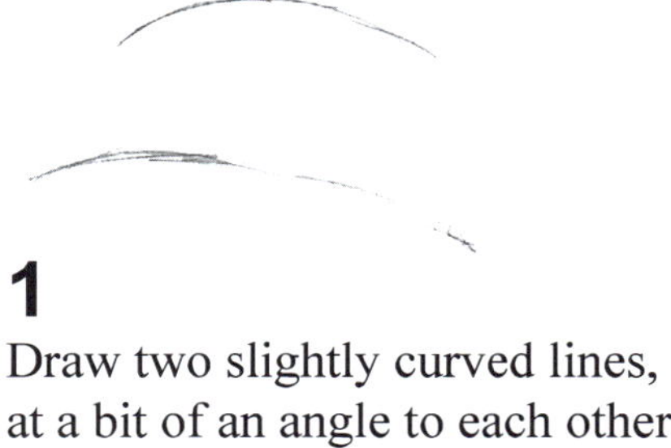

1

Draw two slightly curved lines, at a bit of an angle to each other.

2

Draw circles on the bottom line to help locate knuckles in the main part of the hand.

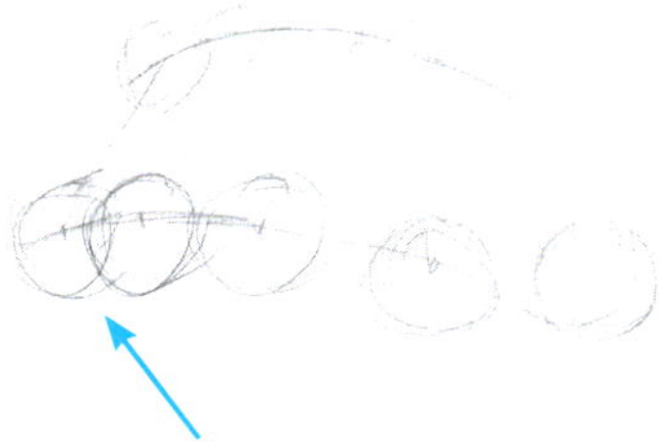

Those on what will be the little finger side appear closer together.

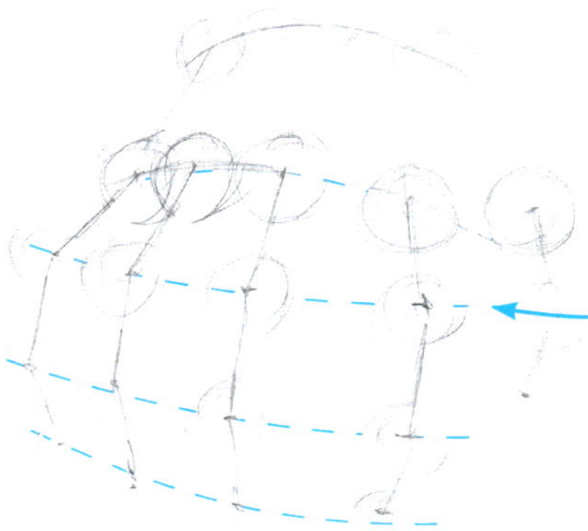

3

Lines and circles represent fingers.

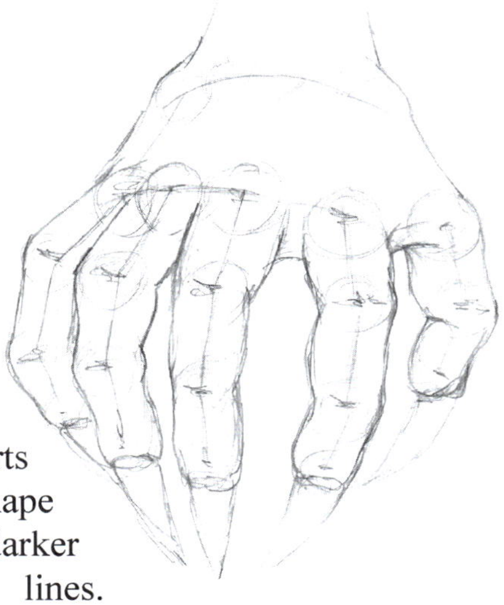

4

Hand starts to take shape with darker lines.

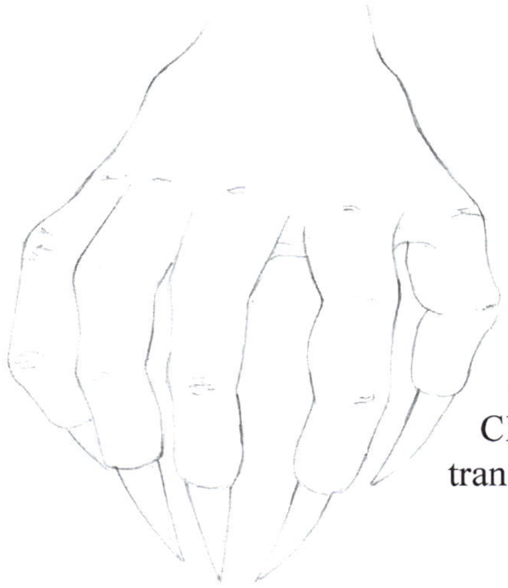

5

Clean up or transfer drawing.

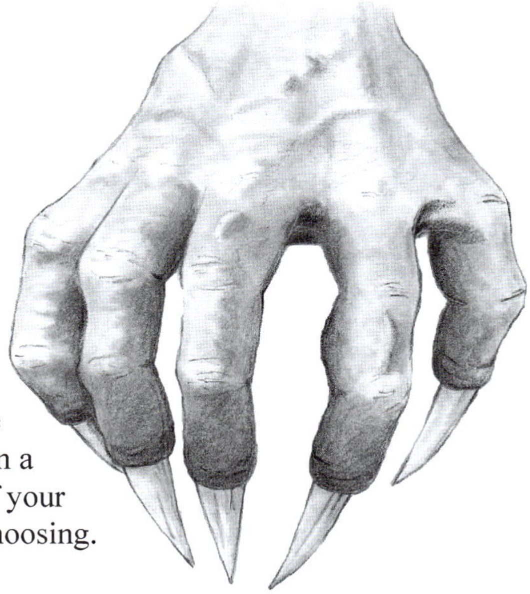

6

Shade (or not) in a style of your choosing.

Fingernails vs. Talons and Claws

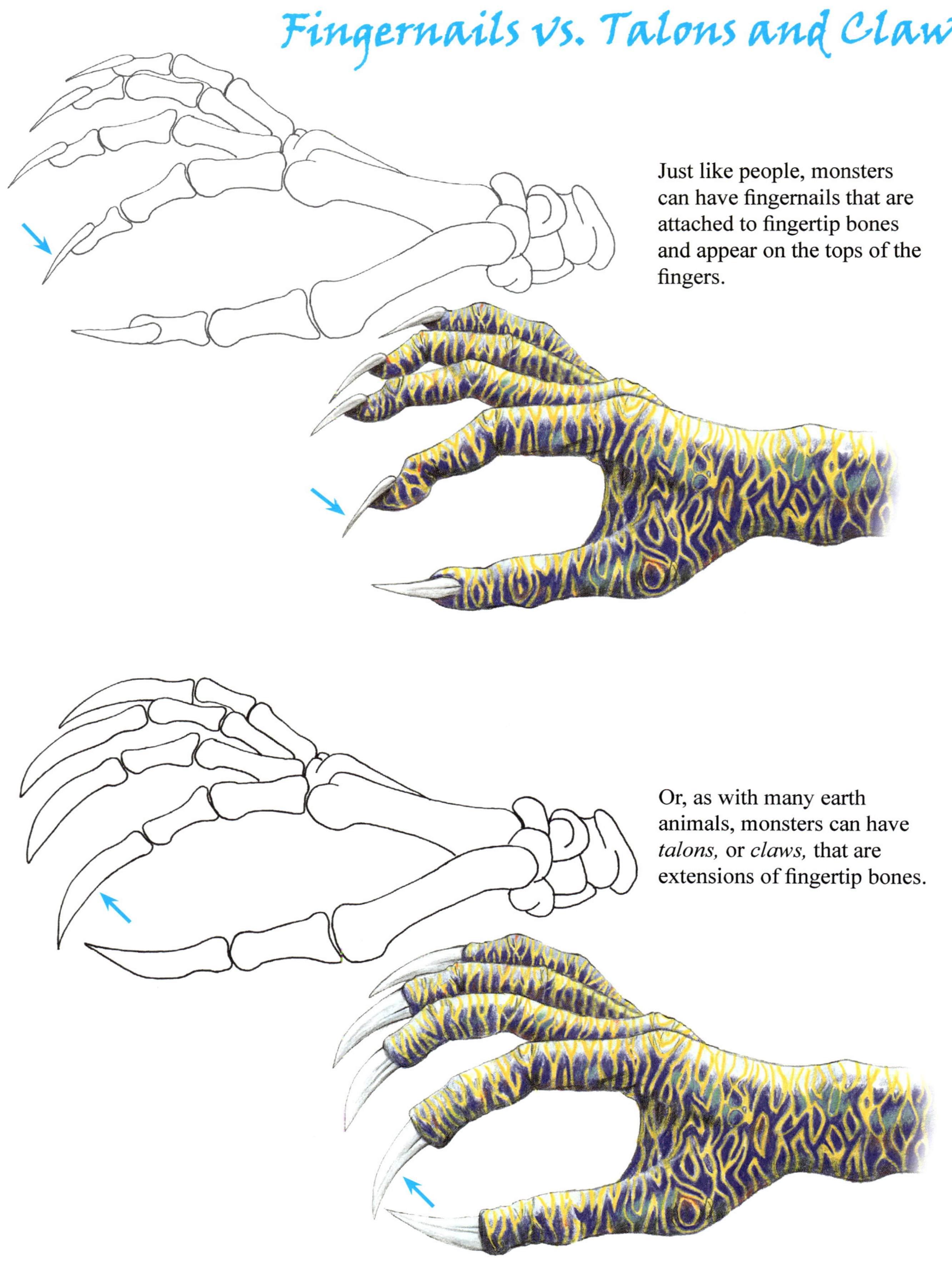

Just like people, monsters can have fingernails that are attached to fingertip bones and appear on the tops of the fingers.

Or, as with many earth animals, monsters can have *talons,* or *claws,* that are extensions of fingertip bones.

TIP

When drawing monster hands, hold your own hand in the desired position, study it and use it as a guide. Or, take a picture of your hand and bring it up on a computer or make a print and use the image as a guide. Your monster's hand will of course look much different than yours, but you'll be off to a good start.

(I used my own hands as a basis for some of the hands on these pages and elsewhere in the book.)

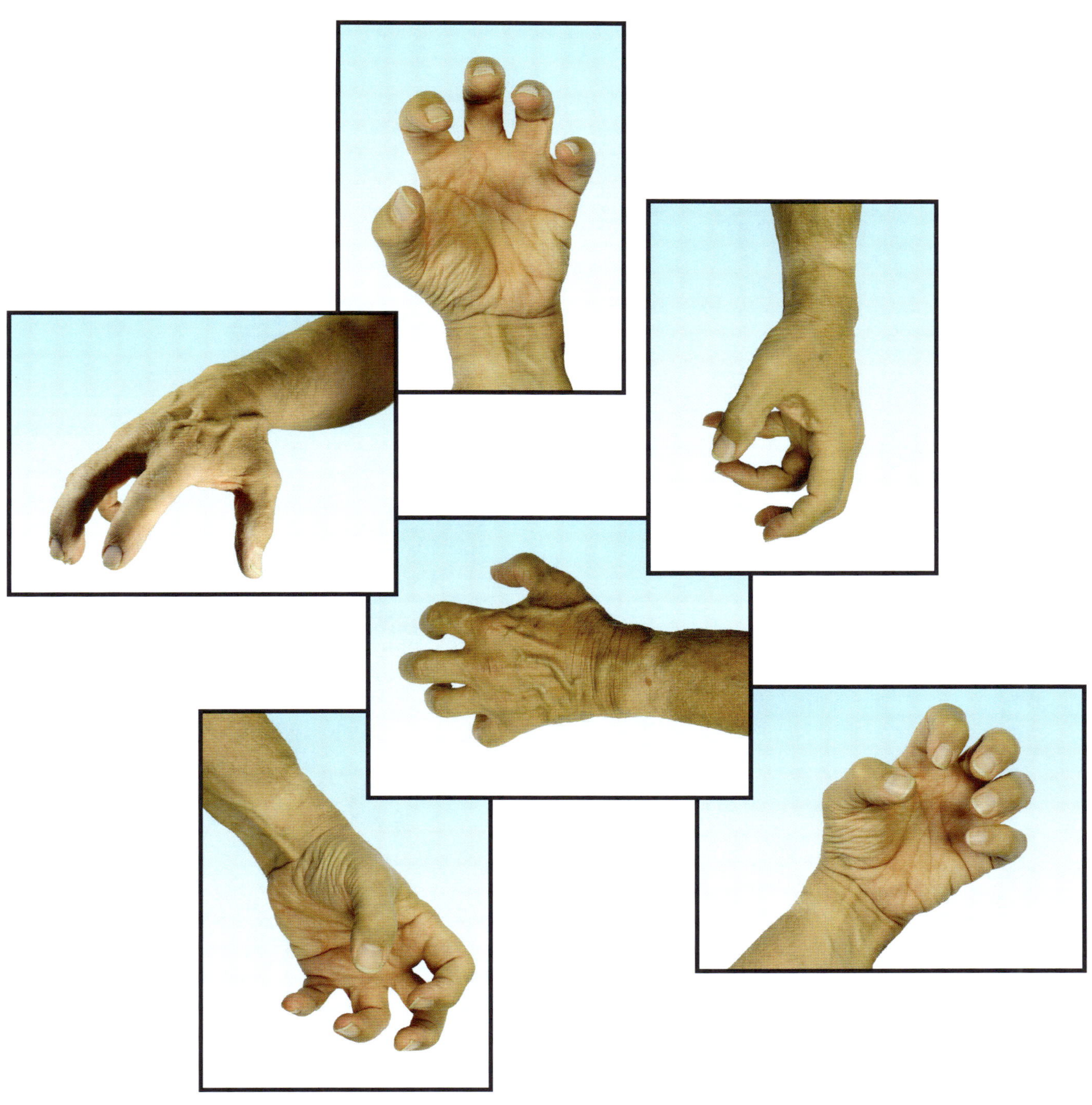

Draw a THREATENING Monster Hand

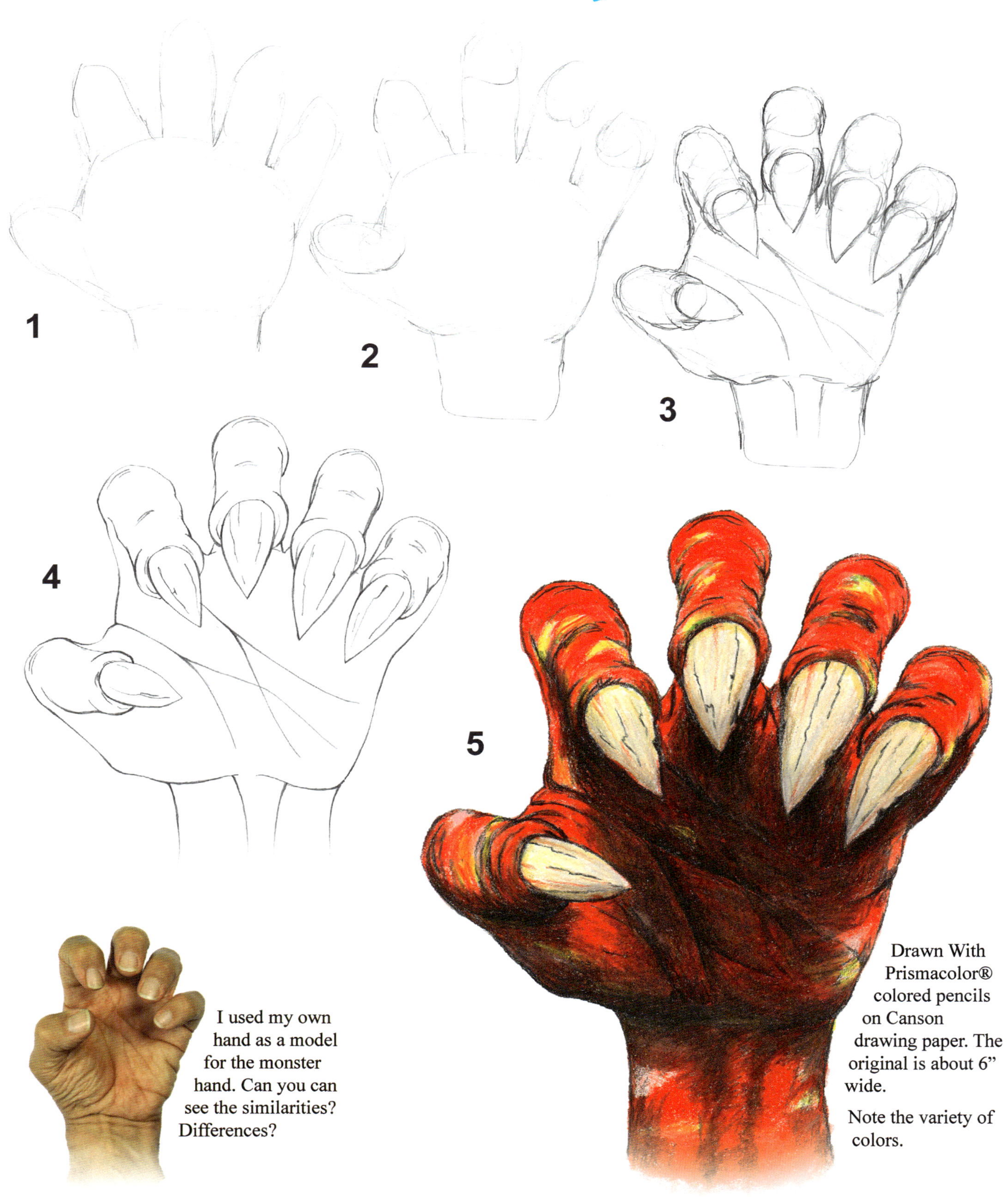

I used my own hand as a model for the monster hand. Can you can see the similarities? Differences?

Drawn With Prismacolor® colored pencils on Canson drawing paper. The original is about 6” wide.

Note the variety of colors.

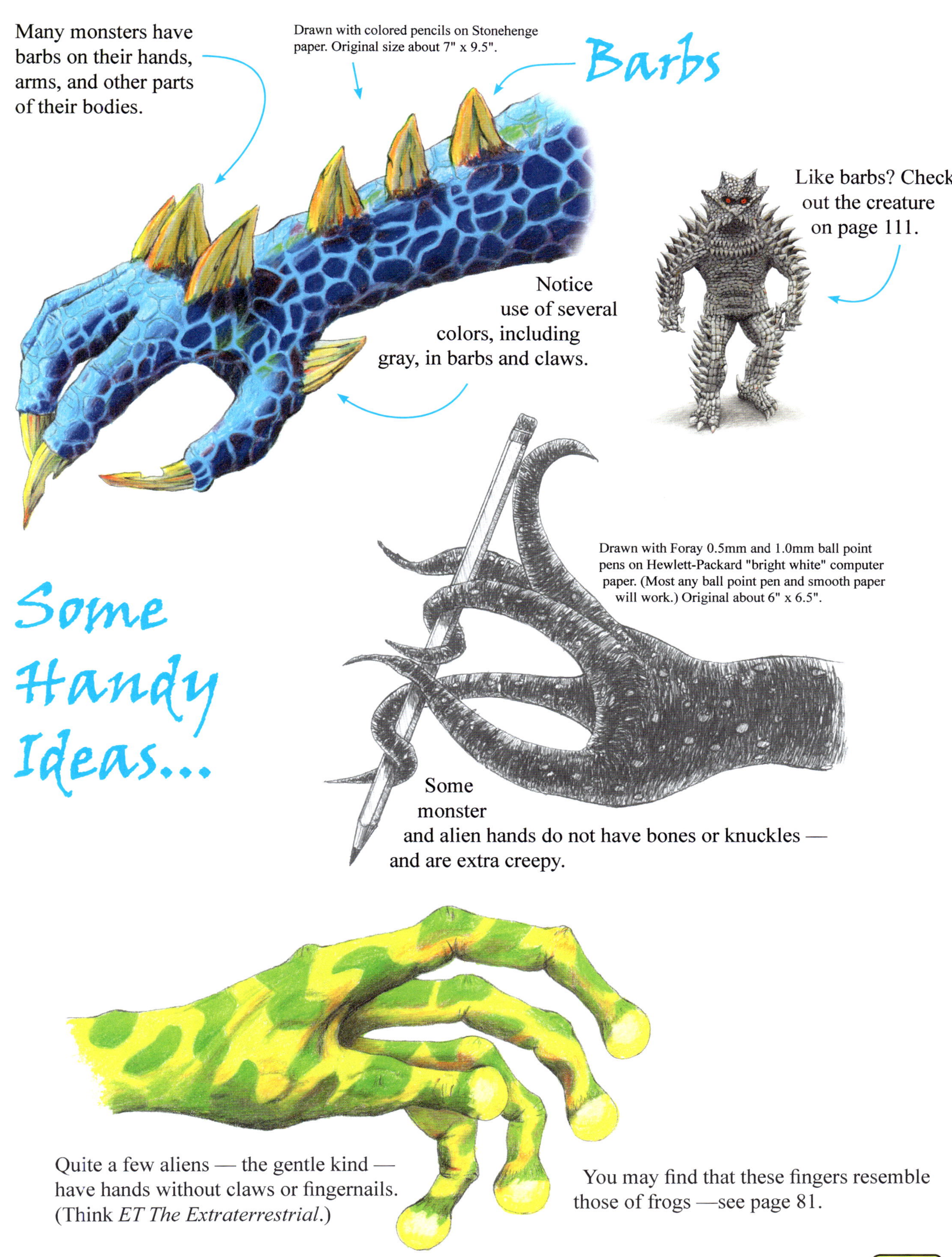
Many monsters have barbs on their hands, arms, and other parts of their bodies.
Drawn with colored pencils on Stonehenge paper. Original size about 7" x 9.5".
Barbs
Like barbs? Check out the creature on page 111.
Notice use of several colors, including gray, in barbs and claws.
Drawn with Foray 0.5mm and 1.0mm ball point pens on Hewlett-Packard "bright white" computer paper. (Most any ball point pen and smooth paper will work.) Original about 6" x 6.5".
Some Handy Ideas...
Some monster and alien hands do not have bones or knuckles — and are extra creepy.
Quite a few aliens — the gentle kind — have hands without claws or fingernails. (Think *ET The Extraterrestrial*.)
You may find that these fingers resemble those of frogs —see page 81.

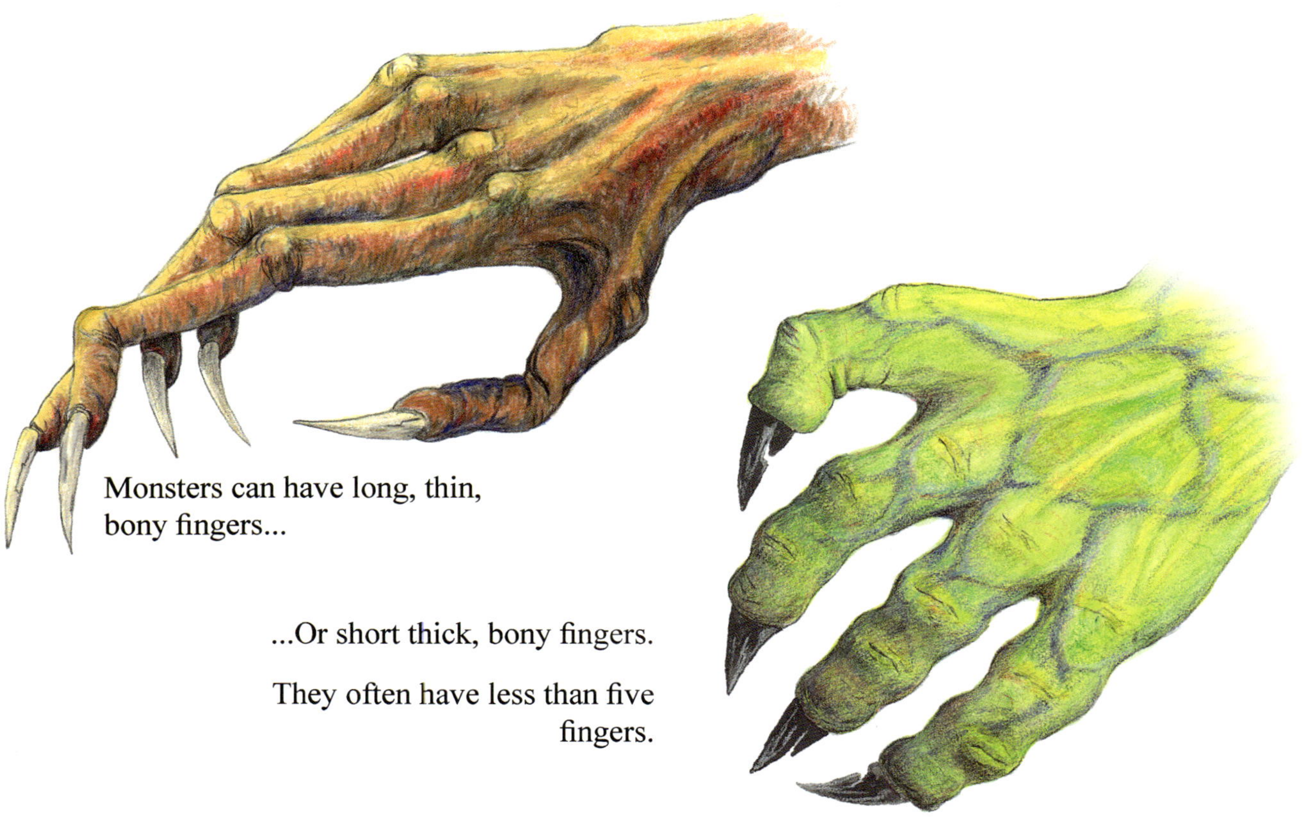

Monsters can have long, thin, bony fingers...

...Or short thick, bony fingers.

They often have less than five fingers.

But What About Feet?

Monsters have feet too, you know...

Yes, they do. And the principles that apply to monster hands usually apply to monster feet: What you see on the surface is influenced by the bones, tendons, and other stuff beneath the surface.

There are some differences: Monster toes tend to be shorter than monster fingers and two or three toes is usually the limit. This is not always the case, of course — there are always plenty of exceptions.

There is an almost infinite variety of monster feet just as there is of monster hands and, for that matter, monsters themselves.

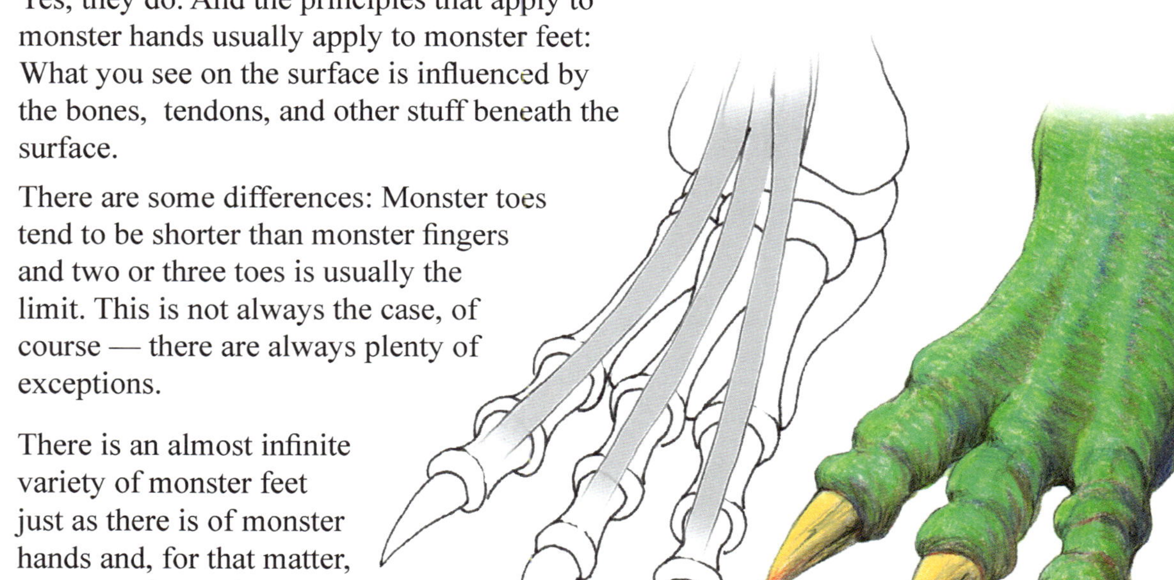

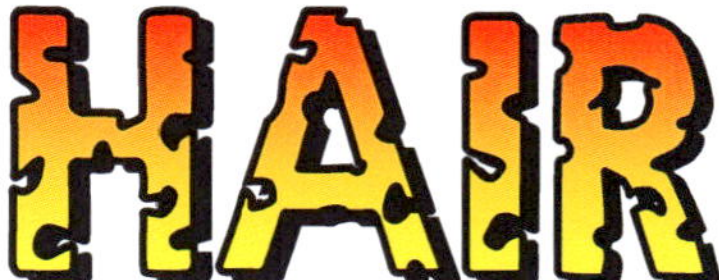

A Practice Session

You may wish to practice drawing hair, as shown in steps 1-6 on this and the next page, before committing to a drawing of a hairy monster.

Remember that the style shown is just one of a few possibilities.

1
Start with very light lines. Assuming you're doing a pencil drawing, I suggest a thin lead mechanical pencil such as a 0.5mm diameter with a hard lead, such as 2H. (More about pencils and leads on pages 9 — 11.)

2
Individual hairs tend to cluster together and come to a point.

3
You can use your eraser to create empty "lines" and areas into which you'll add more hairs going in different directions.

4
Add more hairs, lots of them.

5
Using **short strokes** and a slightly softer lead such as HB, create dark areas by pressing harder with your pencil. HB lead is supplied with most mechanical pencils.

The parts not darkened will appear as highlights, giving the hair a more natural, shiny appearance. Highlights usually appear where clusters bend and are influenced by the direction of light shining on them.

Hairs often appear darker at the ends of the clusters.

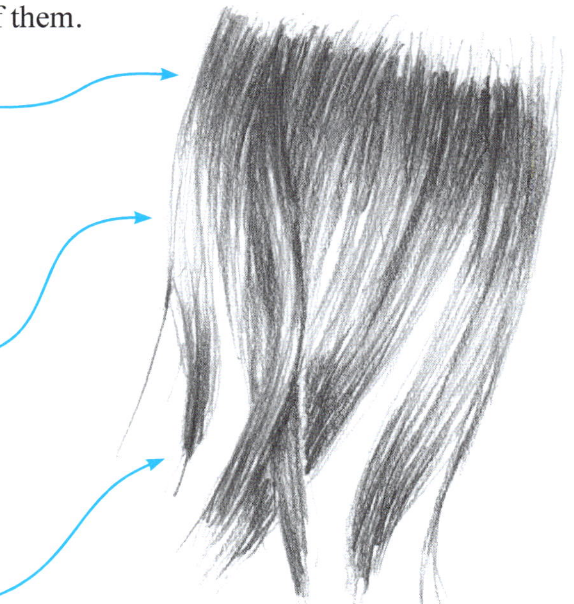

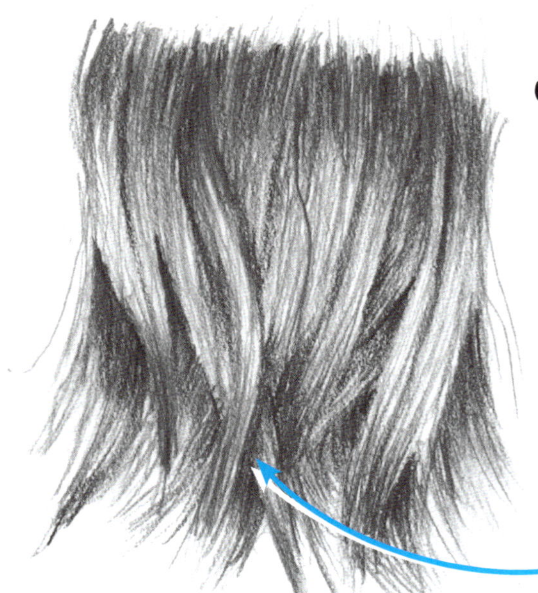

6

Continue adding more strands and clusters of hair. You can use a sharpened regular wood pencil with dark lead, such as 7B, to create darker areas and shadows.

Notice that hairs and clusters of hair often overlap each other.

The illustrations in steps 1-6 are the same size as the originals.

Create a Drawing of a Hairy Monster

Start your drawing with clusters of hair that are nearest the creature's front. This will make it easier to draw additional clusters farther back, behind the first clusters.

Use an eraser to lighten lines that are soon to be covered by hair.

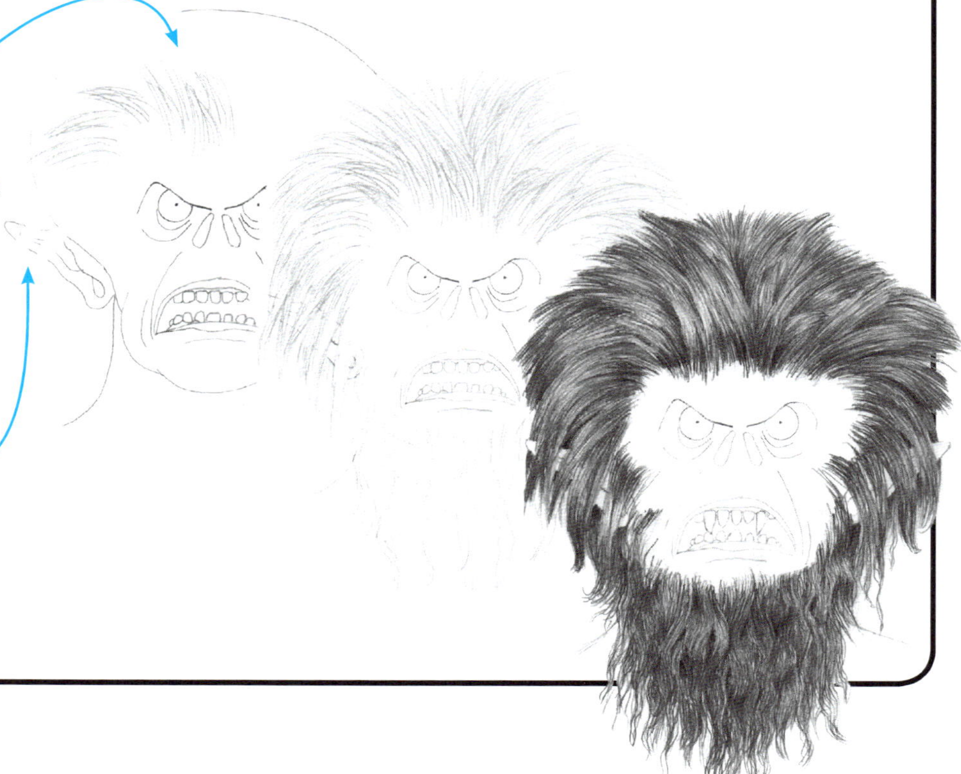

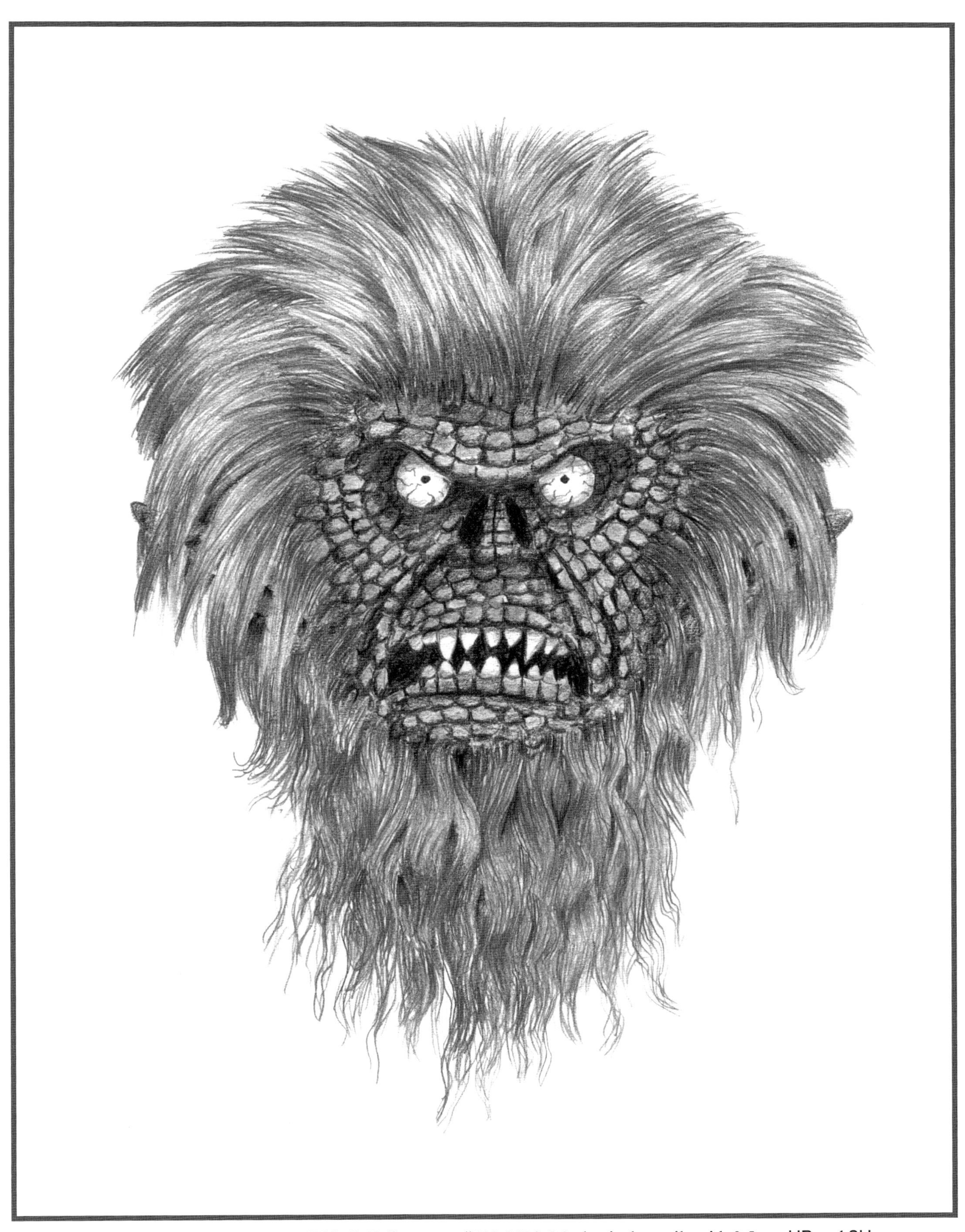

Drawn on Canson "Pure White" 80 lb. paper, #702-2230. Mechanical pencils with 0.5mm HB and 2H lead were used for the hair. A 7B wood pencil was used for facial features and darker parts of hair.

The Skinny On

SKIN TYPES

The variations of skin types found on monsters and aliens are without limits. The next few pages contain a few examples.

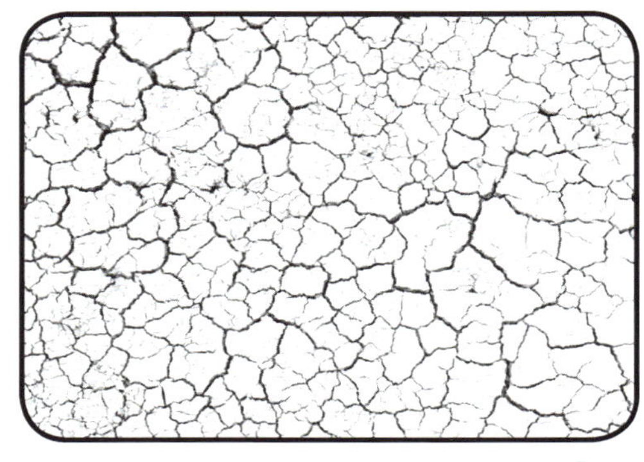

This style is inspired by very dry, cracked, and hardened dirt, as shown in this photo.

"Cracked Dry Skin"

1
It's best that you first shade your drawing.

2
Draw squiggly crack lines and connect them together so they make different shapes and sizes. Use a very dark leaded pencil, such as 7B or 8B.

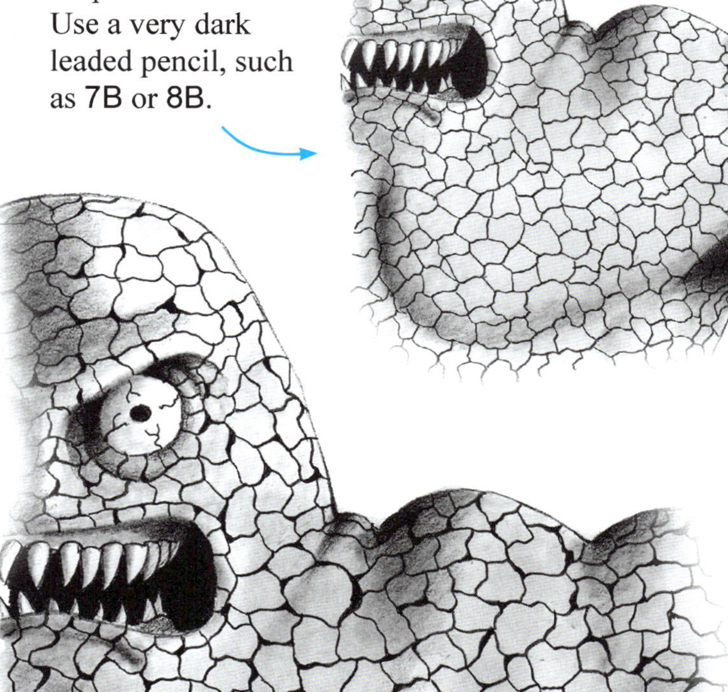

3
Add dark "gaps" between some of the lines.

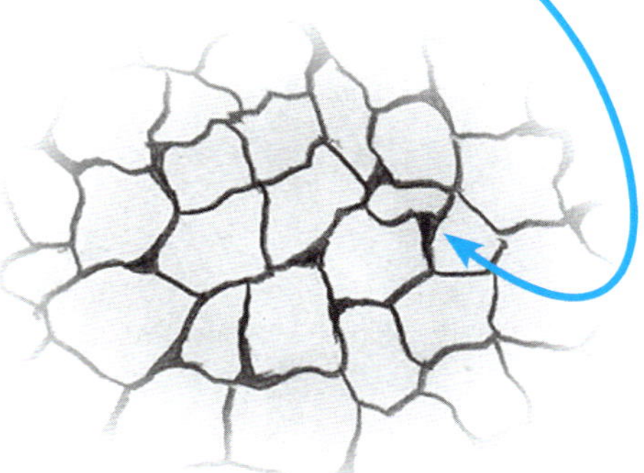

This drawing made on Canson 702-59 drawing paper, using mostly with HB and 7B pencils. The basic shading (Step 1) was blended with a small stump as shown on pages 41-46. The original is about 6.5" wide.

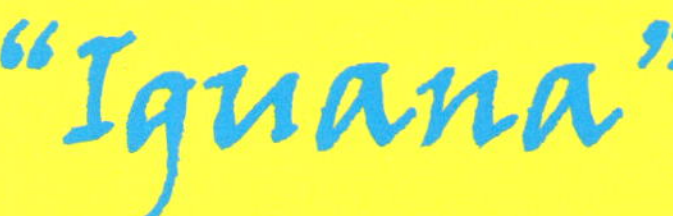

The skin of the monster on this page was inspired by the skin of iguanas — real earth animals shown in these photographs.

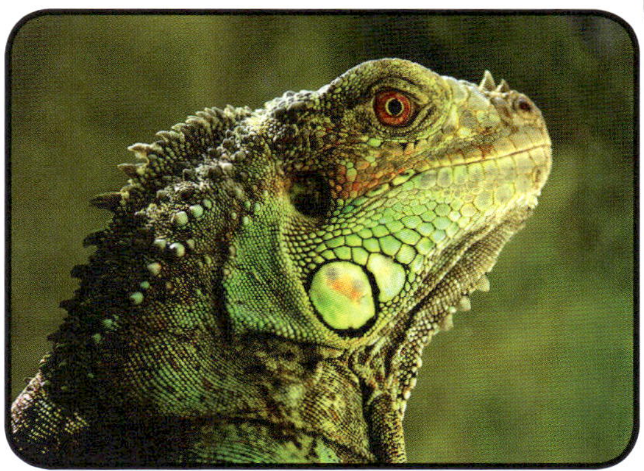

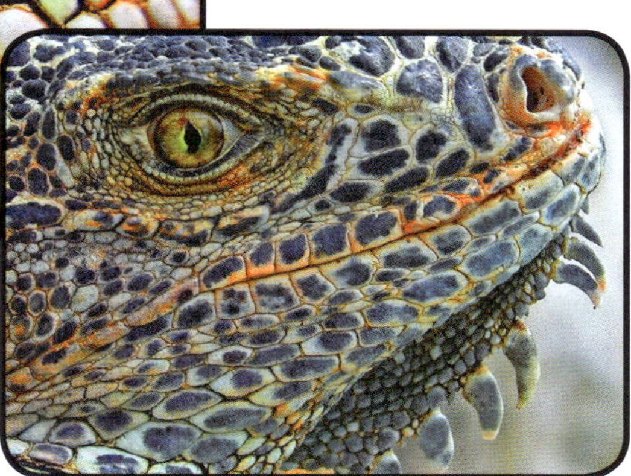

The iguana’s skin is covered with scales.

To Draw Iguana-like Scales...

1

Create various sizes and shapes in different colors. These will become scales. Have some colors overlap if you wish.

2

Put one or two colors in the centers of each scale.

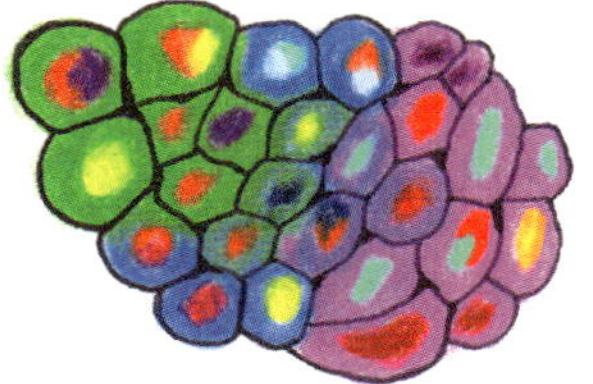

3

Outline scales with a black pencil or Sharpie "Ultra Fine Point" marker or Micron marker (page 19). If you use a marker you may wish to first spray the drawing with fixative in order to make the lines sharper (see pages 77 & 78).

"Honeycomb" scales

1
Draw a bunch of circular shapes — all attached to each other.

As always, keep lines light.

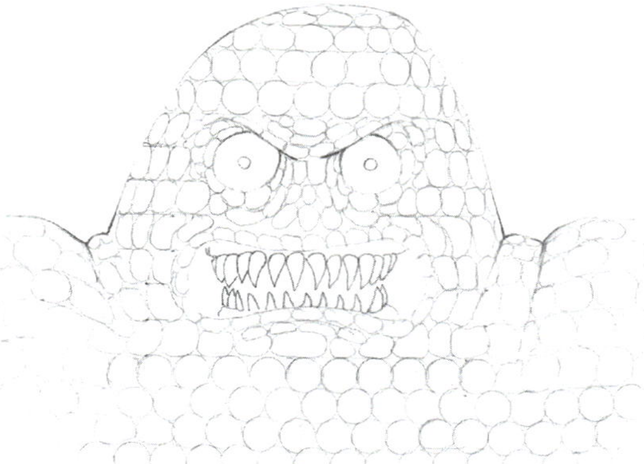

2
Draw somewhat straight lines where the circles touch each other and connect the lines. This will create a honeycomb pattern.

3
Eliminate the guide lines and shade whichever way you like.

As on page 128, draw gaps between some of the scales to make them more realistic.

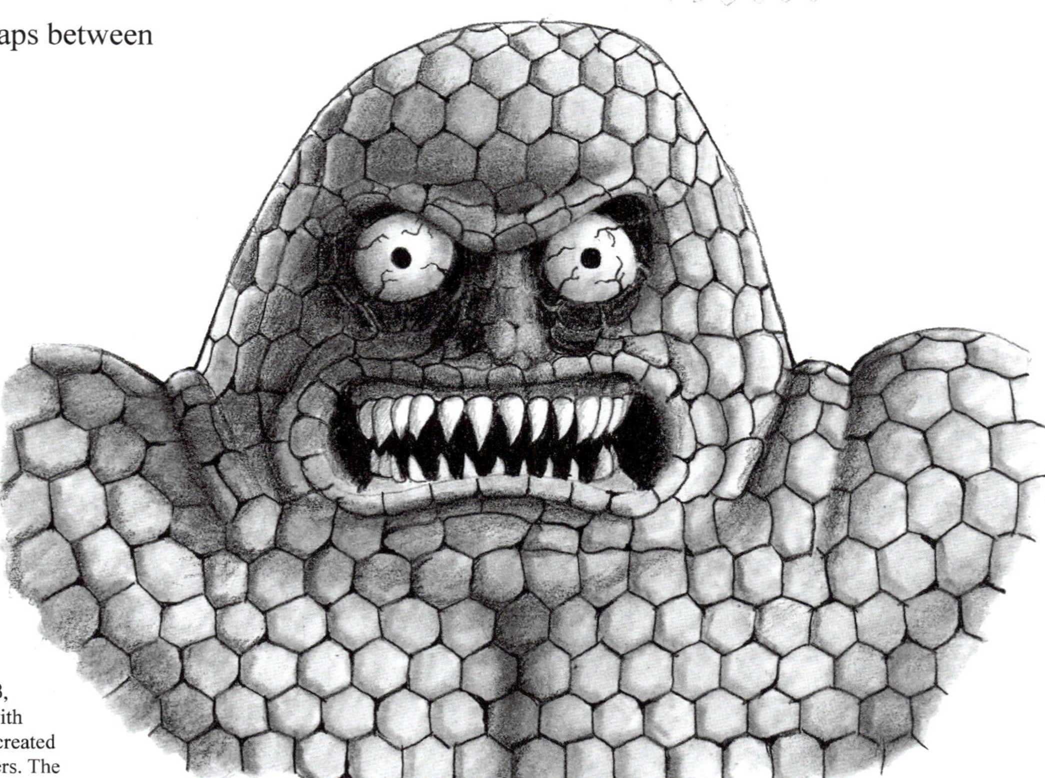

This drawing made on Canson 702-59 drawing paper with HB, 3B, and 7B pencils, blended with a small stump with highlights created with regular and kneaded erasers. The original is about 7.25" wide.

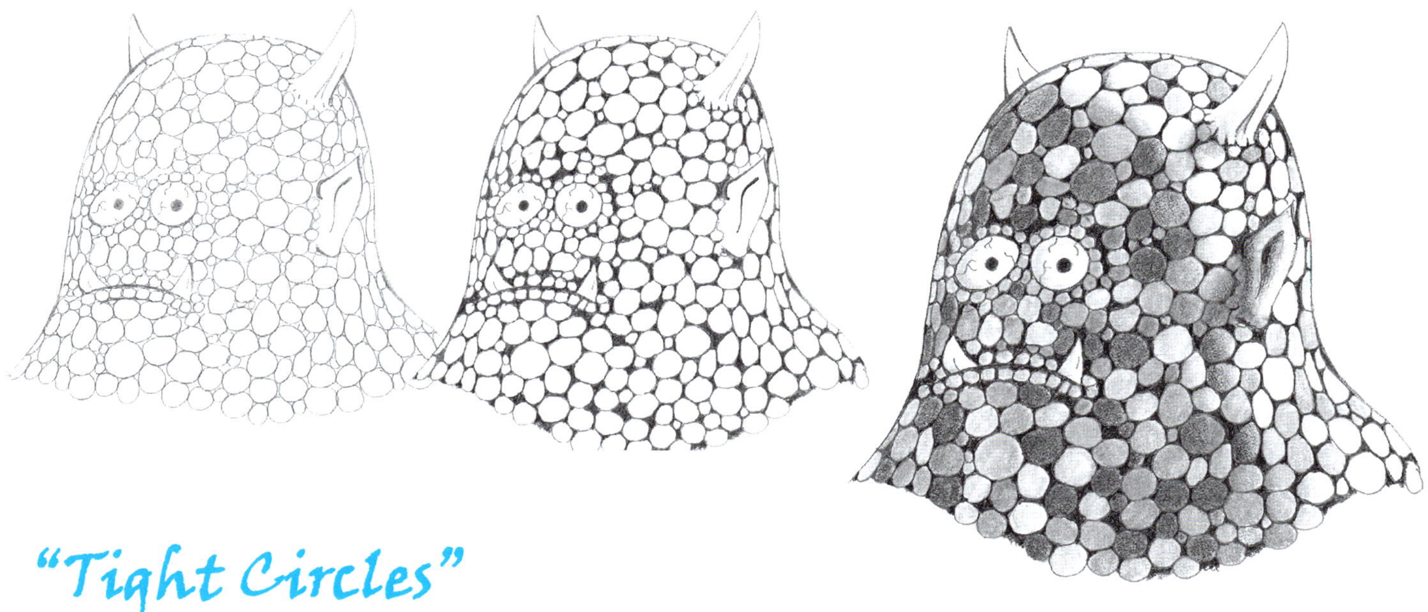

"Tight Circles"

1
Draw a bunch of scales in the shape of different sized circles. Leave as is, or...

2
Fill in gaps between circles. You can also leave this as is, or...

3
Apply shading. Although this guy has different shades of gray, you can shade any way you like, including color.

Lines on this drawing were made with an HB pencil; gaps with a 5B; shading with HB and 5B then smoothed with a stump (pages 41-46).

Make those scales stand out!

1
Notice how flat these scales are.

They were drawn on mixed media paper with Bic Mark-It markers.

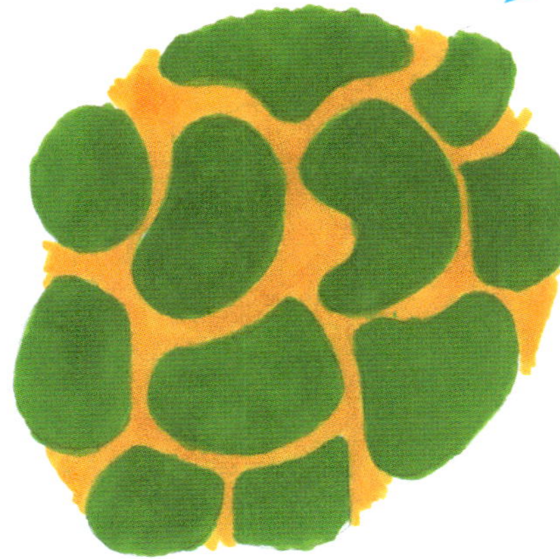

2

Colored pencils were applied on top of the same drawing to make them stand out from the background. They have a more realistic 3D appearance.

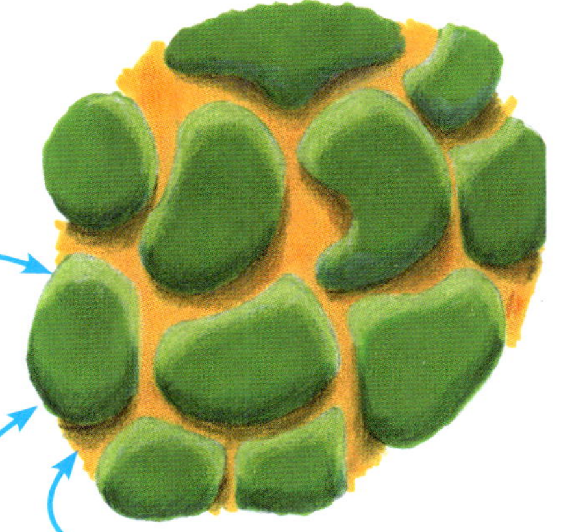

Lighter color on side facing the light.

Darker color on shadow side, the side facing away from the light.

Scales cast shadow on skin. Dark brown — not black — works well with the orange-ish skin.

"Snake Skin"

This style was inspired by the skin of a snake.

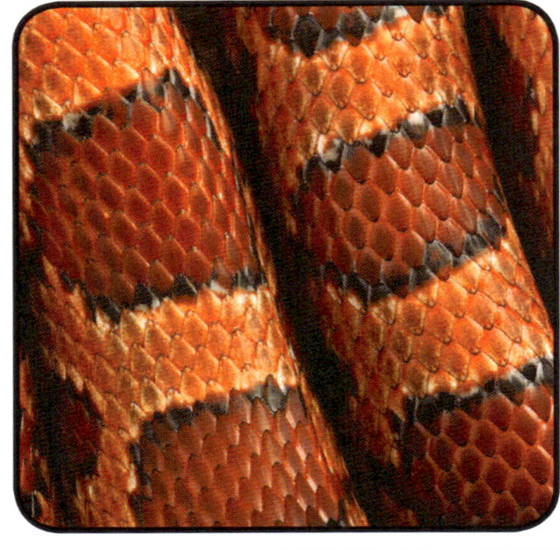

Corn Snakeskin
Courtesy
BigStockPhoto.com

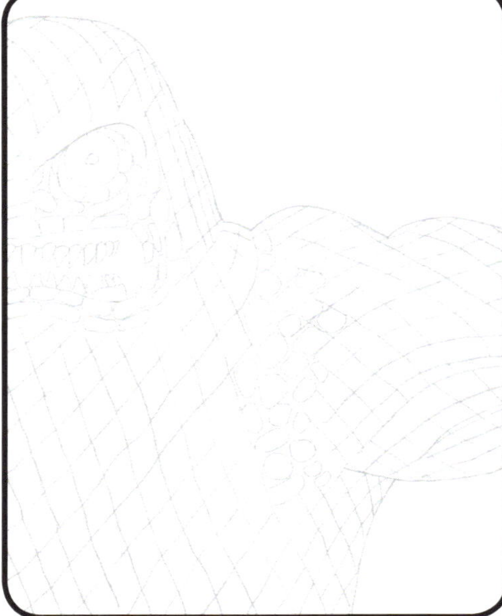

1
As always, I started with guide lines.

They were made as light as possible so they wouldn't mess up the colors to follow.

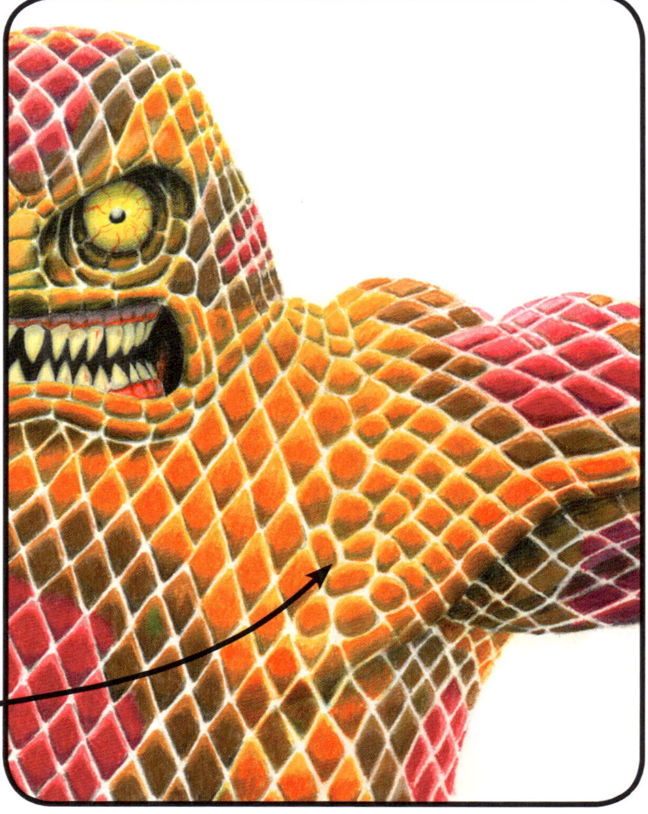

2
Scales and such were drawn with a variety of colored pencils. I didn't worry much about smooth edges — I knew they'd be covered with markers.

It was intended that the scales be mostly vertical on the body and horizontal on the arm. To create a smooth transition, a variety of scales were drawn at random between the two.

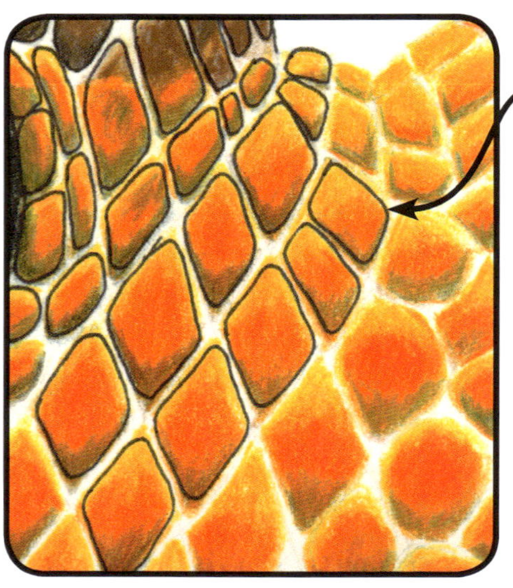

3
Each scale was first outlined with a thin black marker. This made the next step easier, filling in the areas between the scales with thicker black markers.

Note that the scales are rounded at the ends to make them more realistic and appealing.

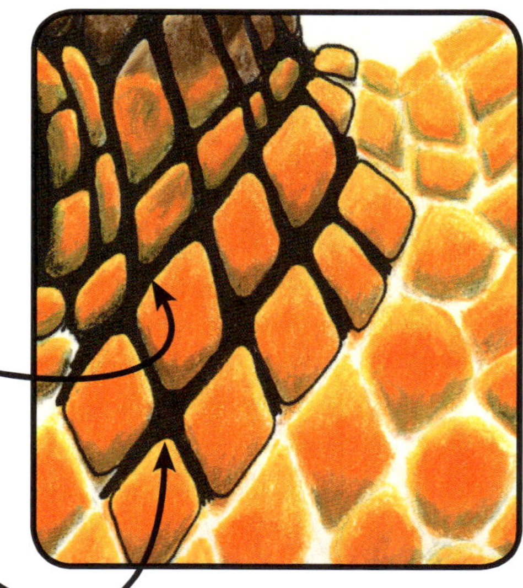

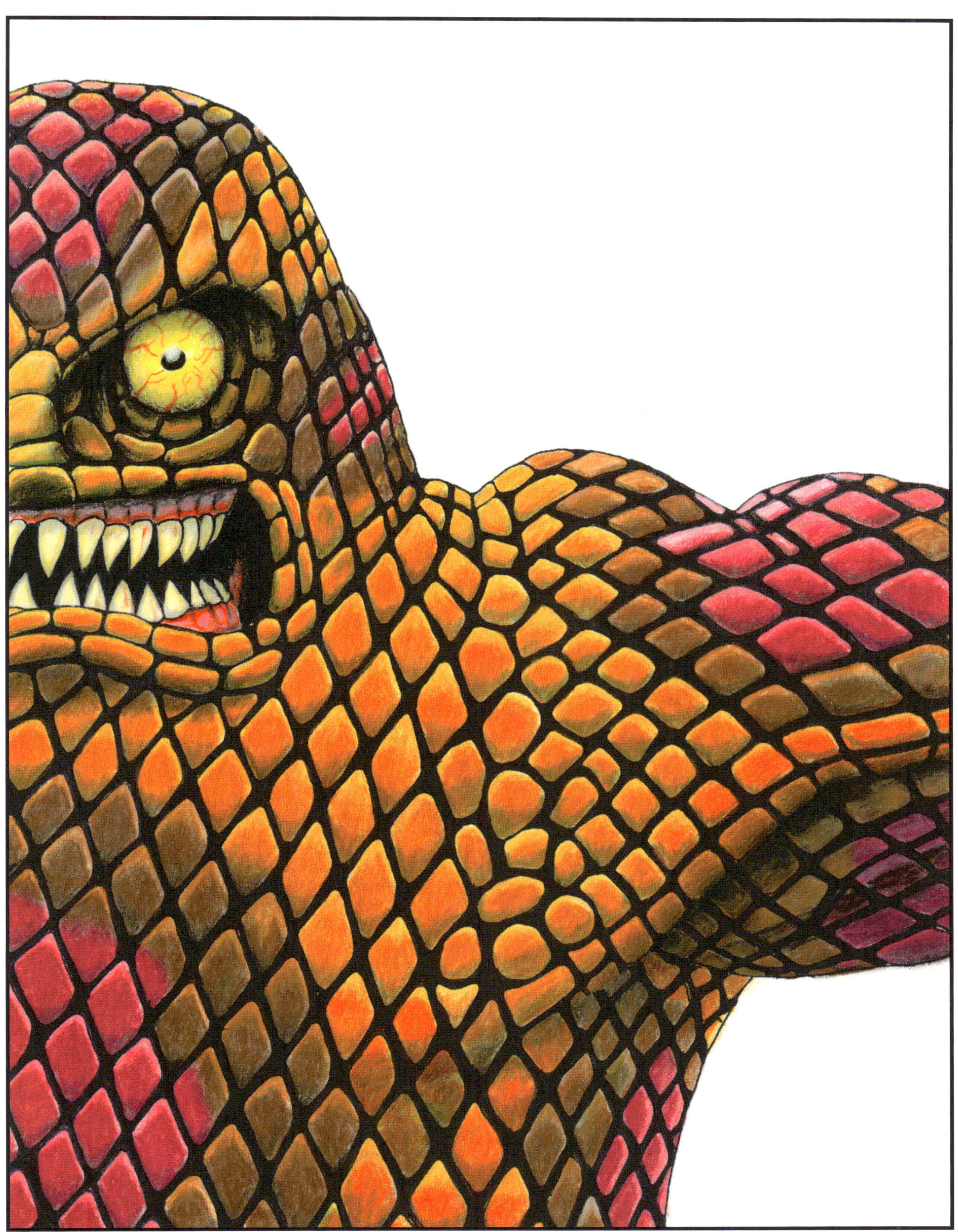

4 Drawing finished with various colored pencils and Sharpie fine and ultra fine point black markers on Stonehenge Rising paper. Original size 11" x 14".

Black is Beautiful

This style is similar to "cracked earth" on page 128, but instead of black lines on white or gray skin, white and gray lines are created on black skin.

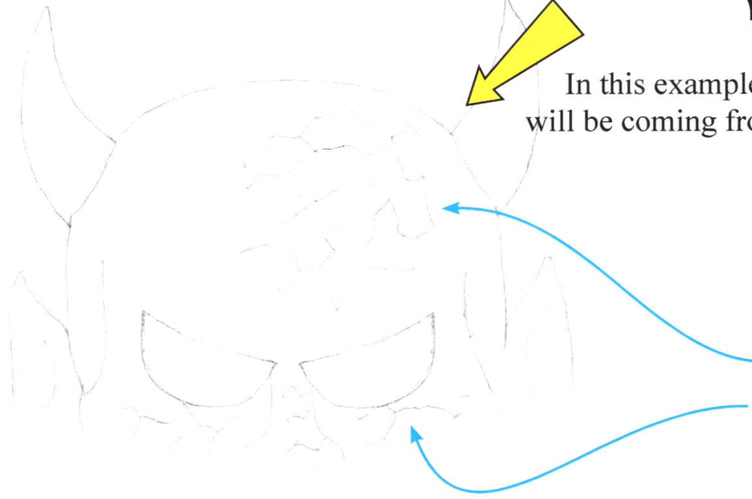

In this example, the main light will be coming from this side.

1

Start with a light pencil drawing.

Create guidelines where you expect to have white "crack lines" that will be in areas most strongly lit by the main light source.

To minimize the spreading (bleeding) of ink on the paper after it is applied, use paper that accepts both watercolor *and* pencil, such as **Aquabee CO-MO sketch, Canson XL mixed media** or **Strathmore Mixed media**.

2

Use a black Sharpie "fine point" or "ultra fine point" marker to color *around* the crack lines created in Step 1. These are lines that you wish to be white. The ink may bleed into the white area; if so, leave a little extra room around the white lines.

Erase pencil lines with a kneaded eraser.

Fill in all areas that will be dark with black ink.

Leave areas white where you expect to apply fairly bright colors, such as the eyes and teeth.

Leave extra white space where you expect to blend a color, such as red into black under the eyes, as shown in step 6.

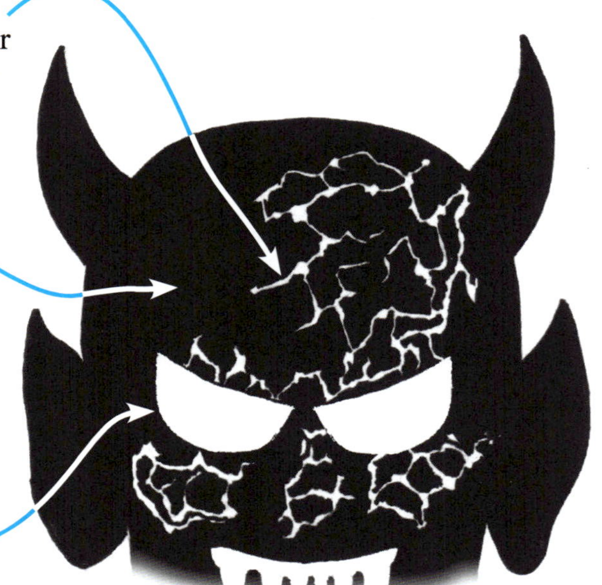

Instead of a marker, you could use black paint or India ink and apply with a brush.

3

Use various shades of gray colored pencils to draw more crack lines on top of the area you painted black. These lines are in the shadow areas of the creature.

5

Start applying other colors to the eyes, teeth, mouth, etc.

Notice coloring applied to this side, to the top of his head, etc. This could be from a blue light source behind the creature.

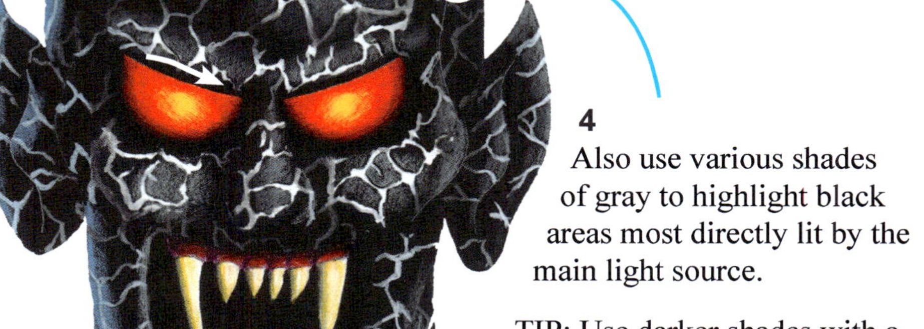

4

Also use various shades of gray to highlight black areas most directly lit by the main light source.

TIP: Use darker shades with a firm pressure rather than white with light pressure.

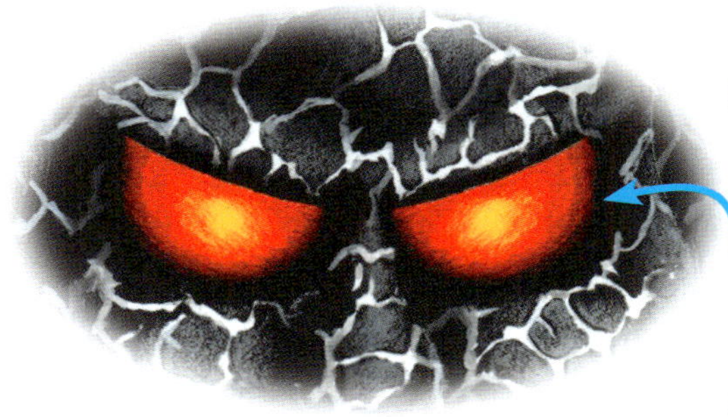

6

You can make smooth blends from red to black near the edges of the eyes to make them slightly blurred so they appear to glow.

NOTE: Rather than using a black pencil, I used dark blue — the color opposite red on the color wheel — plus red to create a richer black.

7

Complete the drawing.

NOTE: One of the few times I "cheated" in this book: Although the background colors in the finished drawing (next page) were created with colored pencils, they were drawn on a separate page, blurred with Photoshop, then digitally "pasted" behind the image of the monster.

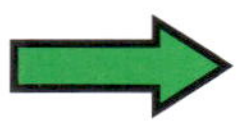

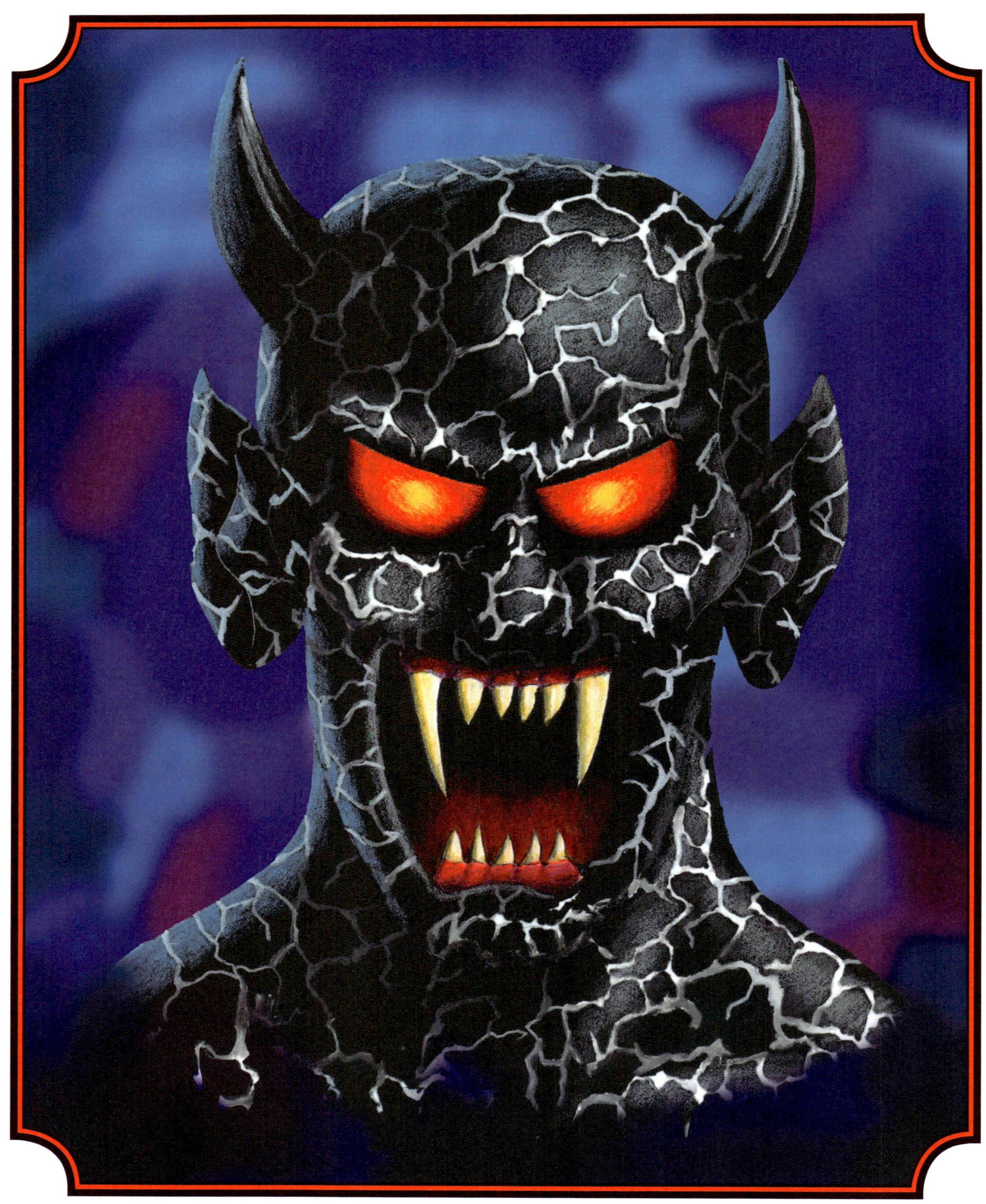

Drawn with a Sharpie marker pen for the black area and colored pencils for the rest on Stonehenge paper. Original size about 8.5" x 11". (Violets and grays in background created with colored pencils, but scanned and applied with a computer, producing smoother blends than can easily be done with pencils alone.)

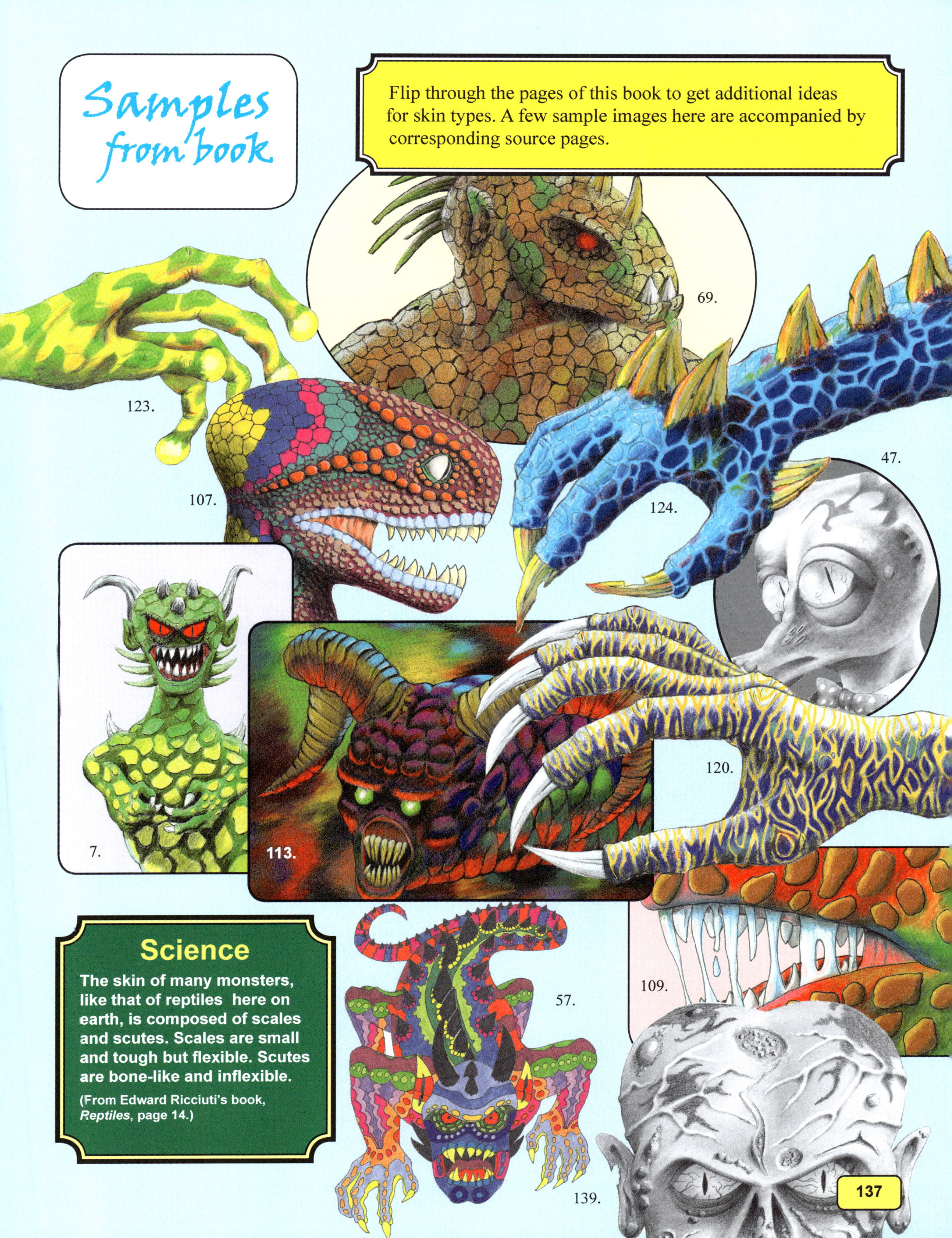

Samples from book

Flip through the pages of this book to get additional ideas for skin types. A few sample images here are accompanied by corresponding source pages.

Science

The skin of many monsters, like that of reptiles here on earth, is composed of scales and scutes. Scales are small and tough but flexible. Scutes are bone-like and inflexible.

(From Edward Ricciuti's book, *Reptiles*, page 14.)

A cool way to draw VEINS ZITS BOILS GASHES and such

You can create skin features (veins, zits, boils, gashes, birthmarks, etc.) by simply drawing them as you draw the creature. However, I often like to draw them *after* the basic drawing has been made, enabling me to first lay down a nice even texture of skin without messing up the features.

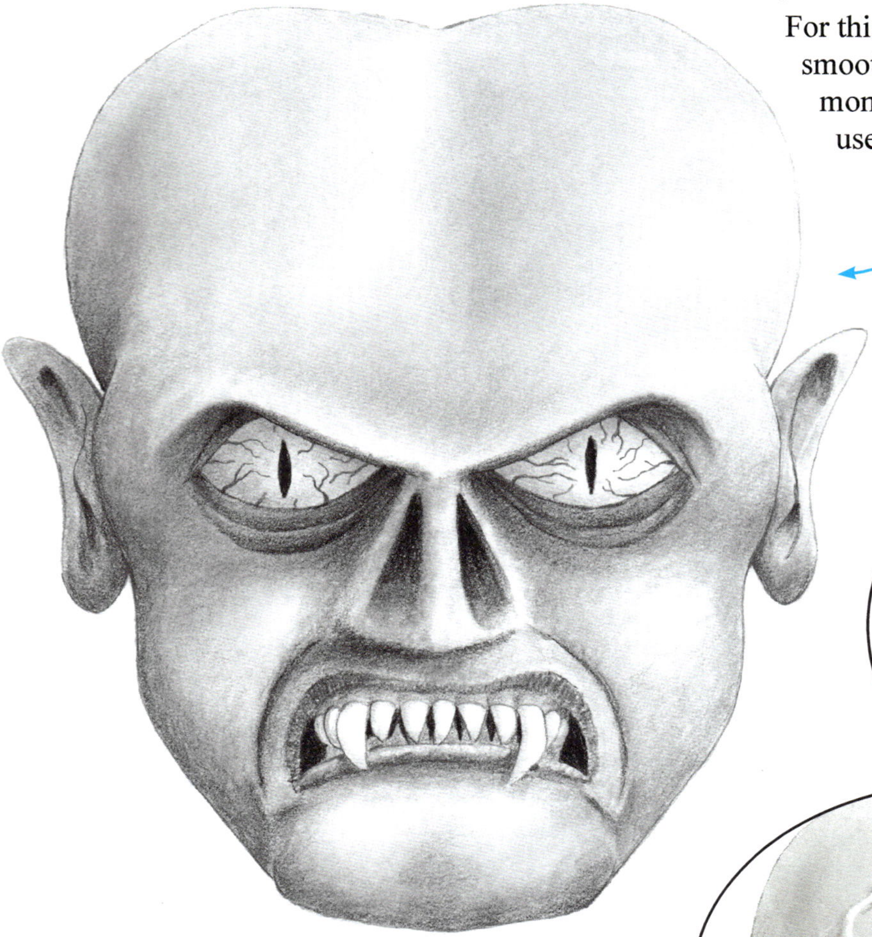

1

For this graphite drawing, I chose to use the smooth shading technique to render the monster's skin (pages 42-47), but you can use any technique you like.

2

If you want parts of the veins to be lighter than the background, "draw" them with an eraser.

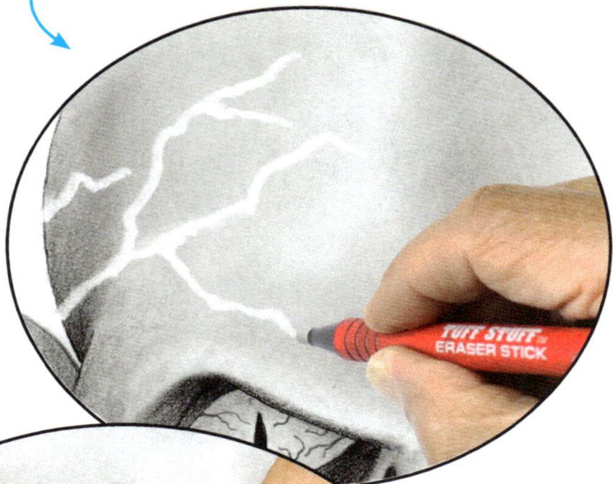

TUFF STUFF ERASER STICK

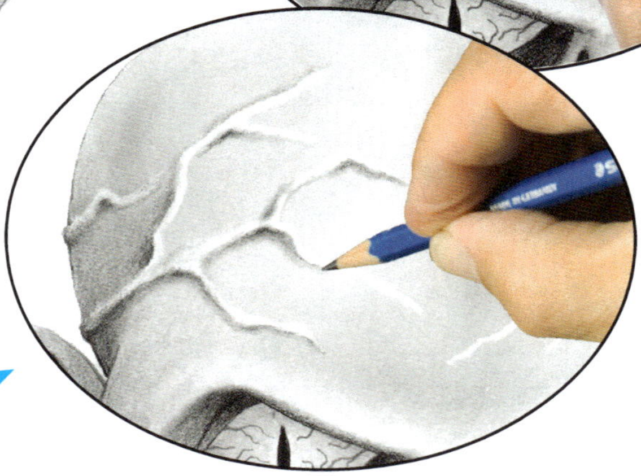

3

Remove eraser crumbs with a soft brush (page 12). Using a pencil and / or stump, draw the veins' shadows. (Learn about stumps on page 42)

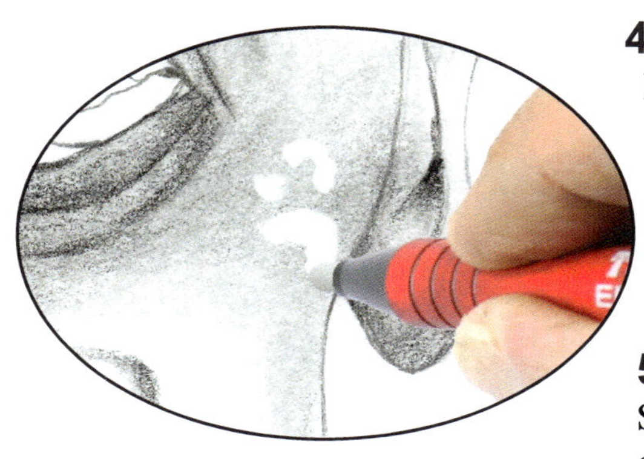

4

Draw a variety of blemishes. Remember to use an eraser *only* when you want to have part of the blemish be lighter than the background.

5

Shade with a pencil and / or stump.

Would you agree that open sores add extra charm?

A white spot makes the boil look shiny.

Dark areas are birthmarks.

The veins could have been darker, but I kept them almost white because, to me, white veins sometimes look extra creepy.

Notch in ear created with eraser & HB pencil.

Note incisors, mentioned on page 107.

Teeth were made to appear cracked, broken, and stained. An eraser was not used.

Drawn mostly with 6B and 8B pencils on Stonehenge paper. An HB pencil was used for lighter, sharper lines. Original is about 7-3/4" x 8-1/2".

Using an eraser to create features in color

When doing color, it is usually easier to create veins and other features as you make the basic drawing; however, you may at times wish to add features as an afterthought, when the basic drawing has already been made, using techniques similar to those shown on the previous pages.

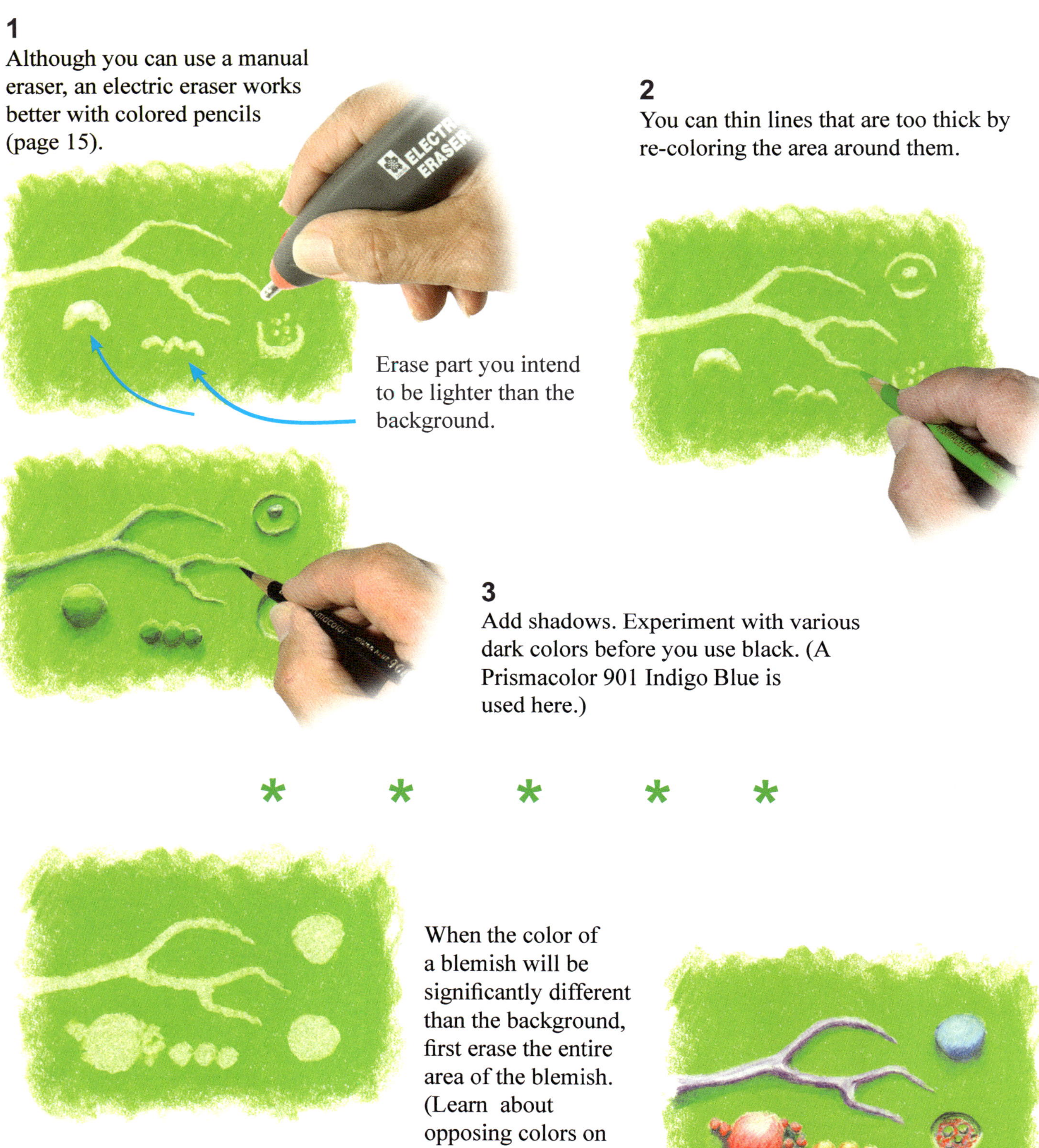

1
Although you can use a manual eraser, an electric eraser works better with colored pencils (page 15).

Erase part you intend to be lighter than the background.

2
You can thin lines that are too thick by re-coloring the area around them.

3
Add shadows. Experiment with various dark colors before you use black. (A Prismacolor 901 Indigo Blue is used here.)

* * * * *

When the color of a blemish will be significantly different than the background, first erase the entire area of the blemish. (Learn about opposing colors on page 48.)

About SIMPLICITY and DRAMA

It is possible to create really cool creatures with simple lighting and a lack of detail. The monster on this and the next page, for example, was rendered with only three colors. There is just one source of light. Because he is little more than a shadow, a silhouette in the misty black of night, he is especially threatening — tapping, perhaps, into the dark unconscious fears of the viewer.

It was my intention to have the picture suggest something *dramatic*, like a poster for a horror film. A creative use of light and shadow was employed to accomplish this.

For all the monster's simplicity, would you agree that he is among the scariest and most interesting in this book?

1. A sketch was first made on white paper.

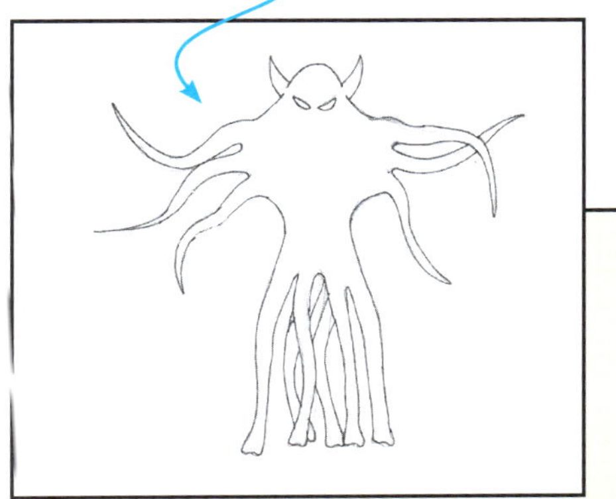

Transfer paper

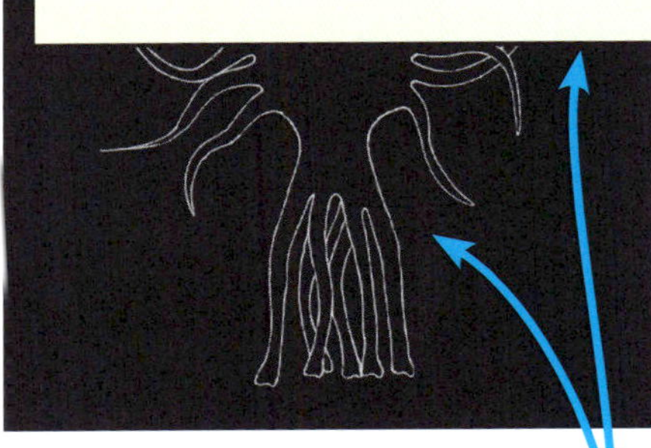

2. White transfer paper was used to copy the sketch onto black paper (previously demonstrated on pages 66-69).

3. The white sketch lines were made less visible with a kneaded eraser (page 11). White colored pencil was first used for the monster's eyes so the red color, applied over the white, would be brighter. Thick light blue lines show parts of his body illuminated by the light source, which is located behind him, near the ground.

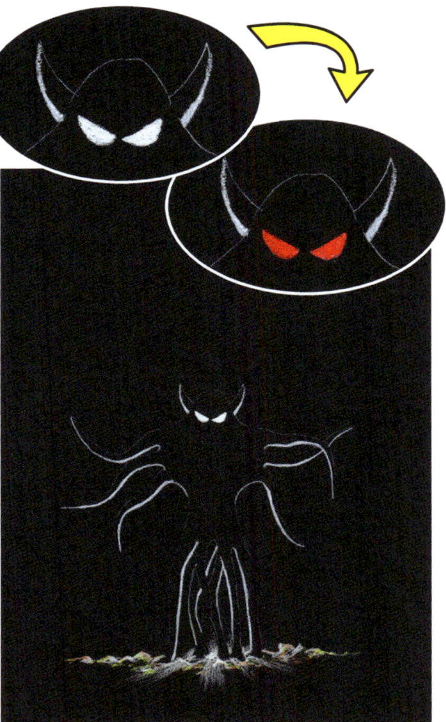

4. White and pale blue were used for the air, or mist, behind the monster that is illuminated by the light. The drawing could be considered done at this point...

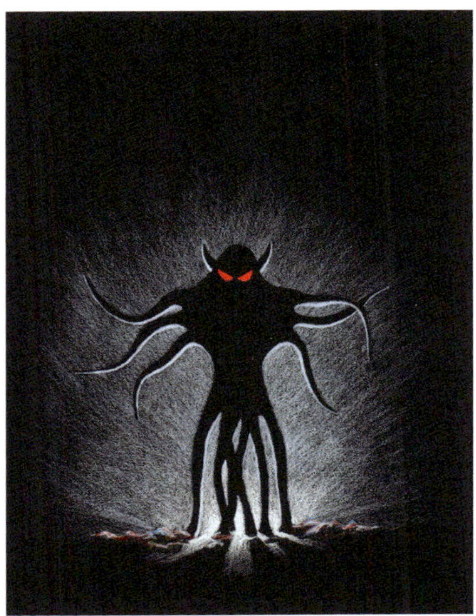

But, as you can see on the next page, I chose to add more white and pale blue in front of the monster to give him more of a mysterious "out of the mist" appearance.

Step 5 next page

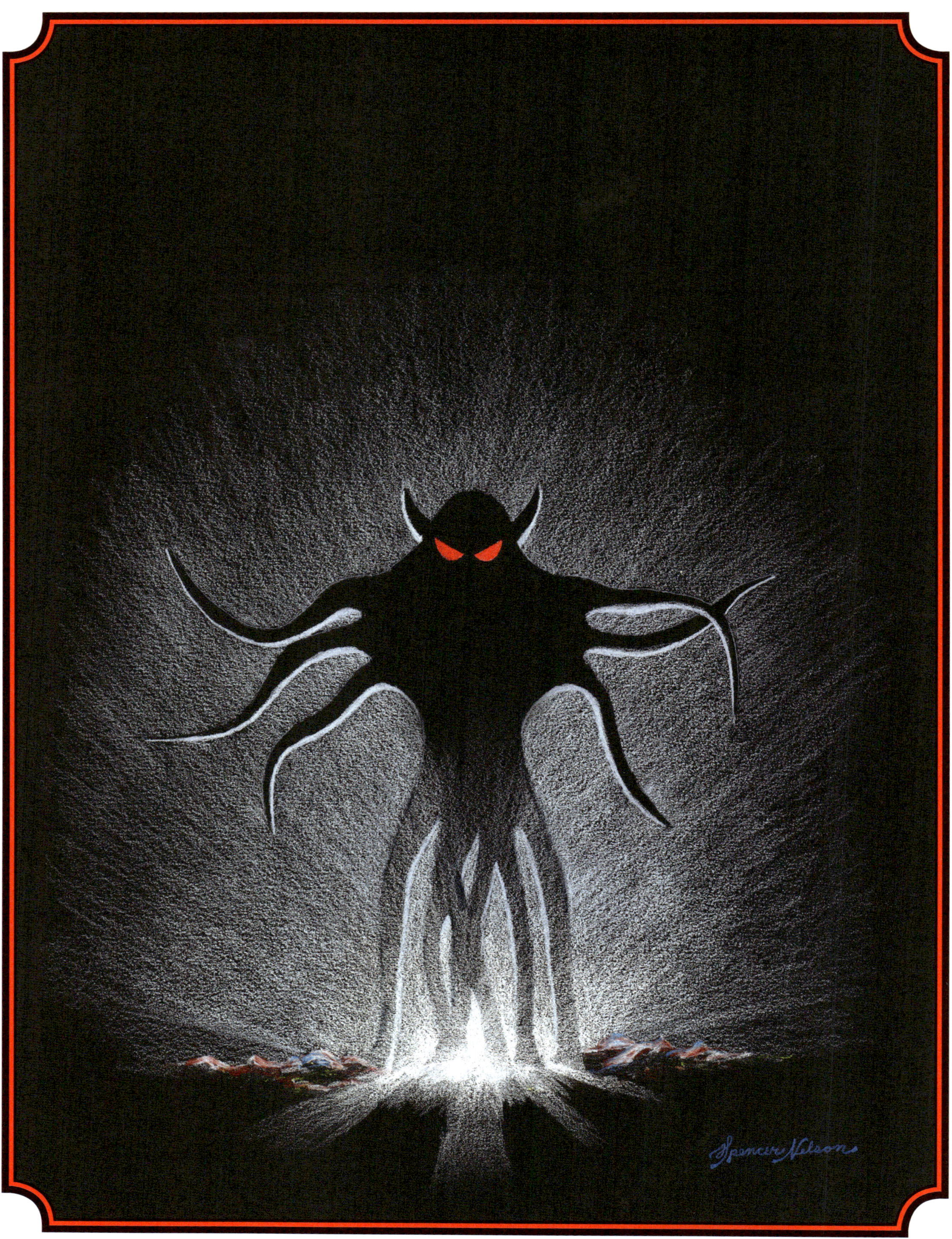

Drawn on Canson Mi-Tientes black pastel paper with Prismacolor colored pencils. 12" x 16".

RESOURCES

* Where to Buy Stuff

* How To Gain More Knowledge & Skills

Stores

Art Supply Stores

Search online or Yellow Pages for "art supplies" in your area. Art supply stores (not to be confused with hobby stores) typically have salespeople — often artists themselves — who can give you helpful advice on products and techniques.

Hobby and "Big Box" Stores

Michael's, *Hobby Lobby* and similar stores have a range of medium and high-quality art materials, though not as much as regular art supply stores and they generally lack salespeople with expertise.

You'll also find inexpensive, but limited, art supplies at places like *Target* and even your local supermarket.

Online Store

www.dickblick.com is an easy-to-use website that lists a wide variety of items with useful descriptions at discounted prices. Seek additional guidance from staff members via the posted 800 numbers.

Online Information

An *awesome* amount of information can be found in cyberspace from manufacturers and organizations.

Visit ***www.prismacolor.com*** for info on colored pencils and a wealth of ideas. Click the "contact us" link and ask about downloadable PDF files on care and sharpening of colored pencils, lightfast color charts, and other issues you may have.

Learn more about acrylics at ***goldenpaints.com*** and ***liquitex.com***. (I'm a fan of Golden paints.)

For Oils, watercolor, and gouache, check out ***mgraham.com***.

Books, Magazines and the Internet

Want some great ideas for monster and alien body types, skin textures, eyes, claws, teeth, and more?

- Browse bookstores and search online for references featuring dinosaurs, reptiles, insects, and other earth creatures as well as fantasy monsters and aliens.
- Take advantage of your local library.
- Online booksellers such as ***amazon.com*** offer discounted prices. They also have sources for very inexpensive **used books**.
- Booksellers like **Barnes and Noble** may send you coupons for significant **price reductions** if you sign up for emails.

Visit www.spencerWnelson.com where you *may* acquire more ideas and info relating to this book, including a list of sources and prices for materials, *and* see more of the author's artwork!

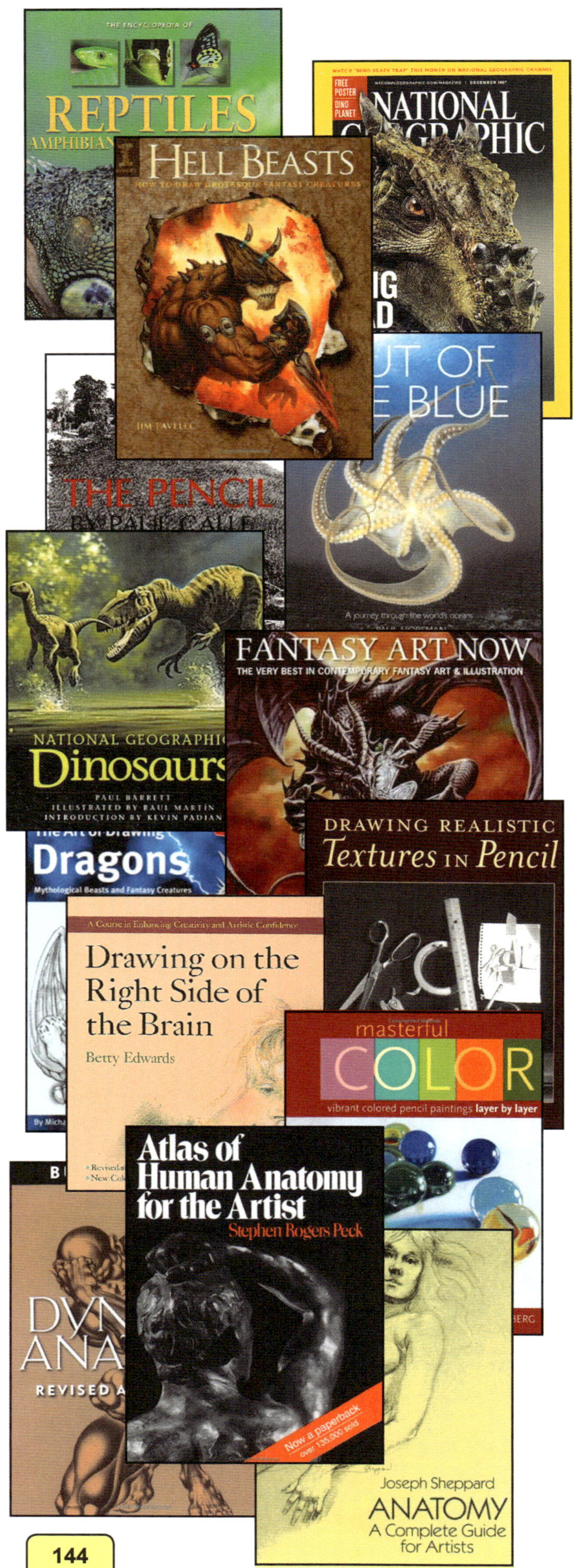

The **National Geographic Magazine** is an excellent source of illustrations of **very strange but real earth creatures**. Past issues are available at libraries. (Check out the December 2007 issue on dinosaurs.)

Search booksellers and online stores for "how to" books on **drawing and painting fantasy creatures** as well as books that feature fantasy artwork.

Many wonderful books are available to **improve your skills** in **drawing with pencils** and **colored pencils**. Among them are:

- ***Drawing on the Right Side of the Brain*** by Betty Edwards: Perhaps the most popular art instruction book ever. May unleash abilities you didn't know you had.
- ***Basic Drawing Techniques***, edited by Greg Albert and Rachael Wolf.
- ***Drawing Realistic Textures in Pencil*** by J.D. Hillberry. Methods for creating smooth blends of grays in pencil drawings. *Highly recommended.*
- ***The Pencil*** by Paul Calle. His unique "engraving" technique is well worth studying.
- ***Masterful Color: vibrant colored pencil paintings layer by layer*** by Arlene Steinberg. Create colored pencil drawings that look like paintings. *Also highly recommended.*

The more you have a knowledge of human anatomy, the better able you'll be to draw realistic monsters and aliens. Two books are recommended: ***Atlas of Human Anatomy for the Artist*** by Stephen Peck, and ***Anatomy a Complete Guide for Artists*** by Joseph Sheppard.

Also consider ***Muscle and Fitness*** magazine and similar publications. They feature guys whose over-sized muscles, together with popping veins, serve as good models for humanoid monsters. Available at your local supermarket.

— Have Fun!!!